a

Robin Nixon's

HTML5 Crash Course

Learn HTML & HTML5 in 20 easy lectures

ROBIN NIXON'S HTML5 CRASH COURSE

Learn HTML & HTML5 in 20 easy lectures

Robin Nixon

Nixon Publishing

ROBIN NIXON'S HTML5 CRASH COURSE

By Robin Nixon

Published by: Nixon Publishing
4 Coast Drive
Greatstone
New Romney
Kent TN28 8NX
United Kingdom

Email: info@nixonpublishing.com
Website: nixonpublishing.com

ISBN: 978-0-9568956-1-5

For Julie

About the author

Robin Nixon is a motivational and technical author who has written over ten books for publishers such as O'Reilly, McGraw-Hill and Wiley, and in excess of 500 magazine articles. He is also the founder of Nixon Publishing.

In 1995 he started the world's first licensed Internet radio station. As well as attracting the attention of Microsoft, who helped him to develop the audio player, as a result of which he was interviewed by BBC2 TV who came to film the operation he had set up.

Robin has been the director of several Internet and software development companies in both the UK and US, and has in excess of 15 years' experience with developing for the Internet.

Robin lives on the South East coast of England with his wife, a trained psychiatric nurse and university lecturer on Autism, five children and three disabled foster children.

Other books by Robin Nixon

- *The PC Companion*, Sigma 1993
- *The Amstrad Notepad Advanced User Guide*, Sigma 1993
- *Learning PHP, MySQL and JavaScript*, O'Reilly 2009
- *Ubuntu: Up and Running*, O'Reilly 2010
- *Plug-in PHP*, McGraw-Hill 2010
- *Plug-in JavaScript*, McGraw-Hill 2010
- *Plug-in CSS*, McGraw-Hill 2011
- *HTML5 For iOS And Android*, McGraw-Hill, 2011
- *Creative Visualization For Dummies*, Wiley 2011

TABLE OF CONTENTS

LEARN HTML5 THE QUICK AND EASY WAY

By following the exercises in this course you will:

- ✓ *Learn what all the fuss around HTML5 is about.*
- ✓ *Understand how to use all the powerful new features.*
- ✓ *Know what other features lie in store for the future of HTML.*

Welcome to this course on using HTML5, which should take you 20 hours or less to complete – so you can even do it in a weekend. As you probably know by now HTML5 isn't any one upgrade to HTML. Rather it's a collection of items from people's wish lists that came together at roughly the same time, and which simply ended up with the moniker HTML5.

Some of the new features are major new technologies, such as the canvas, geolocation, audio and video, while others are more like service updates, such as the extensions that have been made to HTML forms, microdata and web workers.

But collectively all these things have become known as HTML5, and you need to know what they are when your boss or someone else asks you what HTML5 is.

About JavaScript

If you come from a web development background and have little experience with programming you'll be right at home with the HTML extensions that have been introduced in HTML5, but you may find the going a little tough when learning how to implement the HTML5 canvas, due to needing to use JavaScript.

Sorry, but there are no two ways about it. The modern world of web development requires you to be experienced with HTML, CSS *and* JavaScript (and also to have a more than passing acquaintance with PHP and MYSQL, or similar server technologies).

I have tried to make things easy for you if you have limited JavaScript experience by introducing the absolute minimum of code needed to make the HTML5 technologies function, and you'll be able to achieve an awful lot with what you learn, but to get expert results you'll have to become a JavaScript expert at some point. So I recommend you make a note to get a good book on the subject next time you're in a book store.

However experienced JavaScript programmers won't find the examples trivial either, because they reveal in detail how each feature works. It's up to you to take this information and knit it into fast, tight and compelling code.

The Course of The Book

To accompany this book I have also created an online course at *udemy.com*, which contains all the information in this book and also takes you through each lecture with a screencast video tutorial that I have recorded for each.

There's also a forum attached to each lecture in which you can ask questions from me directly and I generally will have an answer within a workday or so (often much sooner). The website for the course is at the following website, where there are often generous discount offers available:

udemy.com/html5-crash-course

***Note**: While at* udemy.com *you may also wish to browse the JavaScript and other courses they offer too.*

Thanks And Good Luck

Thanks again for purchasing this book. I hope you find it teaches you everything you want to know and helps you to the next level in your web development endeavors.

- *Robin Nixon*

LECTURE 1

AN INTRODUCTION TO HTML

By following this lecture you will:

- ✓ *Obtain an overview of what HTML is and how to use it.*
- ✓ *Understand the basic syntax behind HTML tags.*
- ✓ *Know how to use attributes in HTML tags.*

IN HIS FAMOUS play for radio, *Under Milk Wood*, the poet Dylan Thomas chose to start with the words 'To begin at the beginning,' and that seems also the appropriate place to start this course on HTML5, because many of you will be new to HTML, while others will be seasoned professionals who wish to add the new skills of HTML5 to your toolkit.

If you are new to web development simply work your way through the entire course or, if you already use HTML I still recommend that you browse through these early lectures as a refresher before moving onto the HTML5 tags themselves. So let's start at the beginning and look at what HTML is all about.

Note: Each lecture includes examples and screen grabs to illustrate the techniques being explained, and you can download the example files from the companion website, at: tinyurl.com/html5ccexamples. *This is a* .zip *archive file in which each lecture is given its own folder, within which you will find the example files and associated content. For example, the examples from this lecture are all in the* Lecture 1 *folder.*

What is HTML?

HTML stands for Hyper Text Markup Language, and it was invented by Sir Timothy Berners Lee in the early 1990s to solve the problem of quickly and efficiently distributing

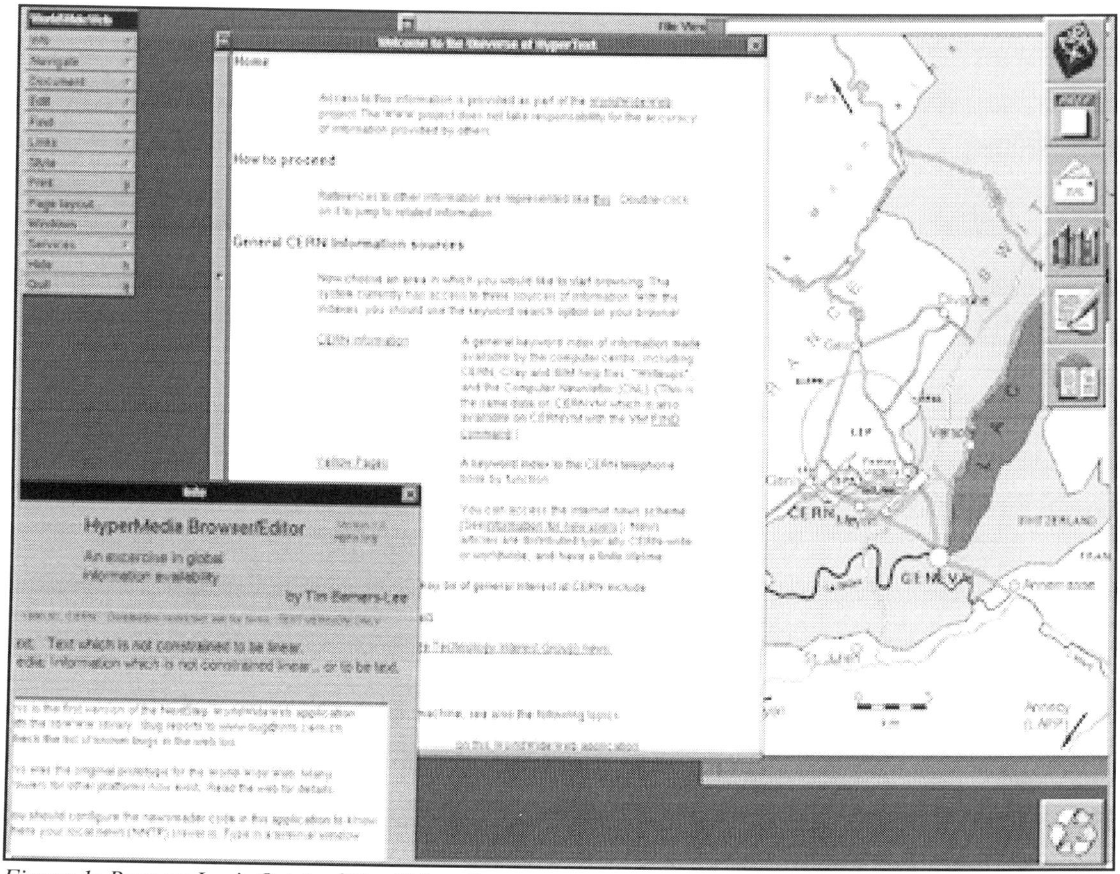

Figure 1: Berners Lee's Original NextEditor Browser

documents between scientists around the world who were working with experimenters at CERN (the European Laboratory for Particle Physics, where the Large Hadron Collider is now also situated).

The Internet was already in place and there were tens of thousands of computers connected to each other using it, but there was no easy means of publishing content for all to see, and in which references to other documents could be easily followed.

So Berners Lee created a hyper linking framework he called the Hyper Text Transfer Protocol, or HTTP (the same set of letters at the front of a web address, such as). He also created a language to use this protocol, which he called HTML (for Hyper Text Markup Language). To utilize both these new inventions he also wrote the world's first web browser, of which Figure 1-1 is a screenshot:

This was a remarkable invention and was widely hailed in the computer press of the time as heralding a new age of communication. Until then the best connectivity computer users had experienced was dialing into a local bulletin board, usually with only one, or at the most just a few phone lines attached.

You could then upload or download files and read and leave messages, but then had to log off again to allow other people to take your place. Occasionally these bulletin boards would swap messages every few days with other boards and so users could interact with people further away, but only with a huge delay.

But right away HTML changed everything because now there was a way for all these bulletin boards and, in fact, any computers to stay in touch with each other and documents could be stored in a multitude of places, which now were only ever a click away.

People all over the world could connect to a local internet host and immediately be in touch with any other person logged into any other web-connected computer. It's hard to feel that way about it now that we've had the net for so long, but at the time it was revolutionary, and within the course of a few years there were three major graphical browsers and more than five million Internet users - while today that has mushroomed into over two billion people who regularly use the web!

HTTP and HTML Basics

Let's look more closely at these two acronyms, starting with HTTP, which is the communication standard used for controlling the requests and responses that occur between a web browser running on your computer and a web server.

The job of the web server is to accept a request from a client such as a web browser and then to reply to it in the most meaningful way it can, generally (as far as you are concerned) by simply returning the contents of a requested document, but in the process many other requests and responses also take place. This returning of a web page is called *serving*, which is why the web server is so named.

In between a client and server there can be a multitude of other computers and devices such as routers, gateways and proxies. A web router chooses the best route to use in order to transfer data the fastest between the client and server.

Gateways are nodes on the edge of one network that act as a connection from it to another. Proxies support indirect connections by acting as if they are the destination (or server), and then fetching the data you request and returning it to you, often employing a cache in which commonly requested documents are stored to save repeatedly fetching them.

These devices generally use an Internet protocol suite called TCP/IP for sending all this information flying across the web, although there are other protocols that could be used to send HTML data (but which generally aren't, and are therefore beyond the scope of this course).

Unlike the bulletin boards mentioned earlier which supported only one user for each connected telephone line, web servers can use a single Internet connection to allow dozens, hundreds or even thousands of simultaneous users at a time (depending on the power of the server).

Each web server spends much of its time simply listening out for incoming requests. When one arrives the server returns a response to confirm safe receipt of the request. It does this by issuing a status message such as the following back to the client:

```
HTTP:/1.1 200 OK
```

After this the server then sends its own message, which generally will be the document that was requested by the client, or it could be an error message if the document was not found.

If a document is returned it can be in any format such as audio, video, images or, most commonly, HTML, which comprises a simple text file within which the text is separated into different sections using a special set of markup tags, and which commonly will have the extension *.htm* or *.html* (although any extension is acceptable, as long as the server knows about it). To indicate that this type of file is being sent to the client, a web server will precede the document with a header telling the client about it, which will look like this:

```
Content-Type: text/html; charset=utf-8
```

Here the type of document is clearly specified to be HTML, and the character set used by the file is set to `utf-8`. But other header types could also be sent. For example, if the requested document has been moved to a new location the web server might, instead, return the following headers:

```
HTTP/1.1 301 Moved Permanently
Location: http://myserver.com/newlocation.html
```

The first header tells the client that the document has moved and, instead of sending the document, the second line states where the document can now be found, and it's then the client's job to go off and request the document from the new location, which could be on the same or a different web server. As you might imagine, there are many more different types of headers and information that can be sent back and forward between web servers and clients, of which the most common one you may encounter is the following:

```
HTTP/1.0 404 Not Found
```

After sending this header the web server will then serve up a page explaining why the document could not be found. Because of the header response code of 404 these pages are often referred to as "404" pages.

The Request/Response Sequence

Following is an example of a web client talking to a web server from which it is requesting a file:

1. You enter a URL such as *http://myserver.com* into your browser.
2. Your browser looks up the IP address for *myserver.com*.
3. Your browser issues a request for the home page at *myserver.com*.
4. The request crosses the Internet and arrives at the *myserver.com* web server.
5. The web server looks for the web page on its hard disk.
6. The web page is retrieved by the server and returned to the browser.
7. Your browser displays the web page.

In *Step 1.* the user enters a URL (Uniform Resource Locator), also known as a web address into the browser's input field. In this instance the root document (or home page) is being requested. Once the browser receives the request it then in *Step 2.* it makes a request to a set of servers on the Internet known as domain name servers.

These translate sequences of letters such as *myserver.com* into an IP address, which consists of four groups of numbers separated by periods, like this: `173.194.66.105`. In fact, all websites reside at IP addresses and you can demonstrate this by entering `http://173.194.66.105` into a web browser, which should take you to Google's website.

However, it's difficult to remember such groups of numbers (and will become even more so when IPV6 is introduced to create extra addresses, and which uses 128 bits instead of 32 bits of data!)

Therefore a system called DNS (Domain Name System) was invented, which simply stores domain names alongside their IP addresses, so that all you need to do is enter *http://google.com*, rather than an obscure set of numbers. Your browser then performs a

DNS lookup, discovers that the IP this domain refers to is `173.194.66.105` and then initiates discussions directly with the web server at that address, as shown in *Step 3*.

In *Step 4*. the request your browser makes to the web server traverses the internet and arrives at the destination server where, in *Step 5*, the page requested (in this instance the home page), is fetched from the server's file system. In *Step 6*. the web server then transmits that page (preceded by a header) back to your web browser, which then displays the page in *Step 7*.

If the page was not found then in *Step 6*. an appropriate error header will be returned to the web browser. Also, web server scripting languages such as Perl and PHP may first manipulate the document and its contents by adding, removing or changing contents according to any embedded scripting commands. Such documents are generally recognizable by their commonly used file extensions of *.pl* (for Perl scripts) and *.php* (for PHP scripts).

The Difference Between GET and POST Requests

When requesting a document it is possible for the web client (or browser) to request additional information or send information to the web server using either `GET` or `POST` requests. A `GET` request is where data is appended to the tail of a URL in the form of a query string, like this:

```
http://google.com/search?q=html5
```

This URL directly sends the search lookup string of `html5` to the Google web servers, by passing it as a string value in the argument `q`. When Google sees this request it knows to return to you all the pages it thinks are relevant to the request. A longer such request might look like the following, in which the + symbol is used in place of spaces:

```
http://google.com/search?q=html5+crash+course
```

Here the search string `html5 crash course` is passed to Google.

In a `POST` request, however, the additional information is passed from the client to the server in the form of headers, which is neater as far as the user goes, because it does not appear as part of the URL. Both `GET` and `POST` requests are discussed in detail later in this course.

HTML Tags

HTML documents are simply text files in which extra commands have been added within angle brackets, like this `<head>`. So, for example, the tag `<i>` tells the web browser that all following text should be displayed using an italic font. And when a `</i>` is encountered the preceding `/` slash character tells the browser to disable the italics. Therefore you frequently find HTML tags in pairs. For example, in the following line of HTML the word `fox` will appear underlined, and `dog` in italics:

```
The <u>fox</u> jumps over the <i>dog</i>.
```

The result looks like this:

The <u>fox</u> jumps over the *dog*.

Some tags don't come in pairs because they are self-closing. One example is the tag `<br />`. This issues a line break to the browser which forces it to move the start point for future display of text to the start of the following line. To be compliant with a standard known as XHTML (eXtensible Hyper Text Markup Language), as used with the RSS (Really Simple Syndication) format accessed by many news reader programs, this tag must have a `/` character before the closing angle bracket, and you might see it used like this:

```
The <b>fox</b> jumps over the <i>dog</i>.<br />
```

***Note**: On many browsers you can omit this final / but because that is not standard HTML there's no guarantee that it will always work in the future.*

Tag Attributes

There is a whole lot more to HTML, though, than simply markup tags, because many of the tags either support or require the use of attributes. These are arguments that you pass alongside the tag to provide further information to the web browser.

Generally an attribute consists of a name followed by the `=` symbol and then either single or double quotation marks enclosing a value. For example, to create a hyperlink that the user can click to navigate to another document you use the `<a>` tag (which stands for anchor), like this:

```
<a href='http://google.com'>Visit Google</a>
```

In a web browser this displays simply as:

Visit Google

In this element the `href` part (which stands for hypertext reference) is the attribute, and the string `'http://google.com'` is its value. The contents between the opening and closing parts of this tag is the text `Visit Google`, which is simply displayed, and if default styling is applied it will be shown in underlined blue (although this is easy to change with HTML or CSS – there's more on this later in the course). The final `</a>` closes the tag ready for displaying in the browser.

There are several types of attributes available, with different tags supporting different attributes, but to give you an overview, here are some of the more common ones you will encounter and use:

- **`id`** This attribute is used to give a name to the object referred to by the tag so that it can be accessed using Cascading Style Sheets (CSS) or JavaScript. For example, `<h1 id='Header1'>` provides the name or `id` of `'Header1'` to the `<h1>` tag. Nothing happens to the contents of the tag (also known as an object) unless either CSS or JavaScript act upon it to, for example, apply a particular font styling.

- **`class`** This attribute lets you supply a group name that may apply to this and other objects. For example `<p class='indent'>` applies the class name `'indent'` to the `<p>` tag, which might be used by a style sheet (with a suitable rule) to indent the first line of all objects using it.

- **`style`** This attribute lets you apply a CSS style to an object by putting it within the quotation marks. For example to apply the Arial font to a paragraph object, you could use the `style` attribute like this: `<p style='font-family:Arial'>`.

- **`title`** Any object may be given a title which most browsers will use to display as a tooltip when the mouse passes over it. For example, the following anchor displays the tooltip 'Go to the Home page' when the mouse passes over it: `<a href='/' title='Go to the Home page'>`.

***Note**: CSS stands for Cascading Style Sheets, a way to separate styling from the textual content of a web page, and JavaScript is a language used within the browser to achieve dynamic effects. Both of these are beyond the scope of this course, although occasionally snippets and brief explanations of their use do appear within it.*

For further information I recommend my books Plug-in CSS, Plug-in JavaScript, *and* Learning PHP, MySQL and JavaScript, *available in all good bookstores and online. If you are developing for iOS or Android you may also be interested in my book* HTML5 for iOS and Android, *which includes tutorials for using HTML5, CSS3, JavaScript, PHP and MySQL on these portable devices.*

Summary

Now that you understand the basics of how an HTML document is put together, in the next lecture I'll introduce the different parts of an HTML document and their associated tags, such as the `<html>`, `<head>` and `<body>` sections.

LECTURE 2

THE LAYOUT OF AN HTML DOCUMENT

By following this lecture you will:

- ✓ *Learn how to use some of the basic HTML tags.*
- ✓ *Understand what style sheets and JavaScript are for.*
- ✓ *Know how to assemble a simple HTML web page.*

DON'T WORRY TOO much if *Lecture 1* has left you scratching your head. If any of it is unclear right now you will soon understand it as I take you section by section through a typical HTML document, and show you how it is laid out. If you've never used HTML before I think you'll be pleasantly surprised because it's actually very straightforward.

In this lecture I explain the different parts of an HTML document such as the `<!DOCTYPE>`, headers, scripts, CSS, meta tags and the body. In it you will gain an understanding of how a document is put together and the things it may contain.

Note*: The examples from this lecture are in the* Lecture 2 *folder of the* examples.zip *file at* tinyurlcom/html5ccexamples.

The `<!DOCTYPE>` Tag

All well formatted HTML pages begin with a line that tells the browser information about the type of content to expect. This line comprises the `<!DOCTYPE>` tag, along with some arguments if the version of HTML used is less than 5. There are a number of different arguments available for this tag, which are listed at *doctype.org* and fully explained at the website: *wikipedia.org/wiki/Doctype*. For example, a typical HTML 4 document of a type known as *transitional* will begin with the following line:

```
<!DOCTYPE HTML PUBLIC "-//W3C//DTD HTML 4.01
  Transitional//EN"
  "http://www.w3.org/TR/html4/loose.dtd">
```

As shown here the tag can be spread over more than one line if it would wrap around in your HTML editor.

In HTML5 documents, the tag has been simplified so that you only need to use the following line:

```
<!DOCTYPE html>
```

You are unlikely to need or very often see the former style of tag because all the latest versions (and some older ones too) of all major browsers will render pages either in standards mode if they do not support HTML5, or using HTML5 styling if they do. Either way, you can probably ignore older style `<!DOCTYPE>` tags except when working with legacy pages that have not been updated.

Note: *`<!DOCTYPE>` tags are unique in that they do not use a closing `</DOCTYPE>` tag, and neither do they self-close by prefacing the final bracket with a / character.*

Internet Explorer Tweak For Local Documents

Because Microsoft's Internet Explorer browser places local documents in a trusted security zone, when you open a web page containing any active content such as JavaScript, you have to click a couple of different things to confirm that you wish to grant the web page access to your computer. Obviously this is quite annoying when you are simply testing a document prior to uploading it to the Internet or using it in an app.

Fortunately there's a simple solution, which is to tell IE that the document was saved from the Internet (even though it wasn't), so that it then automatically assigns the correct security restrictions without being prompted. Therefore you can add the following IE-only tag after the `<!DOCTYPE html>` line when you will be accessing local documents using IE:

```
<!-- saved from url=(0014)about:internet -->
```

Don't worry about leaving it in your documents because it is within comment tags (see the "Using Comments" section), and so all browsers other than IE will ignore this line. You can even leave it in place when you upload documents to the web, because that is the same restricted zone that the command is setting anyway.

The upshot of this is that the HTML examples in this lecture always begin with the following two lines, and it may be useful for you to also get into this habit. But, of course, if you will not be using any active content in your web pages (such as JavaScript), the second line can be omitted:

```
<!DOCTYPE html>
<!-- saved from url=(0014)about:internet -->
```

The `<html>` Tag

This tag notified the web browser that a section of HTML follows. The end of the section should be noted with a matching `</html>` tag to indicate closure.

Any content outside of these tags will be treated simply as text by most browsers unless it is within other tags or comments (explained later).

***Note**: Many browsers are forgiving and do their best to display a page well, even with missing or misplaced `<html>` or other tags. But it's best to get things in the right order to ensure that all browsers display your content well.*

Within a pair of `<html>` tags there are generally two other tags used to contain the header and body text of the document. These are `<head>` and `<body>`.

The `<head>` Tag

This tag indicates that the HTML within it and its closing `</head>` tag contains further information about the document such as its title, metadata, style sheets and JavaScript. At its simplest the head section of an HTML document may look like this:

```
<head>
  <title>Welcome to my website</title>
</head>
```

Creating a Document Title

As you saw in the previous example, setting the title of your document is as easy as enclosing it with a pair of `<title>` and `</title>` tags. The title will appear at the top of the browser in the title bar and will be used by search engines such as Google for indexing your website. Therefore make sure the title is clear, precise, succinct, and contains relevant keywords to the page's contents. So, if your website is about right-handed widgets (for example), a better title might be something like this:

```
<title>
  RH Widgets Inc: Suppliers of Right-Handed Widgets
</title>
```

***Note**: Using phrases such as "Welcome to…" was great in the 1990s when the Internet was new and there were few websites. But in the modern age (when a user might browse dozens of sites in a single session) these phrases are superfluous 'noise' that most people* *ignore. In my view it's far better to get down to the point immediately, before the user surfs off to a competitor's site.*

Including Style Sheets

Cascading Style sheets (CSS) are not really covered in this course but you need to know about them. If you don't already know they are sets of rules used to describe the layout of an HTML document that are kept separately from the content.

This is done to free the content from its layout so that different designs can easily be swapped in according to need. For example, a web page can be restyled with basic CSS to make it more suitable for printing, and some CSS rules can be used to help audio page readers read out a web page to visually impaired people.

More than that, you can change the entire look and feel of a website by altering a few simple CSS rules – something that is very time-consuming to accomplish if the styling is embedded in with the web page's contents.

There are different ways of incorporating CSS rules in a document, including embedding them in with the text, or as a set of rules within the `<head>` section of an HTML document using `<style>` and `</style>` tags, like the following (which tells the browser to display all level 1 headings – explained later – in red):

```
<style>
  h1 { color:red; }
</style>
```

Or, by saving all the CSS rules in a separate document, you can simply include a single line in the `<head>` of a document to include them. The latter is the preferred method of most developers, and you perform it using the self-closing `<link />` tag, like this:

```
<link rel='stylesheet' href='styles.css'
  type='text/css' />
```

***Note**: Since this book only uses a little CSS in passing it will not be discussed in further detail, but you may be interested in reading my books* Plug-In CSS *or* HTML5 for iOS and Android, *which both include in-depth tutorials on the use of CSS (and also CSS3 in the case of the latter).*

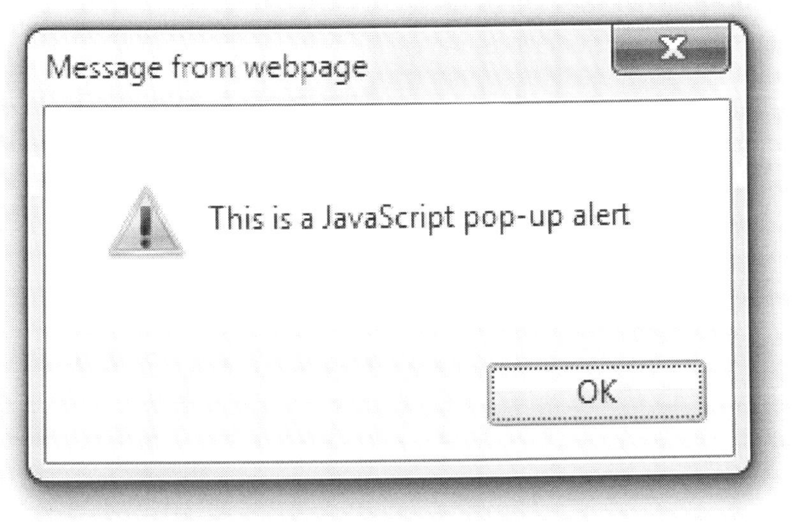

Figure 1: A JavaScript alert window

Incorporating JavaScript

This course doesn't really cover JavaScript, but some elements of HTML5 require its use. Generally JavaScript is included within a web page by either creating a section within `<script>` and `</script>` tags, or by adding a `src` argument to the `<script>` tag to load in an external file.

For example, the following HTML specifies a script that is embedded within `<script>` tags (the result of running this code is shown in Figure 2:1):

```
<script>
  alert('This is a JavaScript pop-up alert')
</script>
```

Like all JavaScript the above example can be placed anywhere within an HTML document, but you will most often find scripts in the `<head>` section of web pages, so that they load in and execute before the body of a document.

If scripts are longer than a few lines they will often be saved as external files that are then loaded in as follows:

```
<script src='ProgramCode.js'></script>
```

The file *ProgramCode.js* is then loaded in from the current folder and its contents are executed as if all its commands were contained within the `<script>` tags. However, the JavaScript examples in this course are short, and for ease of comprehension they are (almost) always inserted alongside the HTML elements upon which they act.

JavaScript `<script>` tags require you to specify the type of script as being JavaScript (for example: `<script type="text/javascript">`) but all major browsers allow you to omit this and so I generally do so to save on typing. But if you find yourself with a strict program editor, or your programming styles at your company require, it then you'll need to use the full string.

You may also see instances of `<script language="javascript">` if you view the source of some websites, but this is deprecated (no longer recommended) and should not be used.

Passing Meta Data

It is possible to provide additional information to an HTML document that the browser can use (if it understands it). Such data is sent using the `<meta />` tag. For example, you can tell a browser to exchange the current page for another one after a set length of time, like this:

```
<meta http-equiv='refresh'
  content='10;url=http://othersite.com' />
```

This meta command uses the `http-equiv` argument with the value of `'refresh'` to tell the browser that a refresh is being requested.

The `content` argument has the value `'10;url=http://othersite.com'`, which states that after 10 seconds the web page at *http://othersite.com* should replace the current one. Note also that this a self-closing tag; instead of using a `</meta>` tag to close it, a `/` is placed before the closing angle bracket.

Other uses of the `<meta />` tag include setting the width of the document for portable browsing hardware such as phones and tablets. This is done using the `viewport` argument, and a common width you see used is 960 pixels, which is the width of the iPhone 4's screen.

However such documents are not restricted to only devices of at least that width because all this setting does is say how many pixels of width your document uses. Devices of differing resolutions will then render at that width but then zoom in or out, or rescale as necessary to enable your pages to display at their best. So, for example, to specify a document with of 960 pixels you might use the following tag:

```
<meta name='viewport' content='width=960' />
```

With both these tags applied, a head section of HTML might look like this:

```
<head>
  <title>Welcome to my website</title>
  <meta http-equiv='refresh'
    content='10;url=http://othersite.com' />
  <meta name='viewport' content='width=960' />
</head>
```

However, as a beginner, on the whole you will probably mostly use only the `<title>` tag in the `<head>` section until you become more proficient at HTML.

***Note**: The `<meta />` tag is an unusual use of HTML (particularly for newcomers) but you need to be aware of it even if you don't use it, as it often crops up containing a variety of different meta data.*

The <body> Tag

You place the contents of an HTML document inside a pair of `<body>` and `</body>` tags. Web browsers then know to display everything they find in there, and the HTML you need can be as simple as this:

```
<body>
  This is the body of the document
</body>
```

As you will learn in *Lecture 3*, there are dozens of tags you can use within the body of a document, but by default you can simply place some text and it will be displayed in your browser's default text font and size.

Summary

When all the parts I have described so far are brought together, but including only the document's title in the `<head>` (without JavaScript or meta data etc.) a basic HTML document will look something like this:

```
<!DOCTYPE html>
<!-- saved from url=(0014)about:internet -->
<html>
  <head>
    <title>The Web Page's Title</title>
  </head>
  <body>
    This is the body of the document
  </body>
</html>
```

As you can see, it's quite simple really and nothing to be frightened of. Each section such as `<head>` or `<body>` is closed with a matching `</head>` or `</body>` tag, and the enclosing `<html>` tag is closed right at the document end with a `</html>` tag.

In the following lecture I'll delve more deeply into the `<body>` tag and show you how to use the various tags it supports.

LECTURE 3

THE HTML DOCUMENT BODY

By following this lecture you will:

✓ *Learn how to document your HTML code.*

✓ *Understand headings, paragraphs and line breaks.*

✓ *Know how to use a variety of styling tags.*

IN THE FIRST two lectures I introduced HTML and explained the different sections it requires. In this lecture I will start to look more closely at the body section of an HTML document, which resides within `<body>` and `</body>` tags.

The `<body>` section of HTML is where you place all the things that the web browser should display. At its simplest you can place plain text in this section and the browser will display it for you.

However, no matter how many spaces, carriage returns or other characters you place within this text, browsers will ignore them and just display the text in one long string. So let's look at how you can format this text to start making it look much more interesting.

Note: *The examples from this lecture are in the* Lecture 3 *folder of the* examples.zip *file at* tinyurlcom/html5ccexamples.

Inserting Comments

To start with let's kick off with comments, probably the simplest type of HTML formatting, and something you place in a document to be seen only in the source, and which is not displayed by the browser.

To do this you place your comment between the opening `<!--` and closing `-->` tags, like this:

```
<!-- This is a comment and will not be displayed -->
```

Comments are useful for detailing the author of a document, and explaining how a document develops. To allow for this, comments may be as long as you like and include as many lines as you wish. They close only when the `-->` tag is encountered, so the following is an example of a legal comment string:

```
<!--
  Created by Joe Brown on July 27th 2014.
  Updated Sept 15 2014 by JB: Improved Ad display.
  Updated  Jan 12 2015 by PB: Updated login script.
-->
```

You can also use comments to temporarily remove sections of HTML that you don't want to display, perhaps because you are highly organized and have written something in advance of a product release, so that you only need to uncomment it on release day (beware of people viewing your source code though).

Comments are also useful for hiding sections from displaying so you can concentrate on debugging only those sections that you may be having a problem with.

***Note**: Although I have waited until this lecture to discuss comments, you should know that you can apply them to any section of HTML, not just the body of a document. This means you can comment out sections in the head or even an entire `<html>` ... `</html>` section if you wish.*

The HTML 4.01 Tags

HTML 4.01 supports almost 100 different tags, but since this is a course on HTML5 I will not go into all of them in detail. Rather, in this lecture I concentrate of some of the main tags and how you use them, and then briefly list the lesser-used ones and the arguments they require.

This includes various text formatting tags, for headings, paragraphs, text emphasis and lists. Then there are the tags for changing text and background colors and font faces, as well as tags for embedding media such as images, creating hyperlinks, building tables and forms, and much more.

By doing this you will get a good grounding in HTML 4.0 before moving onto the new features in HTML5

The <div> and <span> tags

The `<div>` and `<span>` tags were created to help with combining elements into groups Their main purpose is enable the contained elements to be manipulated ensemble from style sheets. The `<div>` tag creates what is called a block element in that by default its width stretches all the way to the browser's right hand edge, forcing any following elements onto the line below. Therefore all `<div>` elements have four sides and are rectangular.

On the other hand the `<span>` tag creates an inline element that flows with the text, and it is therefore particularly suited for applying styles to sections of text. Although this course doesn't teach CSS, it is inextricably entwined with HTML and so, from time to time I may employ either `<div>` or `<span>` tags with suitable CSS styling where standard HTML does not provide the solution required.

You use the tags as follows:

```
<div>This is some text in a div element</div>
<span>This is some text in a span element</span>
```

The main practical difference between the two that you will usually notice is that `<div>` elements by default force a line break before and after them, whereas `<span>` elements do not. You will see how to add CSS styles to them in the *Text Emphasis* section, a little further on.

***Note**: Simply think of each of these two types of elements as invisible containers in which text and/or other elements are placed, and which can be styled with CSS. Remember that* `<div>` *elements are rectangular, while* `<span>` *elements go with the flow of text, line by line along and down the screen.*

Headings

Let's now look at some of the commonly-used tags, those for formatting text, starting with headings. To specify headings in HTML documents you must enclose them in any one of six different pairs of tags, from `<h1>` through to `<h6>`, and their counterpart closing tags `</h1>` through `</h6>`. The `<h1>` heading is the largest, and `<h6>` is the smallest. Headings are also generally emboldened to help them stand out from the body even more.

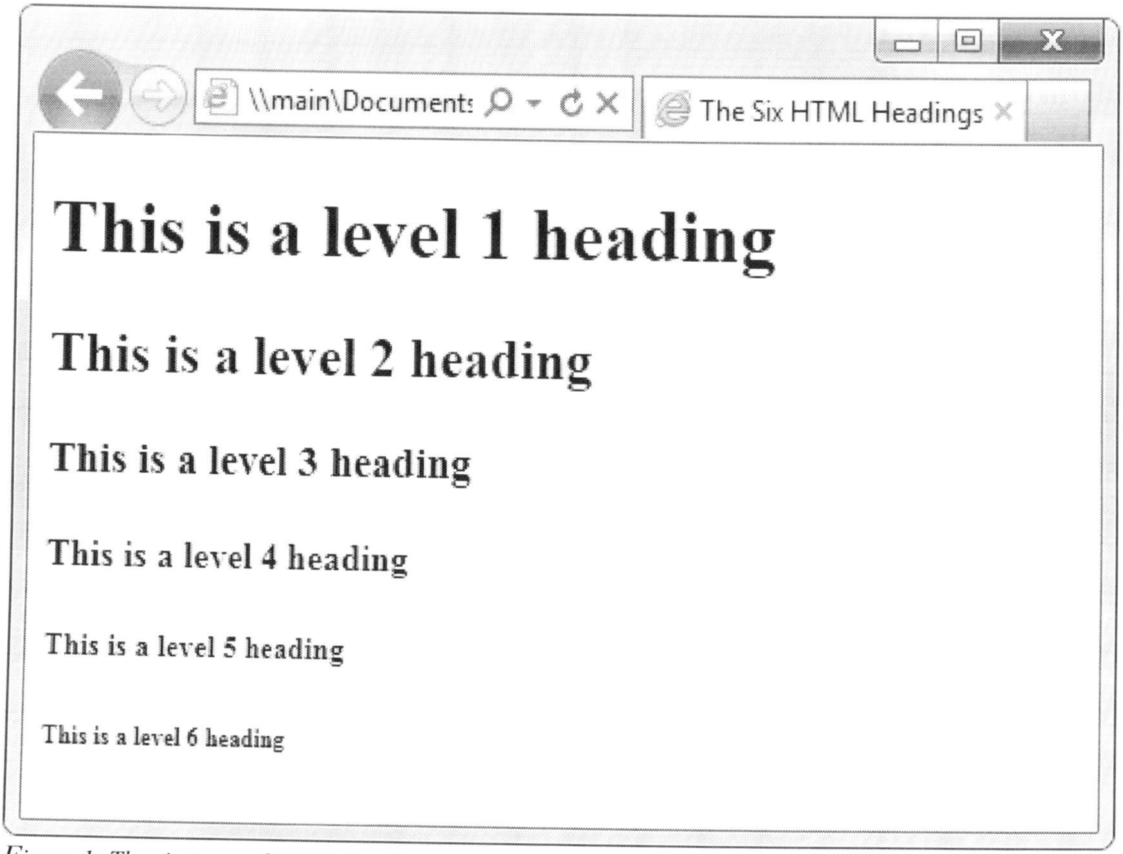

Figure 1: The six types of HTML heading

Here are examples of each heading type, and the result of using them is shown in Figure 3-1:

```
<h1>This is a level 1 heading</h1>
<h2>This is a level 2 heading</h2>
<h3>This is a level 3 heading</h3>
<h4>This is a level 4 heading</h4>
<h5>This is a level 5 heading</h5>
<h6>This is a level 6 heading</h6>
```

***Note**: Interestingly the 5th and 6th level headings are by default displayed smaller than standard body text. However most writers will agree that if you need to go any deeper than four levels you are probably overcomplicating the subject and should consider reworking your content. For this reason (and the previously mentioned reason of small) size I rarely use `<h5>` and `<h6>`.*

Once you have split a web document, with suitable headings inserted in appropriate places using these tags, it is much easier for your readers to comprehend and quickly read it. This is because it is easier on the eye with more whitespace, and each separate topic has its own heading, making it easier to focus in on what interests the reader.

Paragraphs

Each of your paragraphs should be enclosed within <p> and </p> tags so that web browsers know how to handle them.

By default it will ensure the correct default spacing between each paragraph and, with the addition of CSS you can further modify styling by, for example, indenting the first line of each, or by choosing ragged or full justification, and so on.

Here is an example of a simple paragraph taken from Matthew 7:7-8 in the Bible (I like to read English text in examples pages and tend to use that, Shakespeare, Dickens and so on, rather than using Lorem Ipsum Latin text), and formatted as an HTML paragraph:

```
<p>Ask, and it shall be given you; seek, and you
shall find; knock, and it shall be opened unto you:
For every one that asks receives; and he that seeks
finds; and to him that knocks it shall be opened.</p>
```

This paragraph will display as a single line that wraps around only when the text encounters the edge of its containing element. So, for example, it might display like the following ragged justified text:

```
Ask, and it shall be given you; seek, and you shall
find; knock, and it shall be opened unto you: For every
one that asks receives; and he that seeks finds; and to
him that knocks it shall be opened.
```

Line Breaks

What a line break does is interrupt the default flow of text from left to right and then down to the next line (or right to left if that option has been enabled, either with CSS or by modifying the <html> tag to make text read from right to left like this: <html dir='RTL'>), so that the next element displayed is forced to the start of the line below.

Sometimes you have a reason for sending a line break to the browser before the end of a paragraph. This is done using the `<br />` tag which, you will notice, is self-closing and not part of a pair of tags.

So, if you need to make sure some text (or any sequence of HTML elements) displays exactly how you want, you can force its formatting, for example, as with the following reformatting of the Matthew quotation:

```
<p>Ask, and it shall be given you;<br />
seek, and you shall find;<br />
knock, and it shall be opened unto you:<br />
For every one that asks receives;<br />
and he that seeks finds;<br />
and to him that knocks it shall be opened.</p>
```

This HTML will display as follows – as long as its containing element is wide enough:

```
Ask, and it shall be given you;
seek, and you shall find;
knock, and it shall be opened unto you:
For every one that asks receives;
and he that seeks finds;
and to him that knocks it shall be opened.
```

Whatever is next in your HTML to be displayed, whether an image, a video or some text, the `<br />` will always force it down to continue on the next line. There is also a special case of this tag which is used to clear any temporary left or right alignment.

For example, it is possible to display an image with left alignment so that text flows down its right hand side (there's more on how to do this later in the section on including images).

But if you have insufficient text to fill in all the space to the right of the picture before the next paragraph or heading, then that would also appear beside it.

In such cases you can use the `<br />` tag to clear any alignment and force further text (or other elements) to appear not just down a line, but under the image or other object around which the text has been flowing.

There are three versions of the tag to do this, for clearing left alignment, right alignment, and all alignments respectively, as follows:

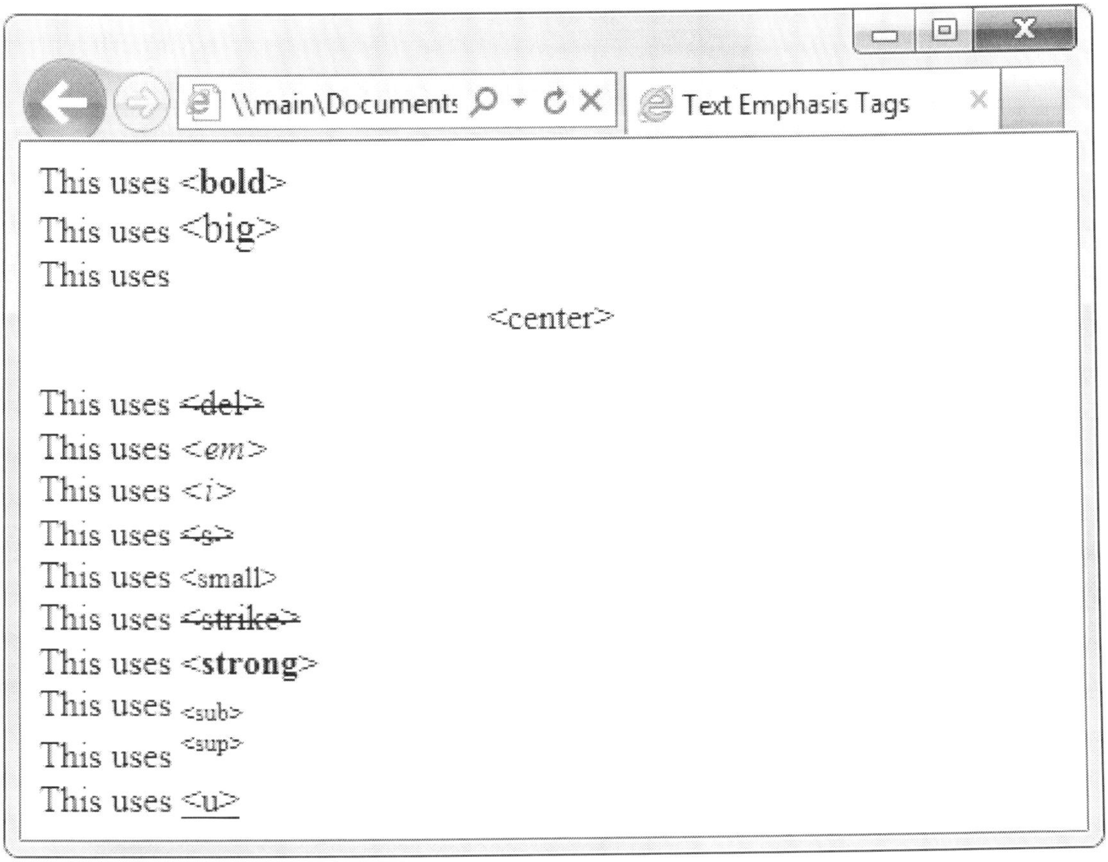

Figure 2: The text emphasis tags and how they display

```
<br clear='left' />
<br clear='right' />
<br clear='all' />
```

Text Emphasis

There are many different ways you can change the emphasis of text in HTML, each with an accompanying tag. For example you can embolden, italicize, underline and strike through text, and you can also display text in superscript or subscript.

Following are the most common HTML tags you will use for this, the results of using which you can see in Figure 3-2. Some of these tags are deprecated, which means that it has been decided that they may be removed from the HTML specification at a later date.

However, the practicality of billions of web pages already employing them means that this is unlikely to ever happen, otherwise too many websites would break.

<b> ... </b>

Text within these tags will appear in bold face. This is the same as using the `<strong>` tag, but it is possible to style this tag differently to `<strong>` with CSS.

<big> ... </big>

Text within these tags will be bigger than that outside.

<center> ... </center>

Text within these tags will appear centered. However, these tags are deprecated and you are recommended to use CSS in their place. Note how in Figure 3-2 you can see that by using this tag, if the text within it is not already at the start of a line, then a line break will automatically be issued first. A line break is also issued after closing this tag, so beware of adding one yourself, which would result in a double line break.

<del> ... </del>

Text within these tags will appear with a ~~strike through~~ line through it. This is the same as using the `<s>` and `<strike>` tags (although they are deprecated and therefore not recommended). It is possible to style this tag differently to `<s>` and `<strike>` with CSS.

<em> ... </em>

Normally text within these tags is displayed in *italics*, and so it is the same as using `<i>`, but it is possible to style this tag differently to `<i>` using CSS.

<i> ... </i>

Text within these tags will appear in *italics*. This is the same as using the `<em>` tag, but it is possible to style this tag differently to `<em>` with CSS.

Figure 3: Using CSS to create text emphasis

<s> ... </s>

Text within these tags will appear with a ~~strike through~~ line through it. These tags are the same as using <strike> but are deprecated, and so you are recommended to either use CSS, or the <del> tag in its place. If you do use this tag you can use CSS to style it differently to both <strike> and <del> if you wish. A CSS alternative might be, for example:

```
<span style='text-decoration:line-through;'> ... </span>
```

<small> ... </small>

Text within these tags will be shown smaller than that outside.

<strike> ... </strike>

The same as <s>, although like <s> it is deprecated and <del> is recommended instead. If you do use it, it is possible to style this tag differently to <s> and <del> using CSS.

<strong> ... </strong>

Normally text within these tags is displayed in **bold** face, and so it is the same as using <b>, but it is possible to style this tag differently to <b> using CSS.

_{...}

Text within these tags will appear $_{\text{subscripted}}$.

^{...}

Text within these tags will appear superscripted.

<u> … </u>

Text within these tags will appear underlined.

The <u> is deprecated and you are recommended to use CSS in its place, for example:

```
<span style='font-style:italic;'> ... </span>
```

Remember, though, that although the deprecated tags are unlikely to ever be removed from the HTML specification because they are so widely used, it *could* happen, so it makes sense to use the alternatives if you can.

Although I have shown ways of embedding CSS rules within <span> tags to achieve strike through and underlined text, it is generally better to create a class containing the rule and to apply the class. Doing so in detail is beyond the scope of this course, but the following snippet shows one way of doing this (using a period symbol in front of the class names in the <style> section):

```
<head>
  <style>
    .italic { font-style:italic; }
    .strike { text-decoration:line-through; }
  </style>
</head>
<body>
  This is <span class='italic'>italic</span>.<br />
  This is <span class='strike'>strike through</span>.
</body>
```

Figure 3-3 shows the preceding example being displayed in a web browser

Summary

Armed with the tags you have learned so far you can already create some quite impressive HTML documents, but in the following lecture I add even more tools to your kit by showing how to change font face and color, and embed images in your documents.

LECTURE 4

FONTS, COLORS AND IMAGES

By following this lecture you will:

- ✓ *Be able to select from a variety of font faces.*
- ✓ *Know how to change a font color by name or number.*
- ✓ *Understand how to display images in your HTML.*

SO FAR YOU have learned about the structure of an HTML document, and how to format and emphasize text to present it well.

In this lecture I will show you how to change the font face and size of any text, as well as how to add coloring to the text foreground or background of, and how to load in and display images in a document, including on-the-fly resizing.

Note*: The examples from this lecture are in the* Lecture 4 *folder of the* examples.zip *file at* tinyurlcom/html5ccexamples.

Changing Font Face And Color

Even without using CSS there are many ways you can use HTML to change the way a font displays by passing different arguments to the `<font>` tag. However, the use of this tag (and another called `<basefont>`) has been deprecated. This means that at some time in the future they could be removed from HTML, but I seriously doubt this will ever happen since they are so widely used on billions of pages worldwide, which would all break if the tags were disabled.

It's true that CSS is a better way to manage colors, but this is a course on HTML, and so I will show you what you can achieve with it. Once you've mastered HTML, though, I strongly advise you learn CSS if you haven't already.

Anyway, let's start off this lecture with the `<font>` tag.

<font color='...'> ... </font>

The color of the text is changed to the value in the quotation marks. This value may be a color name (see the following section *The Named Colors*) or a color number (see the *Coloring By Numbers* section). For example:

```
<font color='red'>This is red text</font>
```

<font face='...'> ... </font>

The font face of the text is changed to the value in the quotation marks. This value should be the name of a font available to the browser. If the font is not found a replacement will be selected. For example:

```
<font face='Arial'>This text is in the Arial font</font>
```

<font size='...'> ... </font>

The font size of the text is changed to the value in the quotation marks. This should be a value between 1 and 7 (from smallest to largest size font, with a default of 3). The value may be preceded with a + or - symbol to indicate a relative rather than absolute change of size. For example:

```
<font size='5'>This is font size 5</font>
<font size='-1'>This is a smaller font size</font>
```

You may combine any or all of the `color`, `face`, and `size` arguments in a single `<font>` tag, for example, like this:

```
<font color='red' face='Arial' size='5'>
  This is red, size 5 text, in the Arial font
</font>
```

<basefont> ... </basefont>

Additionally you can use the global tag `<basefont>`, which has the same attributes as the `<font>` tag but is used to change the default font values for an entire document. In particular, if the size is changed then any use of the `<font>` tag with `+` or `-` values will change the font's size relative to the value specified for the base font.

***Note**: Headings are not affected by the `<basefont>` tag and on some browsers tables do not use this tag's values either.*

<body bgcolor='...'>

You can change the default background color of a web page by specifying your choice of color as an argument to the `<body>` tag, like this, which sets it to cyan:

```
<body bgcolor='cyan'>
```

The Named Colors

All browsers support 16 main color names for the color attribute values, including: `aqua`, `black`, `blue`, `fuchsia`, `gray`, `green`, `lime`, `maroon`, `navy`, `olive`, `purple`, `red`, `silver`, `teal`, `white`, and `yellow`.

Modern browsers support many more color names (up to 147) but they are not part of the HTML standard. Among other options, you can often add the words `dark` or `light` before a color name, but do check that all browsers you intend to support work with these color names. Here are some examples:

```
<body bgcolor='lightgreen'>
<font color='darkblue'>
<font color='navajowhite'>
```

***Note**: Here is the complete list of available color names:* aliceblue, antiquewhite, aqua, aquamarine, azure, beige, bisque, black, blanchedalmond, blueviolet, brown, burlywood, cadetblue, chartreuse, chocolate, coral, cornflowerblue, cornsilk, crimson, cyan, darkblue, darkcyan, darkgoldenrod, darkgray, darkgreen, darkgrey, darkkhaki, darkmagenta, darkolivegreen, darkorange, darkorchid, darkred, darksalmon, darkseagreen, darkslateblue, darkslategray, darkslategrey, darkturquoise, darkviolet, deeppink, deepskyblue, dimgray, dimgrey, dodgerblue, firebrick, floralwhite, forestgreen, fuchsia, gainsboro, ghostwhite, gold, goldenrod, gray, green, greenyellow, grey, honeydew, hotpink, indianred, indigo, ivory, khaki, lavender, lavenderblush, lawngreen, lemonchiffon, lightblue, lightcoral, lightcyan, lightgoldenrodyellow, lightgray, lightgreen, lightgrey, lightpink, lightsalmon, lightseagreen, lightskyblue, lightslategray, lightslategrey, lightsteelblue, lightyellow, lime, limegreen, linen, magenta, maroon, mediumaquamarine, mediumblue, mediumorchid, mediumpurple, mediumseagreen, mediumslateblue, mediumspringgreen, mediumturquoise, mediumvioletred, midnightblue, mintcream, mistyrose, moccasin, navajowhite, navy, oldlace, olive, olivedrab, orange, orangered, orchid, palegoldenrod, palegreen, paleturquoise, palevioletred, papayawhip, peachpuff, peru, pink, plum, powderblue, purple, red, rosybrown, royalblue, saddlebrown, salmon, sandybrown, seagreen, seashell, sienna, silver, skyblue, slateblue, slategray, slategrey, snow, springgreen, steelblue, tan, teal, thistle, tomato, turquoise, violet, wheat, white, whitesmoke, yellow *and* yellowgreen.

If you need a wider choice of colors, you should really use hexadecimal color numbers, which allow very precise color selection, as explained following.

Coloring By Numbers

In place of providing color names to HTML tags you can be much more precise by passing numeric values instead. To do this you start off with a `#` symbol and follow it with six hexadecimal numbers comprising three pairs, which represent the primary colors of red, green and blue.

For example, numbers in hexadecimal go from `0` through to `F`, rather than the `0` to `9` we are used to in decimal notation. Therefore a single hexadecimal digit can represent any of 16 different values (instead of 10 in decimal). This means that two hexadecimal digits together can represent 256 values (16 x 16, between `00` and `FF`), and therefore it is possible to create a color out of any one of 256 levels of red, 256, green and 256 blue – over 16 million colors.

This is done by following the `#` symbol with six hexadecimal digits, like this, for example: `#006699`, which indicates a color comprising hexadecimal (and decimal) `00` red, hexadecimal `66` (102 decimal) of green, and hexadecimal `99` (153 decimal) of blue.

Therefore the value `#000000` specifies the color black because it assigns values of `00` to red, `00` to green and `00` to blue. On the other hand a value of `#FFFF00` specifies the color yellow because it assigns values of `FF` to red, `FF` to green and `00` to blue (on a computer, combining red and green results in the color yellow).

For example, the following tag changes the font color to orange:

```
<font color='#FF8800'>This is orange text</font>
```

***Note**: You may use either the lower case letters* `a-f`*, or the upper case* `A-F`*, or a combination in hexadecimal color values. Also, in some browsers (but not Internet Explorer) if you are prepared to sacrifice the availability of over 16 million possible colors for a more limiting 4,000 or so, you can use a single hexadecimal digit for each primary color in a value, rather than two of them, like this:* `#000`*, or* `#148`*. The former is the color black, while the latter is shorthand for the color* `#104080` *– in other words all the zeros are omitted but some web browsers know to add them back in. However, color values of either length (three or six hexadecimal digits) are accepted by CSS rules (as opposed to HTML) in* all *browsers.*

Font Faces

There are a number of fonts available to a web browser, depending upon their availability in the underlying operating system. Therefore, when you choose a font name, you are permitted to select alternative, or second-best fonts, in order of preference so that a web page will degrade gracefully according to your font preferences.

For example, as a backup in cases where a computer may not have the Arial font installed, you might choose to ask the browser to choose the best sans-serif font it can find by using the following syntax:

```
<font face='Arial, sans-serif'>
  This is Arial, or sans-serif if unavailable
</font>
```

Following is a list of all the main fonts that are likely to be available on most PCs, Macs, Linux boxes or other modern computers, along with one or more suitable substitutes where the chosen font isn't available. Simply enter the entire string as the `face` argument to a `<font>` tag to select it.

- `"Arial, sans-serif"`
- `"'Arial Black', sans-serif"`
- `"'Arial Narrow', sans-serif"`
- `"'Avant Garde', sans-serif"`
- `"Bookman, 'Bookman Old Style', serif"`
- `"'Century Gothic', sans-serif"`

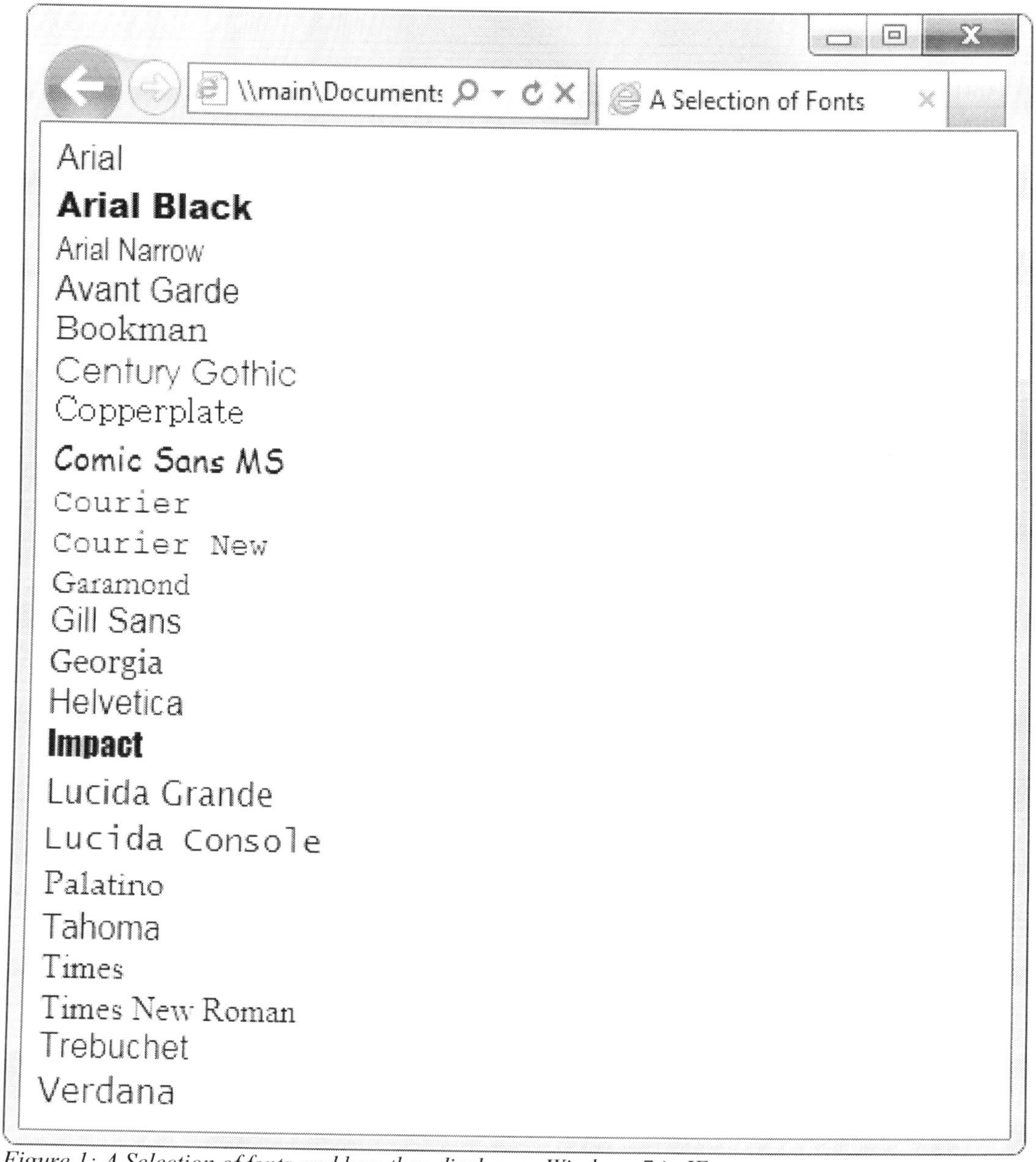

Figure 1: A Selection of fonts and how they display on Windows 7 in IE

- `"Copperplate, 'Copperplate Gothic Light', serif"`
- `"'Comic Sans MS', cursive"`
- `"Courier, monospace"`
- `"'Courier New', monospace"`
- `"Garamond, serif"`
- `"'Gill Sans', 'Gill Sans MT', sans-serif"`
- `"Georgia, serif"`

- "Helvetica, sans-serif"
- "Impact, fantasy"
- "'Lucida Grande', 'Lucida Sans Unicode', sans-serif"
- "'Lucida Console', monospace"
- "Palatino, 'Palatino Linotype', serif"
- "Tahoma, sans-serif"
- "Times, serif"
- "'Times New Roman', serif"
- "Trebuchet, sans-serif"
- "Verdana, sans-serif"

For example, for the Lucida Grande font enter the string shown, like this:

```
<font face="'Lucida Grande',
  'Lucida Sans Unicode', sans-serif">
  This is Lucid Grande, or Lucida Sans Unicode,
  or sans-serif if both are unavailable.
</font>
```

Figure 4-1 shows how these font strings display on a standard Windows 7 computer using Internet Explorer. You can also use these strings without the double quotes (but keeping the single ones) as part of CSS rules for changing a font face, like this:

```
<span style="font-family:Palatino,
  'Palatino Linotype', serif;">
  This is Palatino, or Palatino Linotype, or serif
  if both are unavailable.
</font>
```

***Note**: The single quotation marks are required within the double quotes to encapsulate font face names that contain spaces in them.*

Or, better still employ a CSS class which you create in a separate CSS style sheet or within `<style> … </style>` tags in the `<head>` of your document. For more on using CSS you may wish to refer to my book *Plug-In CSS*, which includes a comprehensive tutorial on CSS.

Displaying Images

Images are easily displayed in a web page and various image types are supported, mainly including *.jpg*, *.gif* and *.png*. Each of these has different features and drawbacks. For

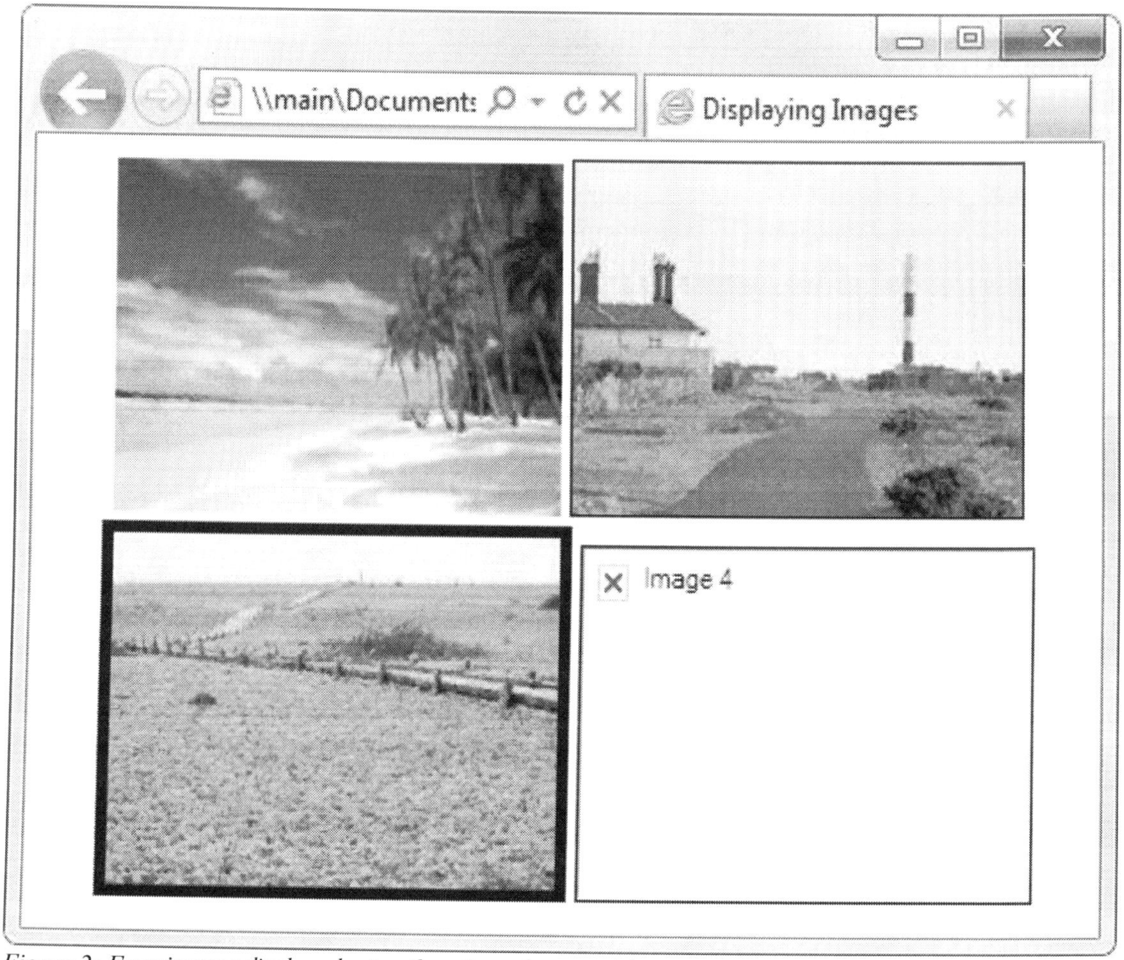

Figure 2: Four images displayed using the `<img />` *tag, with one missing*

example *.gif* images can be animated, but display fewer colors, *.jpg* images display more colors but may employ a lossy compression technique that introduces distortions, while *.png* images offer the best of both worlds, but can be larger. You include an image in your HTML using the `<img />` tag (note that it is self-closing) accompanied by one or more of the following arguments:

- **`src`** The value inside the quotes tells the browser where to fetch the image from. If it is preceded with the string `http://` then the image will be downloaded from the website at the domain following the `http://`. Otherwise the image is assumed to be on the current website (or on the local disc) and is loaded from there.
- **`alt`** Some browsers do not display images or their display may have been disabled so you can use this attribute to provide alternate text describing the image. This is also useful in cases where an image is slow or fails to load, as shown by the fourth

image in Figure 4-2, in which the alternate text is displayed due to the image not being found.

- **width** and/or **height** By default web browsers will look up an image's dimensions and display it using them. But sometimes you may wish to display an image using a different width and height, which you can specify using one or both of these attributes. If only one attribute is used the browser will compute the other dimension such that the image will stay in proportion. Another reason to specify an image's width and height is to ensure page layout is correctly aligned even before the image is loaded. By specifying these values in advance the browser will allocate the space required for the image right away.
- **border** Using this attribute you can specify the width of border (if any) to apply to an image. It accepts the value `0` or any positive number. Unless modified by CSS, if an image has a border and is placed with an anchor, the border color will change when the mouse passes over it. The three images that could be loaded in Figure 4-2 have no border, a `1` pixel border and a `5` pixel border respectively.
- **align** With this attribute you can position an image vertically by aligning it within the current line using any of the values: `top`, `middle`, `bottom`, `absmiddle` or `absbottom`. You can also align it to the left or right of the current line using the values `left` or `right`.

The lines of HTML used to create Figure 4-2 are as follows:

```
<img src='image1.png' border='0'
   width='200' height='150' alt='Image 1' />
<img src='image2.jpg' border='1'
   width='200' height='150' alt='Image 2' />
<img src='image3.gif' border='5'
   width='200' height='150' alt='Image 3' />
<img src='image4.png' border='1'
   width='200' height='150' alt='Image 4' />
```

In *Lecture 3* I introduced the `<br />` tag, which is used for creating a line break, and mentioned that it also had a secondary purpose, which is to clear left or right alignment. Well here's how that works. Figure 4-3 shows an image being displayed using left alignment with some text flowing to its right. It was created with the following HTML:

```
<img src='image1.png' align='left' />

<p>An island or isle is any piece of sub-continental
land that is surrounded by water. Very small islands
such as emergent land features on atolls can be called
islets, cays or keys.</p>
```

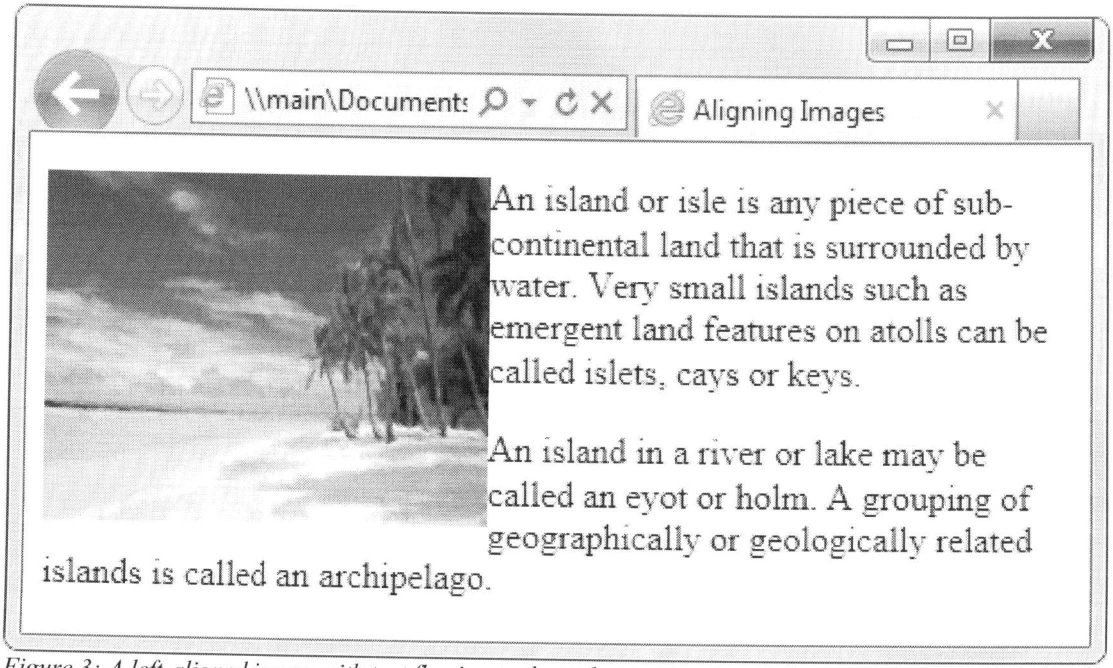

Figure 3: A left-aligned image with text flowing to the right

```
    <p>An island in a river or lake may be called an eyot or
    holm. A grouping of geographically or geologically
    related islands is called an archipelago.</p>
```

Disregarding (for now) the fact that the text butts right up against the image, it also seems rather messy because the second paragraph probably should begin under the image.

To fix this the `<br clear='left' />` tag is used (although `clear='all'` would also work in this instance) prior to closing the first paragraph, as follows, with the result shown in Figure 4-4:

```
<img src='image1.png' align='left' />

    <p>An island or isle is any piece of sub-continental
    land that is surrounded by water. Very small islands
    such as emergent land features on atolls can be called
    islets, cays or keys. <br clear='left' /></p>

    <p>An island in a river or lake may be called an eyot or
    holm. A grouping of geographically or geologically
    related islands is called an archipelago.</p>
```

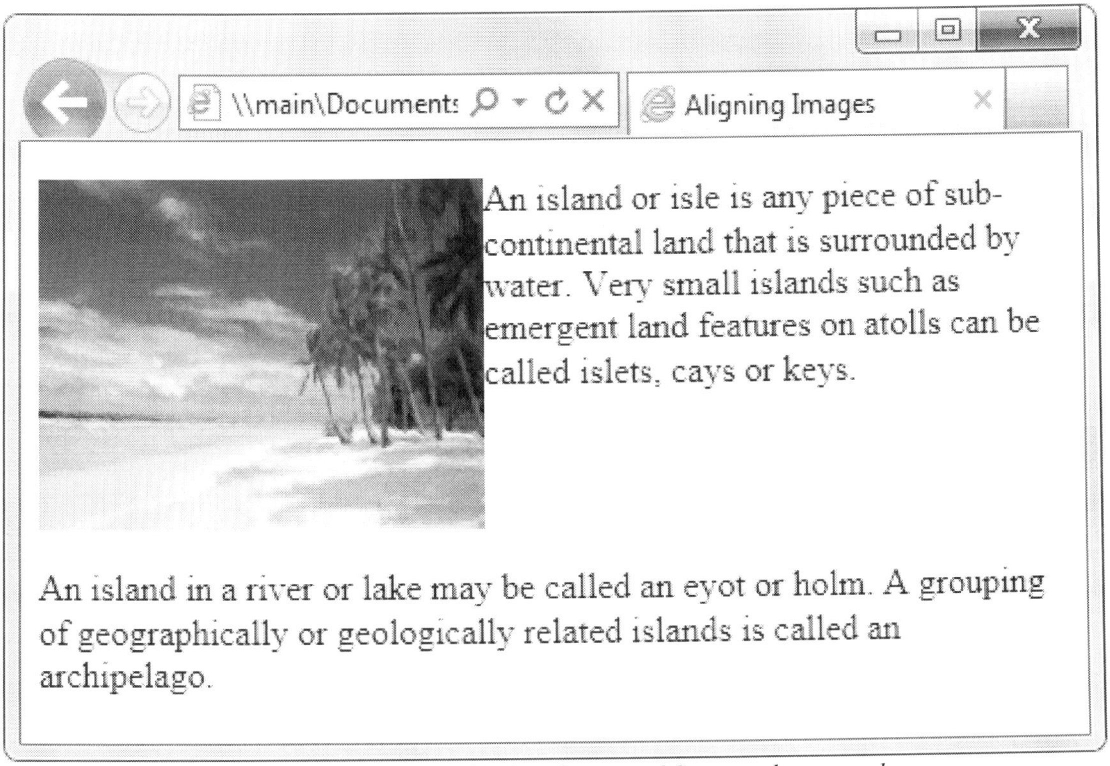

Figure 4: The left alignment has been cleared before the start of the second paragraph

Although better, this display could still do with a little more cleaning up, so in Figure 4-5 I have added a 1 pixel border to the image, a heading to the text, and created a 15 pixel blank margin to the right of the image using a CSS rule, as follows:

```
<img src='image1.png' align='left'
  border='1' style='margin-right:15px;' />

<h1>All About Islands</h1>

<p>An island or isle is any piece of sub-continental
land that is surrounded by water. Very small islands
such as emergent land features on atolls can be called
islets, cays or keys.<br clear='left' /></p>

<p>An island in a river or lake may be called an eyot or
holm. A grouping of geographically or geologically
related islands is called an archipelago.</p>
```

***Note**: Ideally, the CSS styling should be removed from within the body of the web document and into an external style sheet using a class name, which can then be applied*

Figure 5: Now a border, heading and margin have been added

to any left-aligned object. Please refer to your favorite CSS book or website for full details on using CSS.

By default images will line up next to each other unless you use CSS styling or tags such as `<br />` to force a line break, or `<p>` to start a new paragraph. Text will also line up with next to an image, but starting only at the bottom-most possible line, and then wrapping around to the line below. So use the `align` argument to force a full left (or right) align to allow text to flow from the top-most position. If you choose to right-align an image (or any element, in fact), things are just the same, except that text will flow to its left, and you should use either the `clear='right'` or `clear='all'` arguments of the `<br />` tag if you wish to turn of the wrapping prior to reaching the bottom of the image.

Summary

Now that you have mastered managing fonts, colors and images, in the next lecture I will turn to building lists and tables.

LECTURE 5

CREATING LISTS AND TABLES

By following this lecture you will:

- ✓ *Be able to create a variety of different list types.*
- ✓ *Understand how to build HTML tables.*
- ✓ *Know how to introduce color and spacing into tables.*

BY NOW YOU should be really appreciating the power of HTML, and we've only covered a subsection of HTML 4.01, but bear with me if you are new to HTML as you need this background in order to prepare you for all the goodies that have been added in HTML 5.

And even if you are experienced with HTML it may still be a good idea to continue browsing through these early lectures to give yourself a quick refresher on the subject.

***Note**: The examples from this lecture are in the* Lecture 5 *folder of the* examples.zip *file at* tinyurlcom/html5ccexamples.

Building Lists

HTML supports a wide variety of different list types, including bulleted, numbered and definition lists. Numbered lists are known as ordered lists and can be denoted with letters of the alphabet or roman numerals as well as with numbers, and bulleted lists can use squares, or filled or outlined circles. Figure 5-1 shows every possible type of list, all on a single web page, including both the upper and lower case forms that are available. A typical ordered list can be created with HTML such as the following:

```
<ol>
  <li>Apple</li>
  <li>Pear</li>
  <li>Banana</li>
  <li>Plum</li>
  <li>Orange</li>
</ol>
```

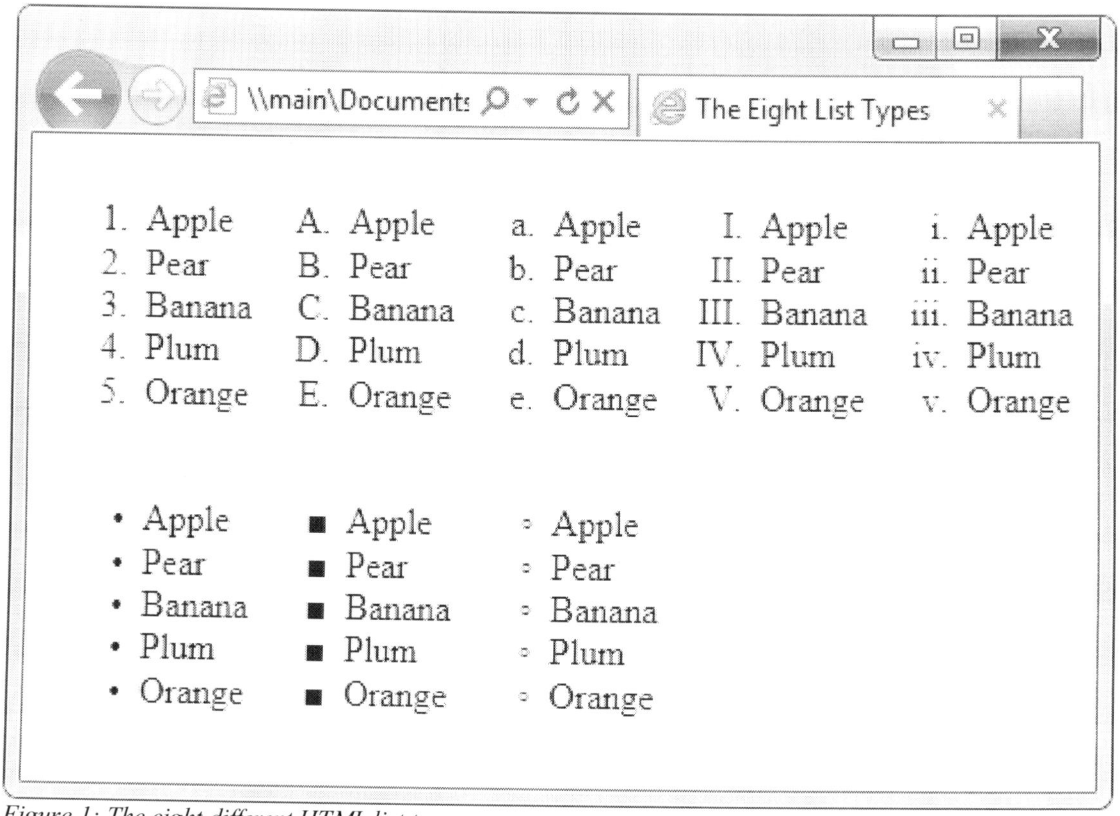

Figure 1: The eight different HTML list types

As you can see, lists are a little more complex than the tags we've used so far because they comprise more than one tag.

To start with there's the enclosing `<ol>` and `</ol>` tags which indicate that their contents is a list (either ordered or unordered). Then each element of the list is itself enclosed in `<li>` and `</li>` tags. The above example displays as the first list in row one of Figure 5-1.

An unordered (or bulleted list) using the default of filled circles could be created like this (which displays as the first list in row two of Figure 5-1):

```
<ul>
  <li>Apple</li>
  <li>Pear</li>
  <li>Banana</li>
  <li>Plum</li>
  <li>Orange</li>
</ul>
```

Lists may also contain sub-lists (and so on), like this:

```
<ul>
  <li>Apple</li>
  <ul>
    <li>Bramley</li>
    <li>Cox</li>
    <li>Golden Delicious</li>
  </ul>
  <li>Pear</li>
  <li>Banana</li>
  <li>Plum</li>
  <li>Orange</li>
</ul>
```

In this example the sub-list of `Bramley`, `Cox` and `Golden Delicious` will appear with a filled square bullet symbol.

This is because the default order of rotation between bullets is filled circle (the outer list level), filled square, outlined circle, and then back to filled circle, and so on. In HTML these three shapes are referred to using the values `disc`, `square` and `circle`.

Overriding The Defaults

You can obtain greater control over your lists by overriding the default values and specifying ones of your own, out of the following arguments:

- **`start`** By default ordered lists start with the number 1 and each additional item in the list is prefaced by the next number in sequence, but you can choose any other starting value, both positive and negative, or zero. This attribute is not used by unordered lists, which always display the same character before each item.
- **`type`** Ordered lists preface digits before each list item by default, but you can change this behavior to displaying upper case or lower case letters, or upper or lower case roman numerals by giving this attribute a value of one of the following: `'A'`, `'a'`, `'I'` or `'i'`, respectively. Unordered lists require any of three words as values for this attribute, out of `'disc'`, `'square'` and `'circle'`, the default being the same as specifying `'disc'`.

So, for example, to use the square bullet (in place of the default disc) in a list, you can use HTML such as this (which displays as the second list on the bottom row of Figure 5-1):

```
<ul type='square'>
  <li>Apple</li>
```

```
    <li>Pear</li>
    <li>Banana</li>
    <li>Plum</li>
    <li>Orange</li>
  </ul>
```

Or, for example, to use upper case roman numerals you could use code such as this (which displays as the fourth list on the top row of Figure 5-1):

```
<ol type='I'>
  <li>Apple</li>
  <li>Pear</li>
  <li>Banana</li>
  <li>Plum</li>
  <li>Orange</li>
</ol>
```

Or, to begin an ordered list at a specified number, you could use code like this (which will commence numbering from the digit 5, instead of 1):

```
<ol start='5'>
  <li>Apple</li>
  <li>Pear</li>
  <li>Banana</li>
  <li>Plum</li>
  <li>Orange</li>
</ol>
```

Definition Lists

HTML also supports another kind of list known as a definition list. This type of list is used in places where it is not appropriate to use either ordered or bulleted lists, for example, when giving definitions of words, which look better if the word being defined is used as the bullet.

In definition lists the first part of each list element is referred to as the *term*, and the second as the *definition*, which gives rise to the HTML tags of `<dl>` and `</dl>` for enclosing a definition list, `<dt>` and `<dt>` for denoting a term, and `<dd>` and `</dd>` for denoting the term's definition, as shown in the following example:

```
<dl>
  <dt>HTML</dt>
  <dd>Acronym for Hyper Text Markup Language</dd>
  <dt>CSS</dt>
  <dd>Acronym for Cascading Style Sheets</dd>
```

```
    <dt>JavaScript</dt>
    <dd>An in-browser programming language</dd>
  </dl>
```

This HTML will display as follows:

HTML
  Acronym for Hyper Text Markup Language
CSS
  Acronym for Cascading Style Sheets
JavaScript
  In-browser programming language

Creating Tables

HTML tables are great for presenting tabular data in a clear and concise way and have also been used for many years as an aid to layout, even though there are more efficient ways of creating good layouts using CSS. However, for knocking together a quick and dirty example, or for laying out rows and columns of data, tables are great.

You create a table using the `<table>` and `</table>` tags, which support the following arguments:

- **`align`** This attribute supports values of `left`, `right` or `center` to align the table according to the surrounding text, although the attribute is now deprecated and use of CSS is recommended instead.
- **`bgcolor`** Using this attribute you can set the background color of a table. However CSS is recommended for this as the attribute is now deprecated.
- **`border`** With this attribute you can specify a border around the table of 0 or any positive number of pixels.
- **`bordercolor`** With this attribute you can specify the color of the border using standard color names or hexadecimal number values.
- **`cellpadding`** This attribute specifies the number of pixels space between cell walls and their content, which can be a value of 0 or any higher number.
- **`cellspacing`** This attribute specifies the number of pixels space between cells and the outer table border, which can be a value of 0 or any higher number.
- **`height`** and / or **`width`** With these attributes you can specify the width and height of a table. When unspecified the browser will resize the table to the best fit for its contents.

For example, the following HTML creates a table that is 450 pixels wide, 200 pixels deep, has a 1 pixel border, 5 pixels of padding inside each cell, 5 pixels of spacing outside the cells, and a background color of cyan:

```
<table border='1' bgcolor='cyan'
  width='450' height='200'
  cellpadding='5' cellspacing='5'>
  <!-- Table contents -->
</table>
```

Table Rows And Columns

Within each table there must be at least one row and one column. These are created using the `<tr>` (for table row) and `<td>` (for table data) tags. In the following example, two rows of three columns each are created:

```
<table border='1' bgcolor='cyan'
  width='450' height='200'
  cellpadding='5' cellspacing='5'>
  <tr>
    <td>Row 1, Col 1</td>
    <td>Row 1, Col 2</td>
    <td>Row 1, Col 3</td>
  </tr>
  <tr>
    <td>Row 2, Col 1</td>
    <td>Row 2, Col 2</td>
    <td>Row 2, Col 3</td>
  </tr>
</table>
```

The `<tr>` and `</tr>` tags are used twice for the two rows, while there are six instances of `<td>` and `</td>` for the six cells (two rows of three).

Both these types of tags also accept the `bgcolor`, `height` and `width` arguments that `<table>` itself does.

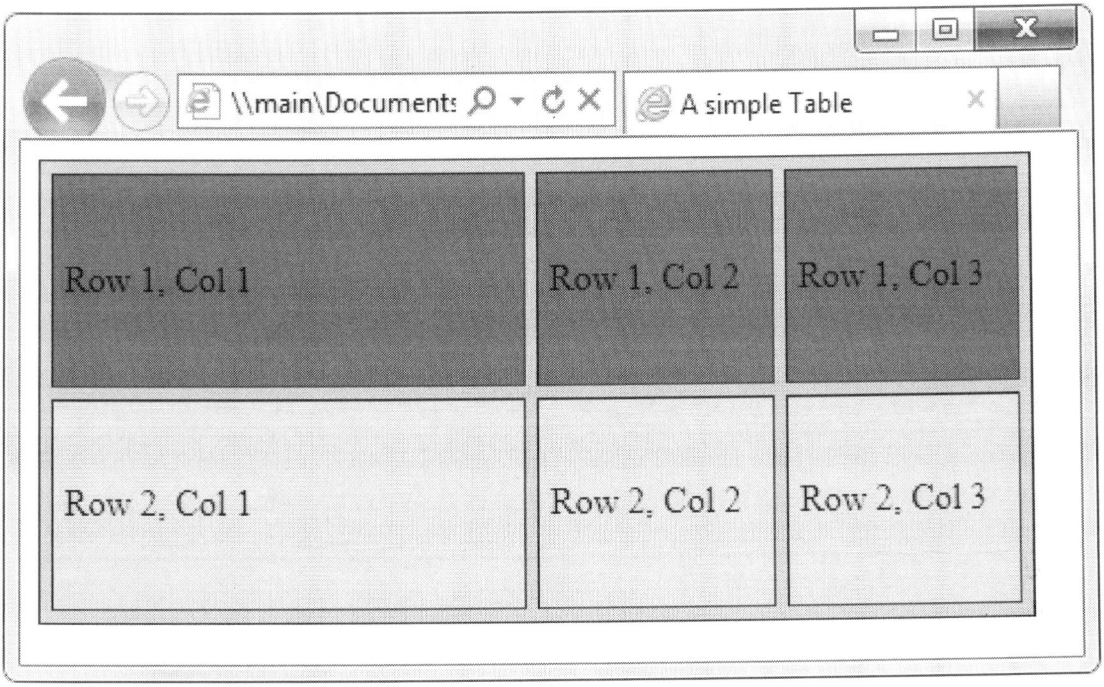

Figure 2: A simple table with two rows and three columns

Therefore the following HTML creates the same table but sets the top row of the table to green and the bottom to yellow. It also sets the first column width to exactly 200 pixels and then the remaining two columns to 25 percent each (by using the `%` symbol) of whatever width remains (in this case 250 pixels, leaving 125 pixels each), as shown in Figure 5-2.

```
<table border='1' bgcolor='cyan'
  width='450' height='200'
  cellpadding='5' cellspacing='5'>
  <tr bgcolor='green'>
    <td width='200'>Row 1, Col 1</td>
    <td width='25%'>Row 1, Col 2</td>
    <td width='25%'>Row 1, Col 3</td>
  </tr>
  <tr bgcolor='yellow'>
    <td>Row 2, Col 1</td>
    <td>Row 2, Col 2</td>
    <td>Row 2, Col 3</td>
  </tr>
</table>
```

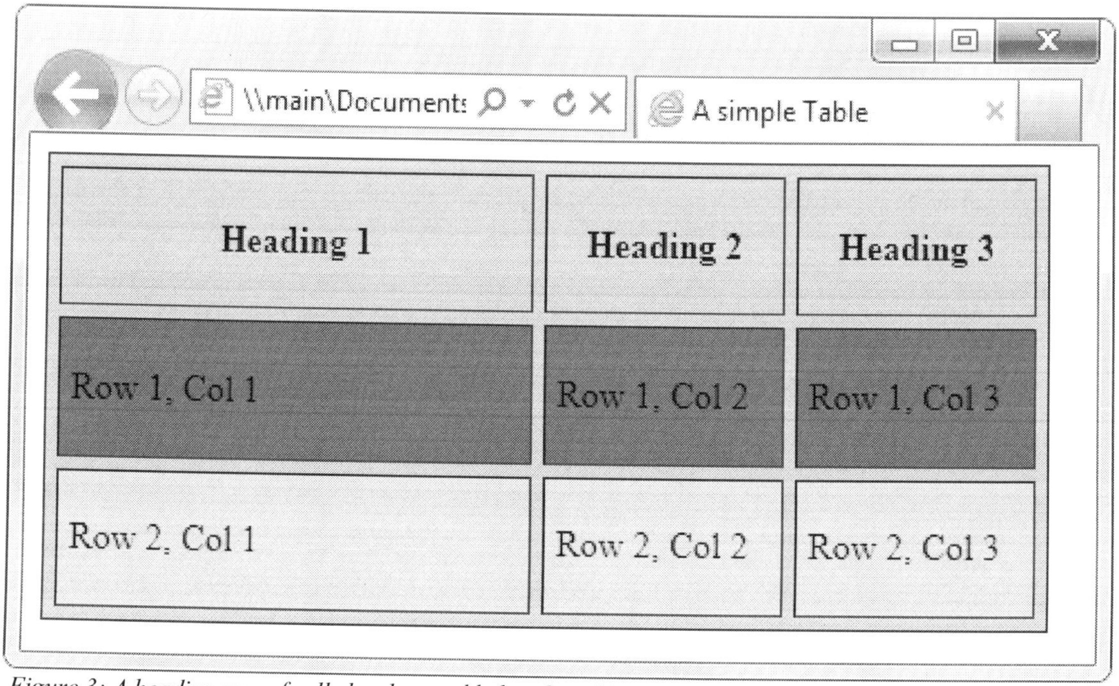

Figure 3: A heading row of cells has been added to the table

***Note**: Because the widths have already been specified in the first row, there is no need to do so again for the second.*

If you want the top row of your table to be a header you can use CSS styling or HTML tags to embolden and otherwise change the headings, or you can use the `<th>` and `</th>` tags (for table heading), in a similar fashion to the `<td>` and `</td>` tags, like this:

```
<tr bgcolor='cyan'>
  <th width='200'>Heading 1</th>
  <th width='25%'>Heading 2</th>
  <th width='25%'>Heading 3</th>
</tr>
```

As you can see from Figure 5-3 (in which this additional code has been inserted before the second two rows), the use of these tags is identical to `<td>` and `</td>`, with the only exception being in the way the cell contents is displayed; it is enlarged, emboldened and centered.

To further enhance the way tables display you can also use the `<caption>` tag to properly caption them

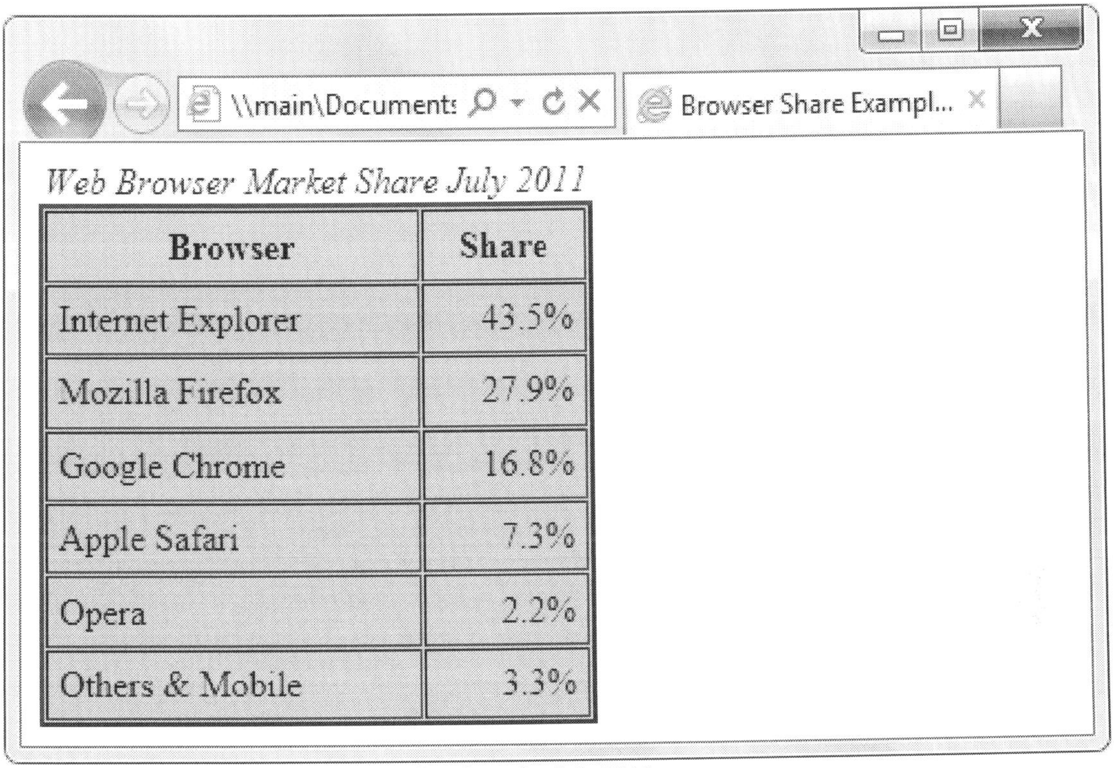

Web Browser Market Share July 2011

Browser	Share
Internet Explorer	43.5%
Mozilla Firefox	27.9%
Google Chrome	16.8%
Apple Safari	7.3%
Opera	2.2%
Others & Mobile	3.3%

Figure 4: A table detailing browser market share for July 2011

So let's bring this tag and all the others together into a real-world example of a useful table, as shown in Figure 5-4, which was created with the following HTML from data at *wikipedia.org*:

```
<table border='2' cellpadding='5' cellspacing='1'
  width='250' bgcolor='lightgreen' bordercolor='blue'>
  <caption>
    <i>Web Browser Market Share July 2011</i>
  </caption>
  <tr>
   <th>Browser</th>
    <th>Share</th>
  </tr>
  <tr>
    <td>Internet Explorer</td>
    <td>43.5%</td>
  </tr>
  <tr>
    <td>Mozilla Firefox</td>
    <td>27.9%</td>
  </tr>
  <tr>
```

```
      <td>Google Chrome</td>
      <td>16.8%</td>
    </tr>
    <tr>
      <td>Apple Safari</td>
      <td>7.3%</td>
    </tr>
    <tr>
      <td>Opera</td>
      <td>2.2%</td>
    </tr>
    <tr>
      <td>Others & Mobile</td>
      <td>3.3%</td>
    </tr>
  </table>
```

Extending Rows And Columns

With HTML tables you are not limited to a fixed number of rows and columns because you can make some cells extend over more than one column and/or more than one row using the `colspan` and `rowspan` arguments.

For example, in the following very simple table the numbers 1 through 10 are displayed in a four rows by three columns table, as shown in Figure 5-5. This means that there are two extra cells that are not used and which are therefore merged into one and grayed out:

```
<table border='1' width='450' height='200'>
  <tr align='center'>
    <td width='25%'>1</td>
    <td width='25%'>2</td>
    <td width='25%'>3</td>
    <td width='25%'>4</td>
  </tr>
  <tr align='center'>
    <td>5</td>
    <td>6</td>
    <td>7</td>
    <td>8</td>
  </tr>
  <tr align='center'>
    <td>9</td>
    <td>10</td>
    <td colspan='2' bgcolor='lightgray'></td>
    <!-- Cell omitted here -->
```

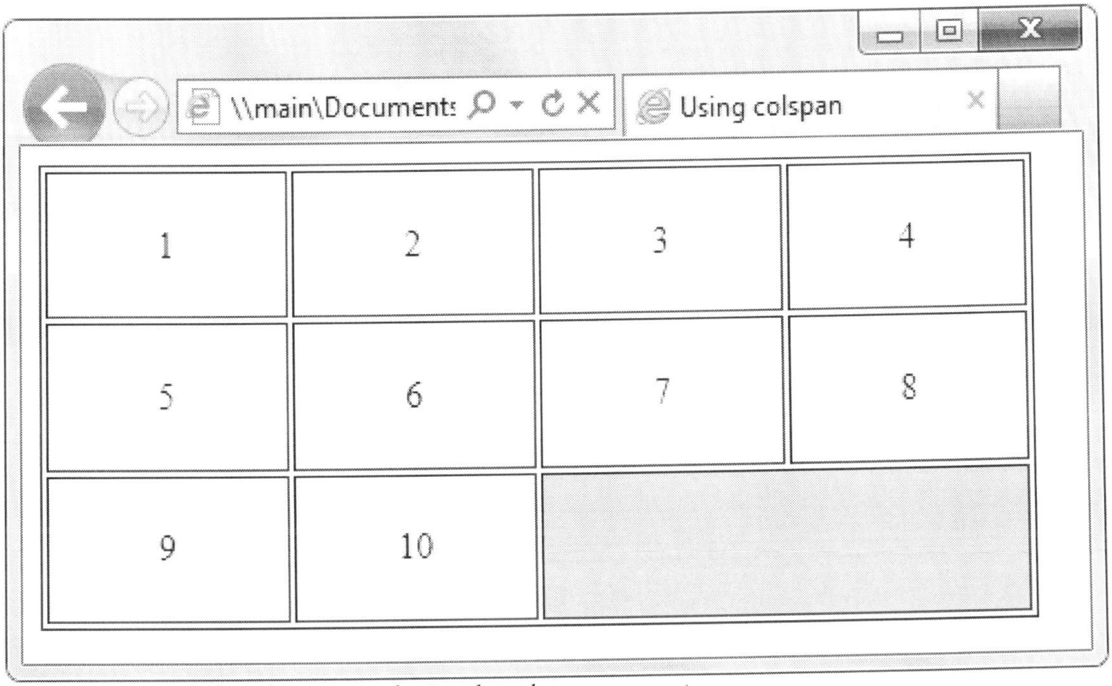

Figure 5: Two cells have been merged using the colspan argument

```
  </tr>
</table>
```

***Note**: I have employed a few other interesting features in this table including setting its width to 450 pixels (and the width of each column to 25 percent of that), the height of the table to 200 pixels, and using the `align` argument with a value of `'center'` to center the contents of each table row. I have also used comment tags to show where the omitted cell would have been.*

Because the third cell on the third line is now two cells wide, there is no fourth cell in that row, and so none is defined.

You can also extend a cell over two rows, as in the following example, which is modified from the previous one using the `rowspan` argument (the result of using which in a browser is shown in Figure 5-6):

```
<table border='1' width='450' height='200'>
  <tr align='center'>
    <td width='25%'>1</td>
    <td width='25%'>4</td>
```

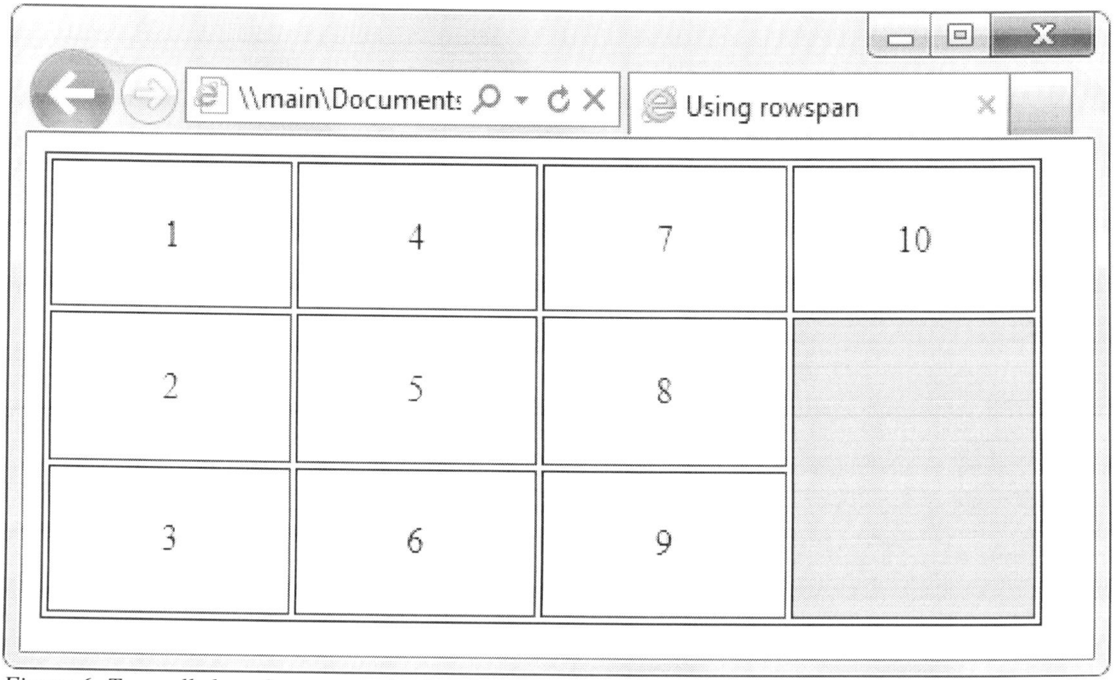

Figure 6: Two cells have been merged using the rowspan argument

```
      <td width='25%'>7</td>
      <td width='25%'>10</td>
    </tr>
    <tr align='center'>
      <td>2</td>

      <td>5</td>
      <td>8</td>
      <td rowspan='2' bgcolor='lightgray'></td>
    </tr>
    <tr align='center'>
      <td>3</td>
      <td>6</td>
      <td>9</td>
      <!-- Cell omitted here -->
    </tr>
  </table>
```

Because the fourth cell on the second line is now two cells deep, there is no fourth cell in the bottom row and so, again, the final cell is not defined. Following is a four rows by four columns table example that could be used as the basis for a simple board game. It combines both the `rowspan` and `colspan` arguments by displaying the numbers 1 through 12 clockwise in small cells, around a larger central cell of double width and height, as shown in Figure 5-7:

```
<table border='1' width='450' height='450'>
  <tr align='center'>
    <td width='25%'>1</td>
    <td width='25%'>2</td>
    <td width='25%'>3</td>
    <td width='25%'>4</td>
  </tr>
  <tr align='center'>
    <td>12</td>
    <td colspan='2' rowspan='2'
      bgcolor='lightgray'></td>
    <!-- Cell omitted here -->
    <td>5</td>
  </tr>
  <tr align='center'>
    <td>11</td>
    <!-- Cell omitted here -->
    <!-- Cell omitted here -->
    <td>6</td>
  </tr>
  <tr align='center'>
    <td>10</td>
    <td>9</td>
    <td>8</td>
    <td>7</td>
  </tr>
</table>
```

Summary

Now that you have lists and tables added to your HTML toolkit you have the ability to really make your web pages stand out. In the following lecture I will show you how to add interactivity to your pages using hyperlinks, forms and frames.

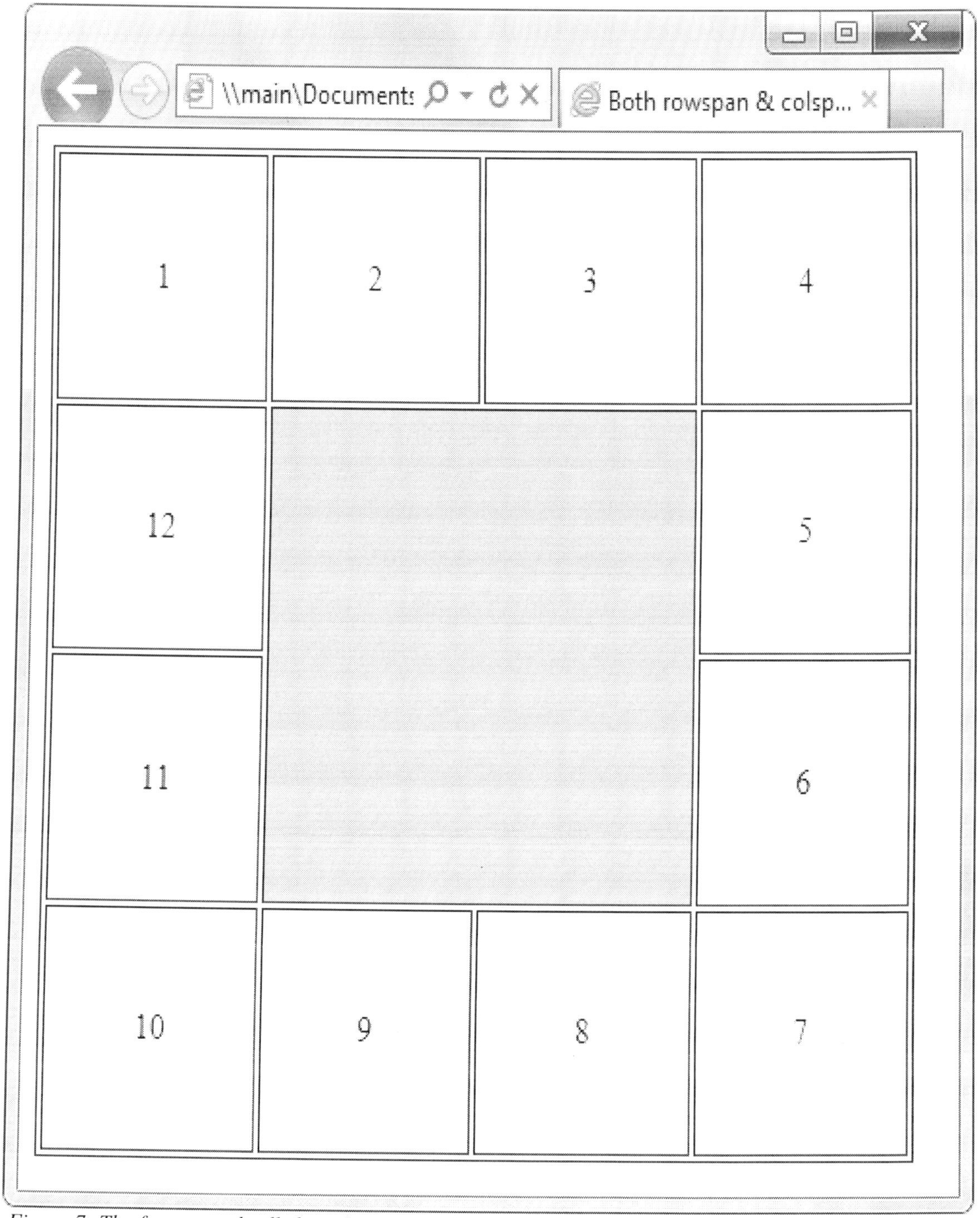

Figure 7: The four central cells have been merged using rowspan and colspan

LECTURE 6

LINKS, FORMS AND FRAMES

By following this lecture you will:

- ✓ *Be able to use Internet hyperlinks.*
- ✓ *Know the difference between absolute and relative URLs.*
- ✓ *Be familiar with using web forms and embedded frames.*

THE GREAT THING about the Internet is the way documents located anywhere in the world can be linked to each other so that you can navigate to them with a single mouse click. This interconnectedness even extends to the ability to embed pages or portions of pages from the same or any other website, anywhere at all, within the current page.

The same goes for sending data to websites and web pages, which is often achieved using forms. The data in a form can be posted to a web server for processing or, if it is sent in the correct way, a simple JavaScript can receive the data and act on it, without recourse to the web server.

In this lecture I show how all these things work and how you can use them to their best effect.

***Note**: The examples from this lecture are in the* Lecture 6 *folder of the* examples.zip *file at* tinyurlcom/html5ccexamples.

Using Hyperlinks

To create a link to another document you must first know where this new document resides; in other words whether it is on the local server or another one.

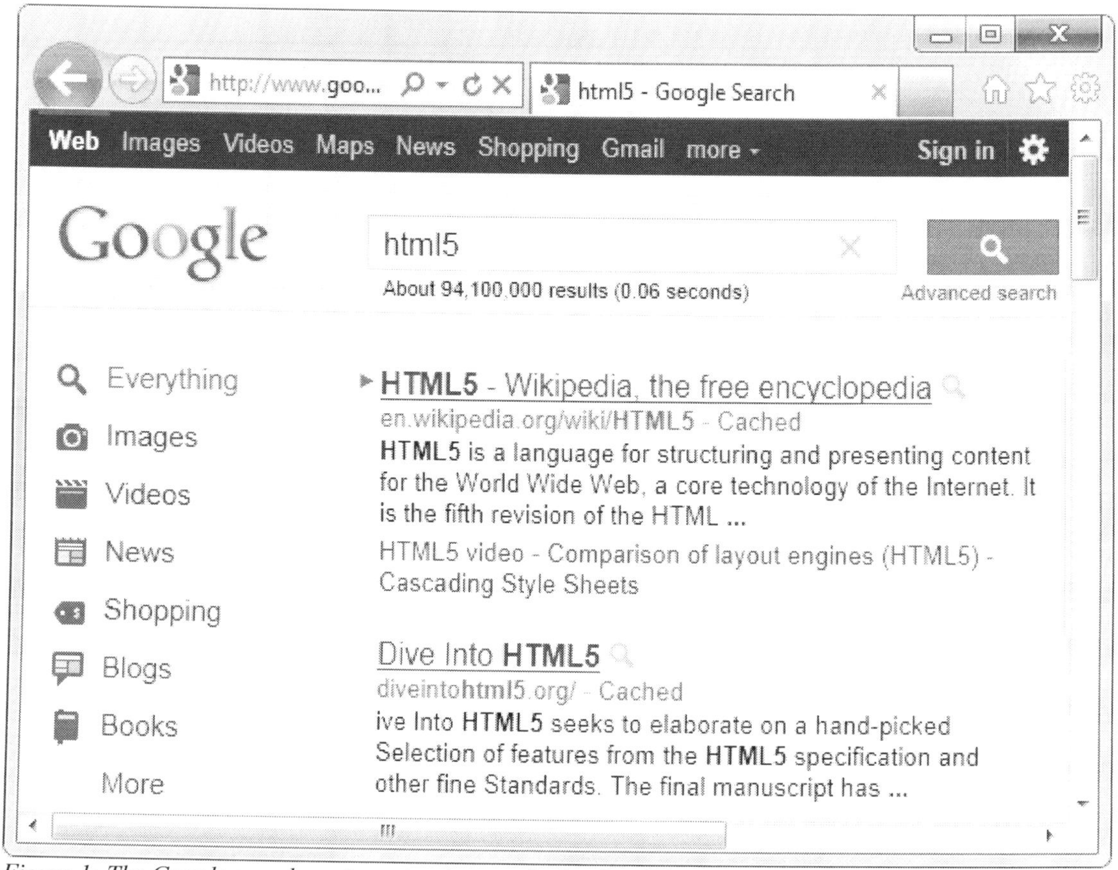

Figure 1: The Google search engine returning results for 'html5'

An external web address (on a different server) uses what is known as an absolute URL (Uniform Resource Locator), which begins with `http://`, such as:

```
http://bbc.co.uk
```

It can be more complicated than that simple URL, by including the folder structure (and sometimes a file name too) within which a web page resides, like this, which accesses the folder `/weather`:

```
http://bbc.co.uk/weather/
```

Some organizations distinguish different servers by adding a prefix before the domain name, the most common of which is `www.`, like this:

```
http://www.bbc.co.uk
```

Because typing `www.` Is an extra four characters most good websites allow you to ignore this prefix (but not all). When it is used it denotes the organization's main web server.

Alternative servers may use prefixes such as `news.`, like this (which leads to the BBC's news service):

```
http://news.bbc.co.uk
```

The Query String

Many websites support the use of a query string, which is a string of data placed after the URL to provide additional information to a web server. For example, the following URL passes the string `html5` to the argument `q` on Google's search page, the result of which is shown in Figure 6-1:

```
http://google.com/search?q=html5
```

Query strings begin with a `?` character, followed by an argument/value pair which is separated by a `=` character. Further arguments may follow if preceded by a `&` character, like this:

```
http://google.com/search?q=html5&hl=fr
```

Here the argument `hl` is set to the string value `fr`, which has the result of changing Google's default language for this session to French, as shown in Figure 6-2. I cover query strings in more detail in the section on forms.

Relative URLs

When documents reside on the current server you can access them more easily and make them more portable by using relative instead of absolute URLs. For example, if you need to link to the file *agenda.htm* in the current folder you can simply use its name as the URL, like this:

```
agenda.htm
```

Or, if the document is in the subfolder `meetings/2011`, you could refer to it like this:

```
meetings/agenda.htm
```

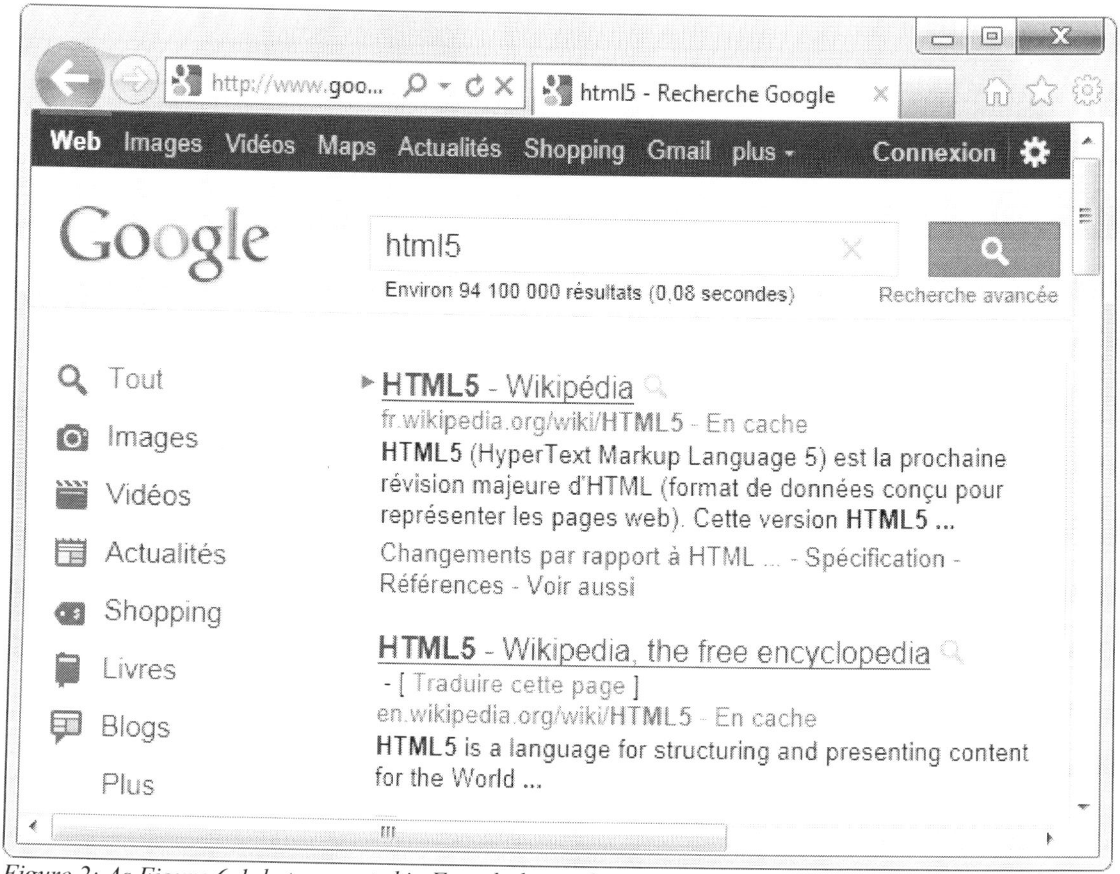

Figure 2: As Figure 6-1, but presented in French due to the query string used

Alternatively, if the file is in the parent folder of the current one you can use the special token `../` which simply specifies that the document can be found one directory higher up, like this:

```
../agenda.htm
```

There again, if the file is in a sister folder, perhaps called `misc`, you can easily refer to it by referencing the folder from the parent one, like this:

```
../misc/agenda.htm
```

Finally, to refer to the root, or uppermost, folder of the current drive or web location you use the `/` symbol. So if the file is in the root folder it can be accessed like this:

```
/agenda.htm
```

***Note**: This root form of accessing is not fully relative to the current folder since it includes a jump all the way to the root folder, and the connection between the root and current folder is not indicated by this form of URL.*

Creating Links

To create a link within an HTML document you apply the `<a>` tag, supplying a value to an argument called `href` (for hypertext reference), like this:

```
<a href='http://google.com'>Visit Google</a>
```

The final `</a>` tag closes the pair of tags, which encompass the text to be displayed for the link, which in the above case simply looks like this:

Visit Google

If linking relatively to the file *agenda.htm*, discussed in the previous section, you might use one of the following forms of the HTML depending on the file's location:

```
View the agenda <a href='agenda.htm'>here</a>.
View the agenda <a href='meetings/agenda.htm'>here</a>.
View the agenda <a href='../agenda.htm'>here</a>.
View the agenda <a href='../misc/agenda.htm'>here</a>.
View the agenda <a href='/agenda.htm'>here</a>.
```

All of these display in the same way, like this:

View the agenda here.

URLs in Images

In Lecture 4 I showed how to embed images in documents, but assumed that the pictures resided in the current folder. But, in fact, they can reside almost anywhere on the current server, or elsewhere on the Internet, and all the following are valid HTML for displaying an image located in different places:

```
<img src='image.jpg' />
<img src='meetings/image.jpg' />
<img src='../image.jpg' />
<img src='../misc/image.jpg' />
<img src='/image.jpg' />
<img src='http://aserver.com/folder/extra/image.jpg' />
```

The target Argument

You can specify whether a linked URL should replace the current web page or open in a new one by supplying a value for the target argument.

For example, if you would like a web page to open in a new blank window (or tab, according to how the user's web browser is configured) you can add the specifier `target='_blank'`, like this:

```
<a href='http://google.com'
  target='_blank'>Visit Google</a>
```

There are three other reserved words you can also supply to the `target` argument: `_self` to replace the current page (the default), `_parent` to replace the parent page or frame (if the current document resides in a frame), or `_top` to ignore any and all frames and replace the entire contents of the current browser window with the new document.

Additionally, if you have already named a frame, window or tab using the relevant HTML or JavaScript, you can specify that name as the target in place of one of the four reserved words.

Creating An Anchor

It is even possible to link to a section of a web page by first specifying an anchor using the name argument of the `<a>` tag, like this:

```
<a name='anchorname'></a>
```

Now you can link directly to that section of the web page using a query string referring to the anchor name, preceded with a `#` symbol, like this:

```
Click <a href='http://server.com/page.htm#anchorname'>
this link</a> to an anchor.
```

When it is passed this URL the web browser will load in the specified page and then scroll it so that the section beginning with the anchor name is at the top of the browser window.

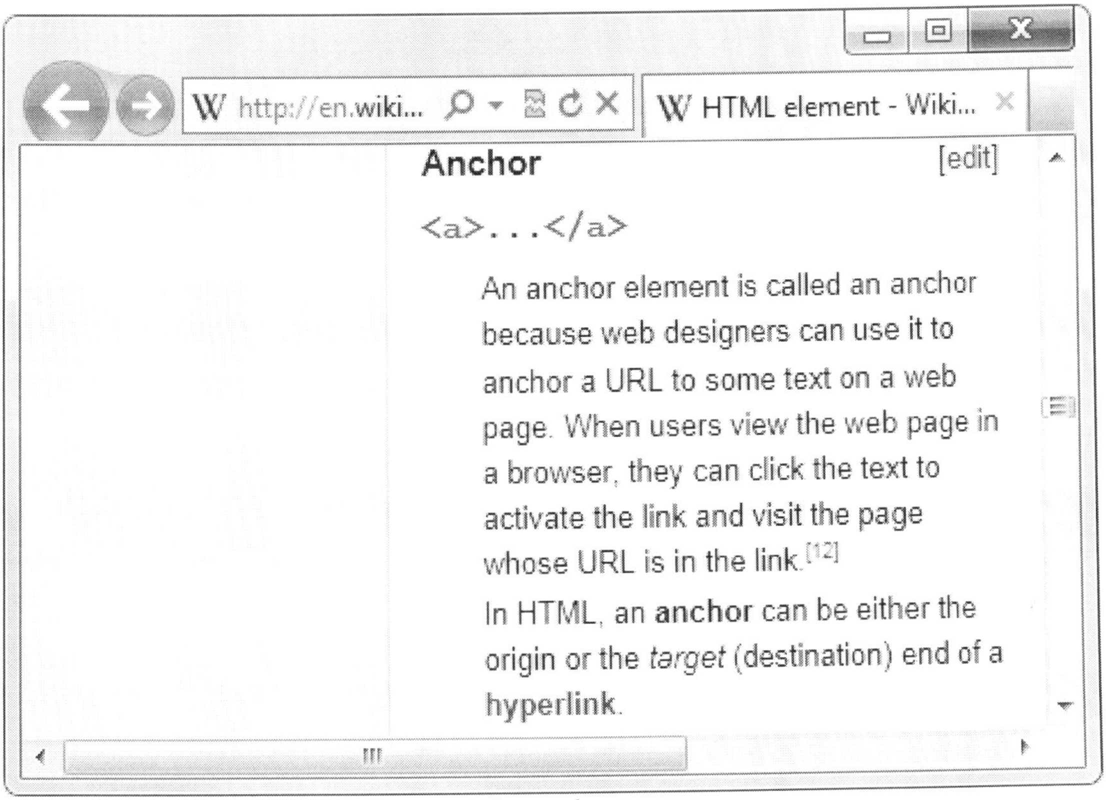

Figure 3: The Wikipedia Anchor section is itself an anchor

***Note**: A good example of anchors in action is the Wikipedia page on the subject. Go to the website at* wikipedia.org *and enter the search term* html anchor. *You will then be taken to the Wikipedia* HTML Element *page, and then scrolled down automatically to the section about anchors, as shown in Figure 6-3.*

Building Forms

Web forms are the means with which you can request input from the user of a web page. Historically web form data has been posted to the web server and then processed but nowadays form data can be pre-processed using JavaScript to ensure that it is in the form required and all fields are correctly completed.

Additionally, through the use of Ajax, a technology whereby JavaScript communicates behind the scenes with a web server, modern forms can even check for the availability of a username you prefer, before you even submit a form.

***Note**: In fact JavaScript can incrementally submit all parts of a form as you fill it in, avoiding the need to use a submit button at all. And where input is used only to control the current web page (and no interaction is required with the web server), JavaScript can read from and write to form fields, and retrieve data from a query string.*

A form definition begins with the `<form>` tag and is closed with `</form>`, and the tag supports three commonly-used arguments, as follows:

- **`method`** There are two values accepted by this attribute: `'post'` or `'get'`. When you select `'post'` all the form data is sent to the web server invisibly (using headers), but when using `'get'` the data is appended to an HTML request in a query string. This can result in messy looking URLs but, among other possibilities, it does enable a form to be posted to a JavaScript program rather than a web server.
- **`action`** This attribute should contain the URL to which the form is to be submitted. If the form is sent using a `'get'` request then a `?` followed by the form data will be tacked onto this value.
- **`enctype`** This attribute tells the program that will receive the form the type of data to expect, out of: `application/x-www-form-urlencoded`, `multipart/form-data`, and `text/plain`. The first encodes all characters before transmitting the form, the second is used when a file is also (or only) being uploaded to a web server, and in the last form text is transmitted, with spaces converted into `+` symbols for use in a query string. By default, if no encoding is specified, `application/x-www-form-urlencoded` is used.

Figure 6-4 shows a range of form elements all incorporated into a single form, using the HTML below:

```
<form><pre>
  Input type: text     <input type='text'
    name='f1' size='26' />
  Input type: password <input type='password'
    name='f2' size='26' />

  Input type: radio    <input type='radio'
    name='f3' value='1' />1
  Input type: radio    <input type='radio'
    name='f3' value='2' />2
  Input type: checkbox <input type='checkbox'
    name='f4' value='1' />1
  Input type: checkbox <input type='checkbox'
    name='f4' value='2' />2
```

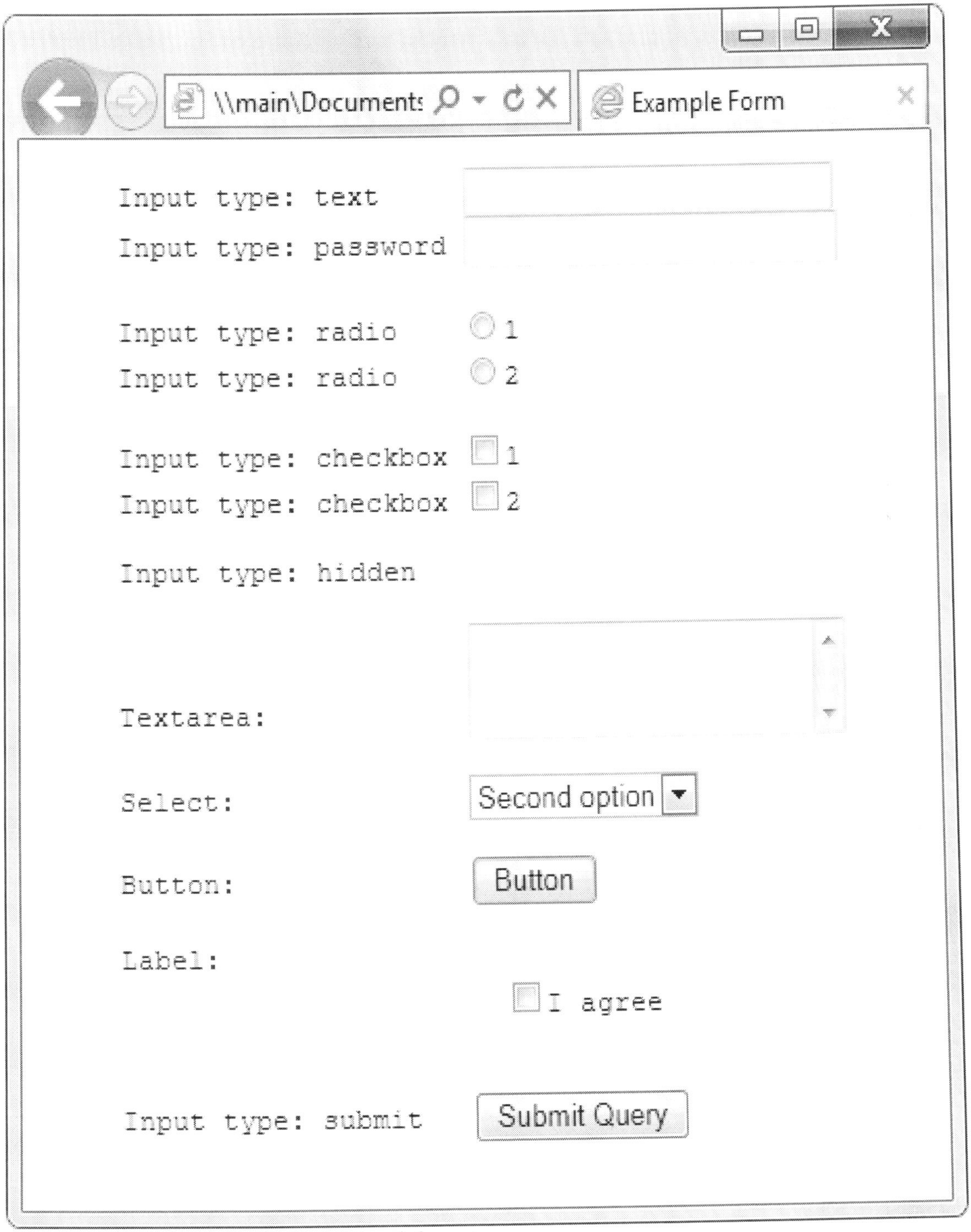

Figure 4: A form incorporating a variety of elements

```
    Input type: hidden   <input type='hidden'
      name='f5' />

  Textarea:   <textarea name='f6' rows='3' cols='20'>
                </textarea>

  Select:     <select name='f7'>
                <option value='1'>First Option</option>
                <option value='2' selected='selected'>
                  Second option</option>
                <option value='3'>Third Option</option>
              </select>
  Button:     <button name= 'f8' value='f8'>Button</button>

  Label:      <label>
                <input type= 'checkbox' name= 'agree'
                  value='yes' />I agree
              </label>

    Input type: submit <input type='submit' />
  </pre></form>
```

***Note**: The `<pre>` and `</pre>` tags are used here simply to help space out the form without having to use CSS or several HTML tags. It tells the browser to display all spaces within the tags as it encounters them, and not to treat them as collapsible whitespace.*

The `<input />` Tag

The code in the preceding section makes use of the following input types of the self-closing `<input />` tag using the `type` argument, like this:

- **`type='text'`** This value creates an input field suitable for entering text. You can change the width of the input field with the `size` attribute and limit the number characters allowed with the `maxlength` attribute.
- **`type='password'`** This value creates an input field suitable for entering passwords in that all typed characters are replaced with the `*` character when displayed, but are properly stored internally. You can change the width of the input field with the `size` attribute and limit the number characters allowed with the `maxlength` attribute.
- **`type='radio'`** Each form may have any number of radio buttons, each created by giving this value to the `type` attribute of an `<input>` tag, but only one can be active at a time. When another radio button is clicked the previously selected one is deselected. Radio buttons are round.

- **type='checkbox'** You use this attribute value to create checkboxes, which are like radio buttons but are square, and more than one may be selected at a time.
- **type='hidden'** Sometimes you may wish to pass a value in a web form that the user shouldn't see such as an identifying token or other data, and doing is accomplished by passing this value. In which case you will also have to provide the value to be posted in the `value` attribute (see below).
- **type='submit'** This attribute value creates a button that will submit the form. By default the button will read *Submit* or *Submit Query*.

The name Argument

When sending data using a form you need to give each item of data a name so that both your form and the receiving program know which piece of data is for what. To do this you use the `name` argument, like this:

```
<input type='text' name='firstname' />
```

Here the field's name is `firstname` and therefore it is clear that this will be used for the input of a person's forename.

The value Argument

You can specify a predefined value for any form field by assigning it using the `value` argument, like this:

```
<input type='text' name='firstname' value='Guest' />
```

Here a default value of `Guest` is given to the input field, which could be useful, for example, if allowing guests to make posts in a guestbook or comment. Such predefined fields can be overwritten or edited by the user so it is not fixed.

The <textarea> Tag

Sometimes the single line of input supplied by the `<input>` tag is insufficient in size, in which case you can use the `<textarea>` tag, which supports adjustable width and height, over more than one line of input.

Unlike the `<input>` tag, however, predefined data is not passed through a `value` argument. Instead, whatever you place between `<textarea>` and `</textarea>` tags becomes the predefined input, which can then be edited or replaced by the user.

Therefore the following lines provide an empty and a predefined textarea input with a default width of 20 characters and height of two lines:

```
<textarea name='summary'></textarea>
<textarea name='summary'>Replace with summary</textarea>
```

You can specify the number of rows and columns to use for the textarea with the `rows` and `cols` arguments, like the following, which creates an area 30 characters wide and five lines high:

```
<textarea name='summary' rows='5' cols='30'></textarea>
```

The `<select>` Tag

If you need a drop down list of options from which a user can select one you can use the `<select>` tag in conjunction with a secondary tag, `<option>`.

Together these tags let you create a list of values and names to display, that will pop down when clicked, like this:

```
<select name='icecream'>
  <option value='b'>Banana</option>
  <option value='c'>Chocolate</option>
  <option value='s'>Strawberry</option>
  <option value='v' selected='selected'>Vanilla</option>
  <option value='w'>Walnut</option>
</select>
```

The fourth element in the list has been set as the default by using the argument `selected='selected'`. When the list is popped down this option will be the one shown as selected and will stay so, unless the user chooses a different element.

The `<button>` Tag

This tag displays a clickable button but I do not recommend its use because Internet Explorer will submit the contents between the `<button>` and `</button>` tags, while other browsers submit the contents of its `value` attribute.

Therefore it is tricky to use consistently, unless you attach to its click events with JavaScript, and so I recommend you steer clear of it unless you know what you are doing.

The <label> Tag

This tag is especially handy for use with radio button or checkboxes (which are small) because you can place one of these elements alongside some explanatory text and if you surround them both with `<label>` and `</label>` tags the user can click either the text or the radio button or checkbox to activate it.

Here's a common example:

```
<label>
  <input type='checkbox' name='agree' value='yes' />
  I agree to these terms and conditions.
</label>
```

This example displays as follows, and clicking any part of it (not just the check box) will check or uncheck the box:

☐ **I agree to these terms and conditions.**

Frames And Iframes

There are two ways in which you can embed entire web pages within other pages: frames and iframes. The first way to do this, and the least recommended, is to use frames to split a web page into the multiple parts and then place them all in frames within the `<frameset>` tag, like this:

```
<frameset cols='20%, *, 20%'>
  <frame src='header.htm' />
  <frame src='body.htm' />
  <frame src='footer.htm' />
</frameset>
<noframes>
  <!-- Alternative content goes here -->
</noframes>
```

***Note**: Note the use of the `<noframes>` and `</noframes>` tags in the example to display alternative content to users whose browser doesn't support frames. Specialist browsers*

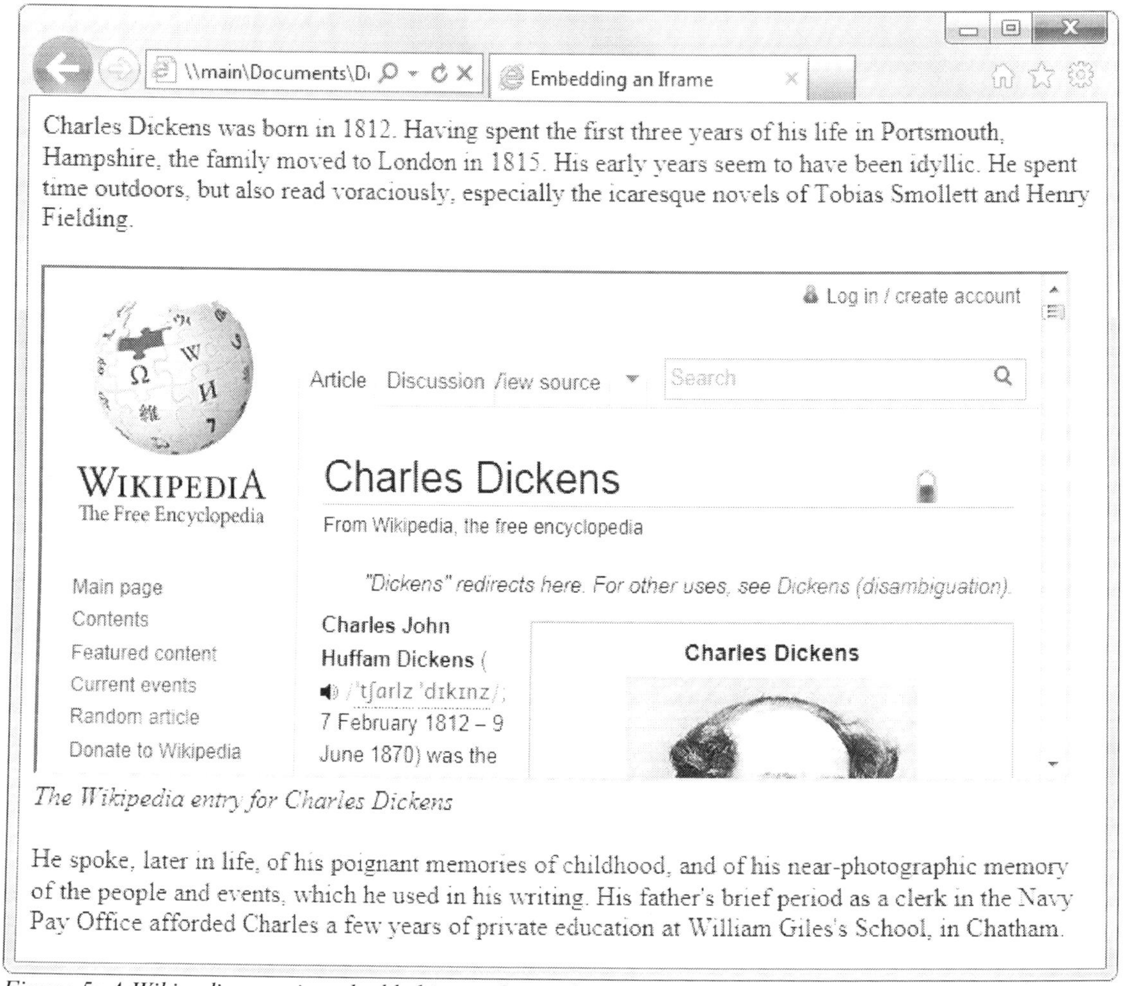

Figure 5: A Wikipedia page is embedded in another webpage

such as audio browsers for deaf people, or text-only browsers may especially benefit from the use of these tags.

This results in a top frame that takes up 20% of the browser height and which is pulled in from the file *header.htm*.

Then there's the main frame which (due to the * argument in the `cols` attribute) will expand to fit whatever space there is after the fixed size frames are in place. It is loaded in from the file *body.htm*. And finally the footer frame is loaded in from *footer.htm* and placed in the bottom 20% of the web page.

The problem with this method is that the entire web page is comprised of frames and there is no content on the page itself. This is obviously not ideal and is not good for ranking in search engines, which will not find such a page very interesting.

Instead I recommend that when you need a frame you use an `<iframe>` tag, as shown in Figure 6-5 (in which a Wikipedia page has been embedded within another webpage), because you can drop a frame of any width and height anywhere in a document as easily as if it were an image, like this:

```
<!-- Some HTML content here -->
  <iframe src='anotherpage.htm'
    width='6400' height='300'>
  </iframe>
<!-- More HTML content here -->
```

Summary

This lecture completes most of your introduction to HTML. The following lecture contains a simple alphabetical summary of all the HTML 4.01 tags, which you can use as a reference if you are new to HTML, or as a refresher if you are a seasoned user.

LECTURE 7

THE COMPLETE HTML TAG LIST

By studying the contents this lecture you will:

- ✓ *Learn all the HTML 4.01 tags if you are new to HTML.*
- ✓ *Review the tags as a refresher if you already know HTML.*
- ✓ *Have a handy reference available when you need it.*

FOR EASE OF reference, the following list contains all the main HTML 4.01 tags in alphabetical order, along with short descriptions for each. It also tells you whether a tag is deprecated and might therefore be removed from future versions of HTML – in which case, for long term stability of your web sites, an alternative should ideally be used instead:

Note: There are no examples for this lecture in the accompanying examples.zip *file.*

- **<!-- ... -->** A comment
- **<!DOCTYPE>** Document type

- **<a> ... </a>** Anchor for a link
- **<abbr> ... </abbr>** Abbreviation
- **<acronym> ... </acronym>** Acronym
- **<address> ... </address>** Author contact details
- **<applet> ... <applet>** Embedded applet
  (Deprecated: use <object> *instead)*
- **<area />** Area within an image-map

- **<b> ... </b>** Bold text
- **<base />** Default link address or target
- **<basefont />** Default font, color, or size
  (Deprecated: use CSS instead)

- **<bdo>** ... **</bdo>** Text direction
- **<big>** ... **</big>** Big text
- **<blockquote>** ... **</blockquote>** Long quotation
- **<body>** ... **</body>** Document body
- **
** Line break
- **<button>** ... **</button>** Clickable button

- **<caption>** ... **</caption>** Table caption
- **<center>** ... **</center>** Centered text
  (Deprecated: use CSS instead)
- **<cite>** ... **</cite>** Citation
- **<code>** ... **</code>** Computer code text
- **<col />** Attributes for table columns
- **<colgroup>** ... **</colgroup>** Group of table columns

- **<dd>** ... **</dd>** Definition list description
- **<del>** ... **</del>** Deleted text
- **<dfn>** ... **</dfn>** Definition term
- **<dir>** ... **</dir>** Directory list
  (Deprecated: use <ul> instead)
- **<div>** ... **</div>** Block section of a document
- **<dl>** ... **</dl>** Definition list
- **<dt>** ... **</dt>** Definition list term

- **<em>** ... **</em>** Emphasized text

- **<fieldset>** ... **</fieldset>** Border around form elements
- **<font>** ... **</font>** Font name color and size
  (Deprecated: use CSS instead)
- **<form>** ... **</form>** Form
- **<frame />** Frameset frame
- **<frameset>** ... **</frameset>** Set of frames

- **<h1>** ... **</h1>** Level 1 Heading
- **<h2>** ... **</h2>** Level 2 Heading
- **<h3>** ... **</h3>** Level 3 Heading
- **<h4>** ... **</h4>** Level 4 Heading
- **<h5>** ... **</h5>** Level 5 Heading
- **<h6>** ... **</h6>** Level 6 Heading
- **<head>** ... **</head>** Document header

- **<hr />** Horizontal rule
- **<html>** ... **</html>** HTML document

- **<i>** ... **</i>** Italic text
- **<iframe>** ... **</iframe>** Inline frame
- **<img />** Image
- **<input />** Input field
- **<ins>** ... **</ins>** Inserted text
- **<isindex>** ... **</isindex>** Searchable index
  (Deprecated: use `<input>` instead)

- **<kbd>** ... **</kbd>** Keyboard text

- **<label>** ... **</label>** Label for an input element
- **<legend>** ... **</legend>** Caption for a `<fieldset>` element
- **<li>** ... **</li>** List item
- **<link />** Link to supporting file

- **<map>** ... **</map>** Image map
- **<menu>** ... **</menu>** Menu list
  (Deprecated: use `<ul>` instead)
- **<meta />** Document metadata

- **<noframes>** ... **</noframes>** Alternative content for frames
- **<noscript>** ... **</noscript>** Alternative content for scripts

- **<object>** ... **</object>** Embedded object
- **<ol>** ... **</ol>** Ordered list
- **<optgroup>** ... **</optgroup>** Group of list options
- **<option>** ... **</option>** Option in a select list

- **<p>** ... **</p>** Defines a paragraph
- **<param />** Parameter for an object
- **<pre>** ... **</pre>** Preformatted text

- **<q>** ... **</q>** Defines a short quotation

- **<s>** … **</s>** Strikethrough text
  (Deprecated: use `<del>` or CSS instead)
- **<samp>** … **</samp>** Computer code
- **<script>** … **</script>** Script (generally JavaScript)
- **<select>** … **</select>** Select drop down list
- **<small>** … **</small>** Defines small text
- **<span>** … **</span>** Inline section of a document
- **<strike>** … **</strike>** Strikethrough text
  (Deprecated: use `<del>` or CSS instead)
- **<strong>** … **</strong>** Strong text
- **<style>** … **</style>** Style information
- **_{** … **}** Subscript text
- **^{** … **}** Superscript text

- **<table>** … **</table>** Table
- **<tbody>** … **</tbody>** Group table body cells
- **<td>** … **</td>** Table cell
- **<textarea>** … **</textarea>** Multi-line text input
- **<tfoot>** … **</tfoot>** Group table footer cells
- **<th>** … **</th>** Table header
- **<thead>** … **</thead>** Group table header cells
- **<title>** … **</title>** Document title
- **<tr>** … **</tr>** Table row
- **<tt>** … **</tt>** Teletype text

- **<u>** … **</u>** Underlined text
  (Deprecated: use CSS instead)
- **<ul>** … **</ul>** Unordered list

- **<var>** … **</var>** Variable text

Summary

Congratulations. You have now completed the first part of this course comprising an introduction to HTML 4.01, and should now either have a basic understanding for what you can do with it, or if you already knew HTML you will have refreshed all its tags in your mind.

In the following lecture we'll start to get into the nitty-gritty HTML5 and learn exactly what all the fuss is about.

LECTURE 8

AN INTRODUCTION TO HTML5

By following this lecture you will:

- ✓ *Learn all the technologies and enhancements that comprise HTML5.*
- ✓ *Get a brief introduction to each new aspect of HTML5.*
- ✓ *Be ready to learn how to use these technologies on your websites.*

HTML5 IS A specification that's still under development and is not expected to be complete before 2012-13. Therefore it's important for you to know about all the tags (both current and future), and how they work on various platforms and browsers, so that you will know just what you can do with HTML5 right now, and also what will become available to you in the future.

But what exactly is HTML5? Is it's a new standard different from the previous 4.01 version? Surprisingly, the answer is no, because HTML5 is simply a loose collection of enhancements that have been (or will be) made to the HTML 4.01 specification, covering a wide range of differing areas; it has simply been found convenient to label these additions as HTML5.

This is why I made sure that you had a thorough grounding in HTML 4.01 before beginning this section, because that means that you now actually already have over 75 percent of the full HTML 5 specification under your belt. Now let's start to look at the remaining 25 percent or so that constitutes the HTML5 enhancements.

Note*: When an older browser comes across an HTML5 tag that it doesn't recognize, the tag will simply be ignored, in the same way as if you use made up tag names such as* `<newtagname>` *and* `</newtagname>`*. However, any text or HTML between such tags is* *displayed. This ensures that backward compatibility is retained for users with older browsers.*

Canvas

***Note**: The examples from this lecture are in the* Lecture 8 *folder of the* examples.zip *file at* tinyurlcom/html5ccexamples.

The `<canvas>` element was introduced by Apple to the Webkit rendering engine (the power behind the default iOS and Android web browsers, and also used by the Apple Safari and Google Chrome browsers), to provide a means of drawing graphics from within a web page, without having to load a plug-in such as Java or Flash. It was later standardized and has since been adopted by Opera and Gecko-based browsers, as used in the Mozilla Firefox browser, and is also included in Google Chrome and Microsoft Internet Explorer 9.

A canvas is a region within a web page that can be drawn on using JavaScript. Because there can be more than one canvas in a web page, it is necessary to provide an `id` for each so that the drawing commands know which canvas they should apply to. So, to create a canvas you use HTML such as the following, which (in this instance) creates a 400 x 300 pixel canvas with the `id` of `'canvas1'`:

```
<canvas id='canvas1' width='400' height='300'>
  This web page uses the HTML5 canvas element, which is
  available on most modern browsers. If you wish to view
  this page at its best, please upgrade your browser to
  the most recent version.
</canvas>
```

***Note**: This is a course on HTML5. However, many HTML5 features can only be accessed using JavaScript. Therefore in these lectures I provide illustrations of how to perform certain functions and give examples in JavaScript, but do not teach the JavaScript language itself. You will be able to use and modify the examples since they are simple and clearly explained, but if you wish to achieve more complex results you may wish to read either of my following books, each of which contains a comprehensive JavaScript tutorial:* Learning PHP, MySQL & JavaScript, *or* HTML5 for iOS and Android, *both of which are available in good bookstores and online.*

Older browsers that do not recognize the `<canvas>` tag will ignore it and simply display the text between the opening and closing tag which, in this instance, provides information to users about upgrading their browser.

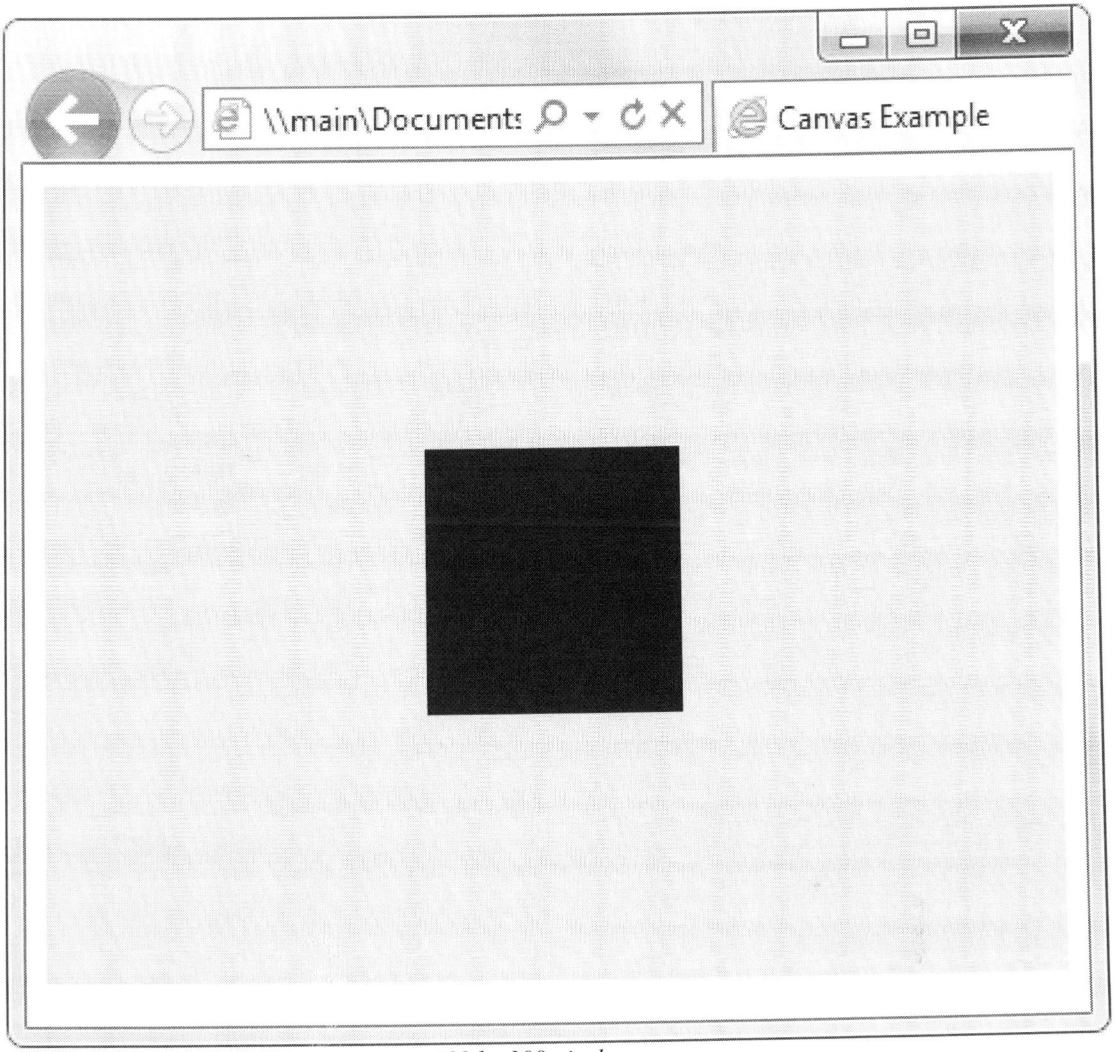

Figure 1: A 100 by 100 pixel square in a 400 by 300 pixel canvas

The great thing about the HTML5 canvas is that you can now draw anything you like in a web browser, in a similar way to using a plug-in such as Flash, but using simple HTML and JavaScript syntax. This makes your web pages far more dynamic and able to display on a wider range of operating systems and devices. For example the iOS infrastructure does not support Flash on iPhones and iPads, but does support the HTML5 canvas.

In figure 8-1 I have created a 400 by 300 pixel canvas and drawn a square in its center using the following combination of HTML and JavaScript:

```
<canvas id='canvas1' width='400' height='300'>
  This web page uses the HTML5 canvas element,  which is
```

```
    available on most modern browsers. If you wish to view
    this page at its best,  please upgrade your browser to
    the most recent version.
  </canvas>

  <script>
    canvas = document.getElementById('canvas1')
    canvas.style.background = '#DDD'
    context = canvas.getContext('2d')
    context.fillRect(150, 100, 100, 100)
  </script>
```

The first part of this example is a repeat of the `<canvas>` creating HTML snippet and the four lines within the `<script>` and `</script>` tags do the work of placing the square on the canvas. Let's look at them in turn, starting with:

```
canvas = document.getElementById('canvas1')
```

This creates a JavaScript object (an element capable of holding different types of information) which refers to the `canvas1` canvas. In the following line the background of the canvas is set to a light gray color (`#DDD`) by altering its CSS `style` property:

```
canvas.style.background = '#DDD'
```

Next it is necessary to decide the way in which the canvas is to be accessed. For example, in future it will be possible to access a canvas using 3D, which will enable professional looking games to be written. But for now 2D is the only option available, and that is what I have used, as follows:

```
context = canvas.getContext('2d')
```

Finally a square is drawn onto the canvas by using the context and the JavaScript function `fillRect()`. The square has its top left corner at 150 pixels in by 100 down and has a width and height that are both 100 pixels:

```
context.fillRect(150, 100, 100, 100)
```

As you can see, even if you are not a JavaScript programmer, this is relatively straight forward, and will become more so when I explain the canvas element in more detail in Lectures 9 through 14.

Figure 2: A circle and some text have been added to the canvas

In the meantime, Figure 8-2 shows the addition of a circle and some text to the canvas, achieved using the following extra statements added into the `<script>` section of the example:

```
context.arc(60, 60, 50, 0, Math.PI * 2, false)
context.stroke()
context.font = '70px Times'
context.fillText('Hi!', 300, 280, 100)
```

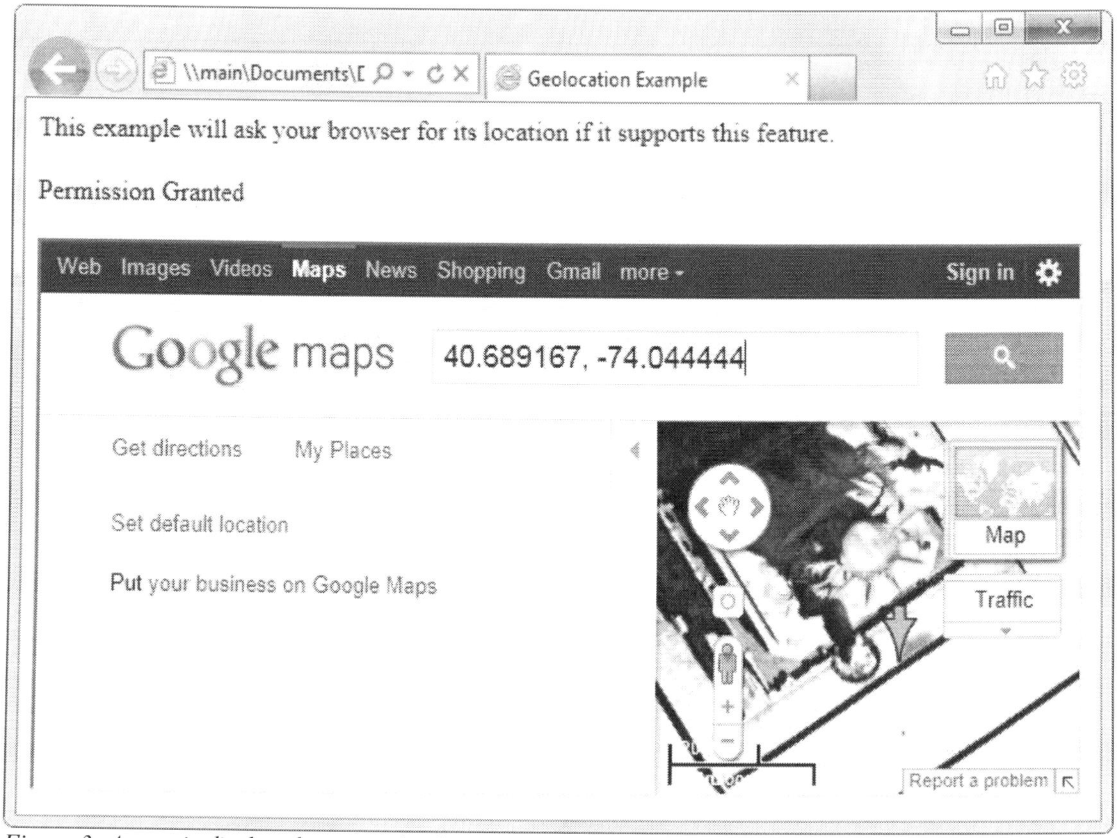

Figure 3: A map is displayed as a result of returning geolocation data

Geolocation

Geolocation is a technology that is used to determine the location of a computer or mobile device, which can be returned to the web server in order to provide relevant information. For example, a local map can be displayed, or details of local stores such as restaurants or gas stations can be provided.

Geolocation can also be used to help improve web connectivity by notifying you of nearby Wi-Fi access points, or to alert you of the proximity of friends, acquaintances or colleagues.

Different methods are used to obtain your location, starting with your IP (Internet Protocol) address IP address, which can reveal which country you are in, and programs that do this can often get very close to your locality. There's nothing you can normally do about this because all websites need to know your IP address in order to send you data.

However, there are third party services that will act as a proxy for you, replacing your IP address with theirs when communicating with a web server.

With HTML5 geolocation, if Wi-Fi is enabled on your computer it is also possible to send more precise location information by scanning your locally accessible Wi-Fi hotspots to pinpoint your location, using databases containing millions of hotspot names and MAC (Media Access Control) addresses, along with their locations. Also, if you are using a mobile

device, triangulation of the mobile antenna masts you can connect to reveals your location quite accurately.

Finally, if your computer has GPS (Global Positioning System) functionality, this can reveal your exact location to within just a few feet, as long as your device is in range of the GPS satellites that orbit the earth.

In Figure 8-3 permission has been granted by the user to return the geolocation data of a device at the location 40.689167, -74.044444, which is a point close to the Statue of Liberty in New York City, USA.

Geolocation is explained in greater depth in Lecture 15, and JavaScript code is supplied which you can use without needing to learn the language.

Forms

Forms have been provided with a number of new enhancements in HTML5, and in my view they are long overdue (and still only partially supported by some browsers).

To start with you can now place `<input>` tags outside of `<form>` and `</form>` tags as long as the new `form` attribute is used to identify the form ID to which the input refers. Similarly you can change the method (either `GET` or `POST`) of a form with the new `formmethod` attribute.

There are also enhancements letting you change the encoding type of a form, or create or override a new `novalidate` attribute. You can also use the `formaction` attribute to change the action (destination) of a form, and you can use `formtarget` to change the target frame, tab or window. At the same time it is now possible to change the height and width of the image type of the `<input>` tag using `height` and `width` attributes.

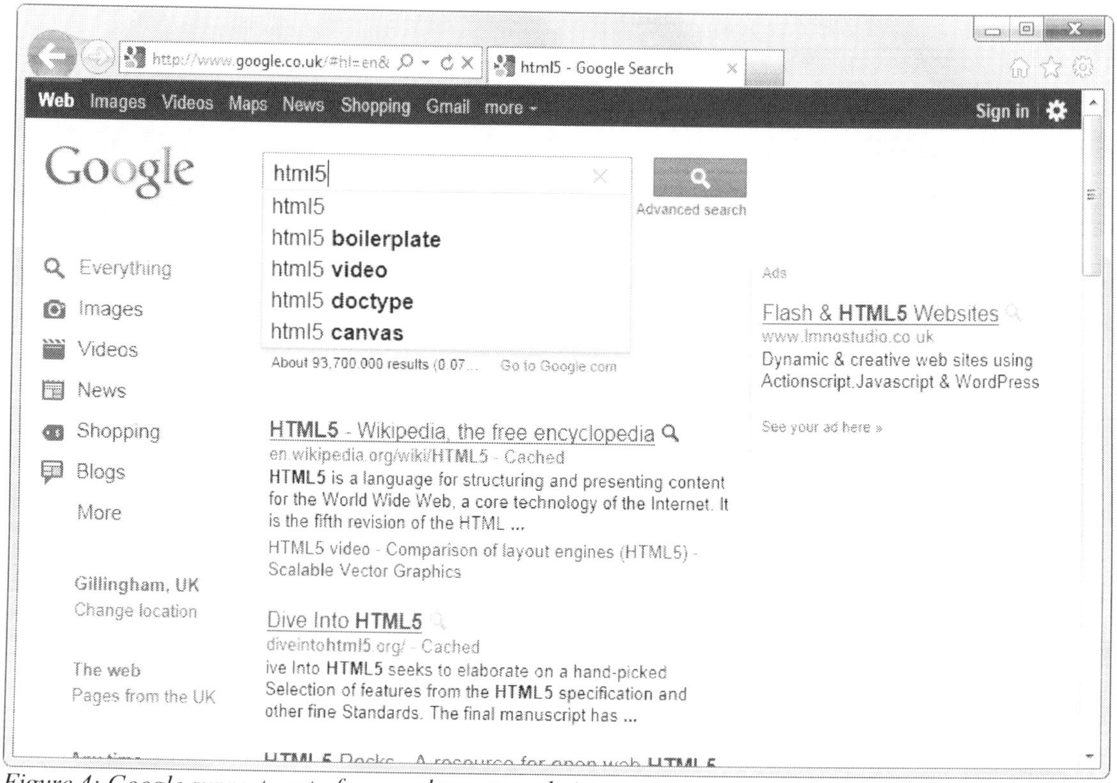

Figure 4: Google supports auto focus and auto completion

Two particularly handy new attributes are `autocomplete` and `autofocus`. The former allows previously entered values for a field to be offered as suggested values, while the latter is used to tell the browser to automatically focus a particular form field ready for input.

This is what happens when you go to a search engine such as Google (see Figure 8-4), where you can begin to enter your search immediately. In the good old days before the use of these tags and JavaScript, you had to click in a field first before it would obtain focus, and you would not be offered suggestions as you typed.

Data lists can also now be included in a form such that you can create a list of labels and values to which you assign an `id`. Then you can use that `id` as the value for the new `list` attribute to easily offer a selection of choices to an input. This is especially useful when you wish to use the same list more than once as it avoids unnecessarily duplicating it.

New `min`, `max` and `step` attributes have also been added for inputs that contain numbers or dates, and there's a new `multiple` attribute with which you can allow an `<input>` tag to accept multiple values. This is especially useful, for example, when selecting groups of files to upload to a server.

Pattern matching is now supported in forms via the new `pattern` attribute, the `placeholder` attribute lets you display some hint text in a field that disappears once the field is selected, and you can use the `required` attribute to tell a form that a field must be completed.

Several new values are now supported for the `type` attribute, including `color`, `date`, `month`, `time`, `week`, `number`, `range`, `tel`, `url` and `email`. These allow the browser to check such input fields for proper syntax and sensible data being entered. There's also a powerful `type` value of `search` which enables a field to provide search suggestions in a similar fashion to the instant results that appear when entering a request into the Google search engine. All these and more are fully detailed in *Lecture 16*.

Local Storage

Before HTML5 the only way that data could be stored on a local device was via the use of cookies, which are small bundles of data generally used to help retain the contents of a shopping basket or more controversially by advertising websites to track your browsing.

But it has long been realized that the web could be significantly speeded up of a local data store were made available which could be used, for example, for storing longer documents as you edit them, prior to them being sent to the server for safe keeping. With HTML5 this is possible and even large chunks of data (up to 5MB per website) can be stored locally, but only if the user agrees to it, so your retain full control.

What's more, on some browsers local storage can be accessed like a database using Web SQL, providing the possibility of creating advanced local web apps for handling data such as your music collection, or personal exercising and dieting, and so on. Lecture 17 fully explains what you can and can't do with local storage.

Audio & Video

Possibly the most interesting and popular enhancements in HTML5 other than the canvas are the ability to now play audio and video directly from within HTML, with no need to embed Flash or any other type of object as a player.

Figure 5: Embedding a YouTube Flash video

To do this the new tags `<audio>` and `<video>` have been provided, but how to use them is still a bit up in the air as it can depend on the browser and operating system being used. In addition there is still a big hoo-ha going on about the use of the H.264 video codec (the software algorithm used to compress all the video data down to a manageable size for the Internet), which is not free for products that encode or decode the video (such as browsers), although it is free for end users.

Because of this Google, Firefox and Opera do not natively support the codec, and opt for the open Theora codec instead. Fortunately there are workarounds and tweaks you can employ to ensure that just about all your users can play HTML5 audio and video, and all is explained in *Lectures 18* and *19*.

The <embed> Tag

while on the subject of embedding objects (such as video players) in a web page, the `<embed>` tag which was officially deprecated in HTML 4.01 has now been restored and made official again. Therefore, for example, you can officially use code such as the following to play a YouTube video in a non-HTML5 browser using flash:

```
<object width="480" height="385">
  <param name="movie"
    value="http://www.youtube.com/v/ILUcxHG-Tw8">
  </param>
  <param name="allowFullScreen" value="true"></param>
  <param name="allowscriptaccess"
    value="always"></param>
  <embed src=http://www.youtube.com/v/ILUcxHG-Tw8
    type="application/x-shockwave-flash"
    allowscriptaccess="always"
    allowfullscreen="true" width="480" height="385">
  </embed>
</object>
```

Code such as this can be inserted between `<video>` and `</video>` tags so that browsers that do not recognize them will use Flash to display a video, as shown in Figure 8-5, in which musician Priscilla Ahn sings "Masters in China" by Benji Hughes.

Microdata

Microdata is a subset of HTML designed for making a document have meaning to machines by providing meta data, just as it has meaning to a reader of the document.

What it does is make available the following new tag attributes: `itemscope`, `itemtype`, `itemid`, `itemref` and `itemprop`. Using them you will be able to clearly define the properties of an item such as a book, providing a range of information that a computer can use to understand, for example, its authors, publishers, contents and so on. Further information on microdata is in *Lecture 20*.

Web Workers

Normally, to achieve background processing in JavaScript, you need to set up a timer that is constantly called, supplying slices of processor time to one or more functions, and these functions must then quickly do a small piece of work and return, in order to not slow down the browser and make it seem sluggish.

Web Workers are not yet widely implement but will provide a standard way for browsers to run multiple JavaScript threads in the background that can pass messages to each other, in much the same manner as the threads running in an operating system. You will simply call up a new worker script which will sit there in the background waiting for messages to be sent to it, which it will then act upon.

On the whole the aim of this is to achieve a 2-3 times speed increase over regular background JavaScripts, although getting to grips with programming them is likely to require a longer rather than shorter learning curve. *Lecture 20* discusses web workers in more detail.

Web Applications

The idea of offline web applications is that once you visit a website, it tells your browser about all the files it uses so that the browser can download them all and you can then run the web application locally, even without an Internet connection.

There is a complication with web Applications in that they require a web server to set up with the correct MIME types (originally known as Multipurpose Internet Mail Extensions, but the word *Mail* has since been replaced with *Media*), in order for a browser that understands Web Applications to make use of the feature and fetch the files it needs. Lecture 20 goes into web applications in greater detail.

Summary

This lecture has introduced you to all the new goodies in HTML5. In the following lectures I will explain each of these main areas in depth so that you can begin to use the tags that have been widely supported in your own web pages, and will be prepared to also include the lesser-supported ones as browsers pick them up.

LECTURE 9

AN INTRODUCTION TO THE HTML5 CANVAS

By following this lecture you will:

- ✓ *Get a basic understand of how JavaScript works.*
- ✓ *Be shown a couple of powerful and invaluable JavaScript functions.*
- ✓ *Learn the basics of the* `<canvas>` *tag.*

IF I'M GOING to show you how to use the HTML5 Canvas then I'm also going to have to give you and ultra-crash course on JavaScript, or at least on those aspects of it required for manipulating the canvas.

So here goes (if you already know JavaScript you can briefly skim the following section, before moving onto the *Accessing The Canvas* section).

***Note**: The examples from this lecture are in the* Lecture 9 *folder of the* examples.zip *file at* tinyurlcom/html5ccexamples.

An Ultra-Crash Course in JavaScript

Although I'm going to teach you a few parts of JavaScript it is by no means the entire language, but it will be sufficient for you to complement your use of HTML for manipulating the canvas. Along the way I also touch upon a few elements of CSS (Cascading Style Sheets) too.

JavaScript was created to allow you to directly access various parts of the HTML DOM (Document Object Model). To explain the DOM take a look at the following example web page:

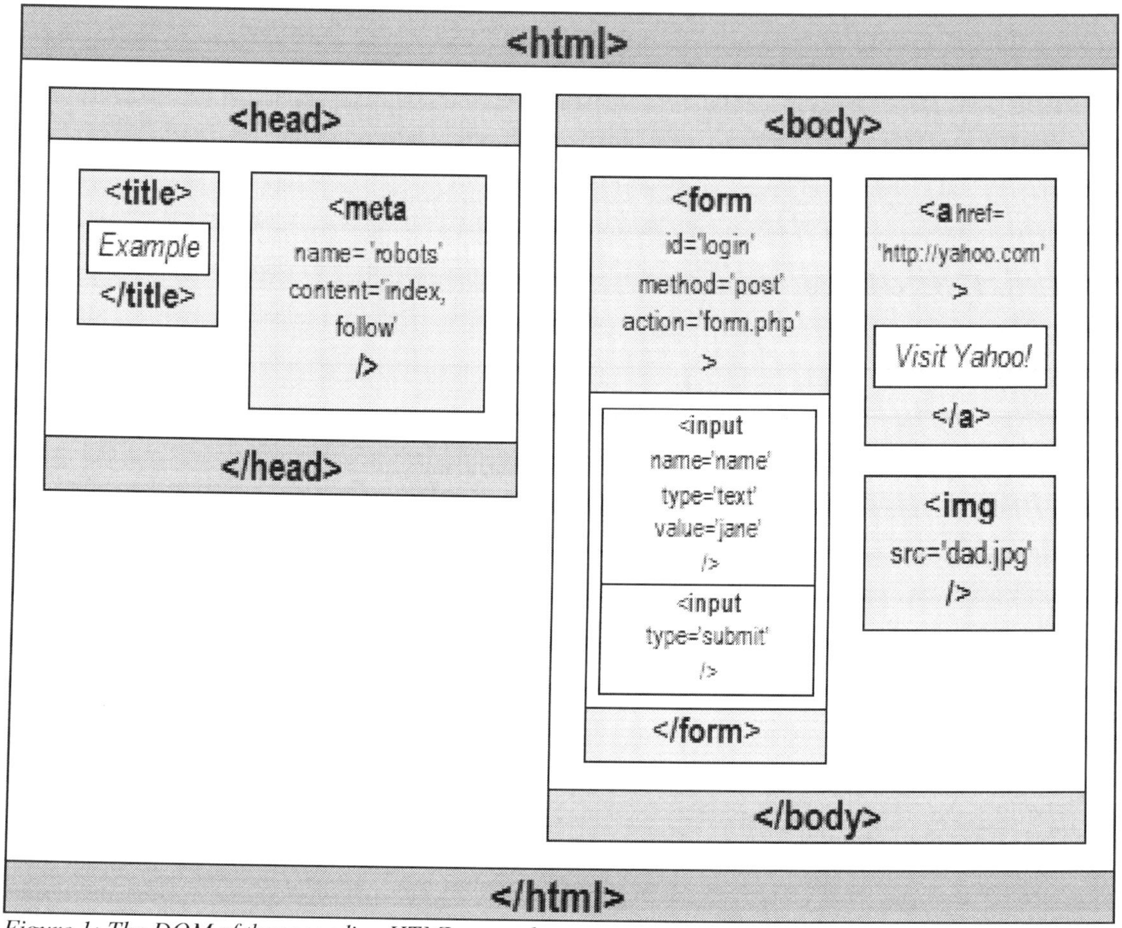

Figure 1: The DOM of the preceding HTML example

```
<html>
  <head>
    <title>Example</title>
    <meta name='robots' content='index, follow' />
  </head>
  <body>
    <a href='http://yahoo.com'>Visit Yahoo!</a>
    <form id='login' method='post' action='form.php'>
      <input name='name' type='text' value='jane' />
      <input type='submit' />
    </form>
    <img src='dad.jpg' />
  </body>
</html>
```

This is a simple page that displays a link to the Yahoo! Website and has a form underneath that submits a username to PHP script with the filename *form.php*. Beneath that an image is included. In terms of this web page's DOM, it looks something like Figure 9-1, in which the entire contents is contained with `<html>` and `</html>` tags.

Looking at the `<head>` section in Figure 9-1 you can see that there are two elements. The first is the document's title of *Example*, contained within `<title>` and `</title>` tags, while the second is the meta tag that tells search engine crawlers that the document may be crawled, its contents indexed and any links can be followed. This is done by passing the value `robots` to the `name` attribute, and `'index, follow'` to the `content` attribute. Meta tags are self-closing so there is no </meta> tag. The section is then closed with a `</head>` tag.

To the right of the figure is the body of the document, which is contained within `<body>` and `</body>` tags. There are three elements in this section, a link to *yahoo.com* in `<a>` and `</a>` tags, an embedded image that uses a self-closing `<img />` tag, and a form contain within `<form>` and `</form>` tags.

The form passes a value of `login` to the `id` attribute, `post'` to the `method` attribute, and the program name `'form.php'` to the `action` attribute. This is the program that is to process the form when it is submitted. The opening `<form>` tag is then closed and inside the form there are two self-closing `<input>` tags. The first passes the value `name` to the `name` attribute, `text` to the `type` attribute, and the value `jane` to the `name` attribute. This pre-populates the input field with the word `jane` but it can be altered by the user.

After this a second `<input>` tag creates a submit button by passing the value `submit` to its `type` attribute. Finally the form is closed with a `</form>` tag. When opened in a browser the document looks something like Figure 9-2.

Accessing Form Elements From JavaScript

Now let's look at how these elements can be manipulated from JavaScript, which should always be placed within `<script>` and `</script>` tags. For example, the following code changes the document's title from *Example* to *This is an example web page*:

```
<script>
  document.title = 'This is an example web page'
</script>
```

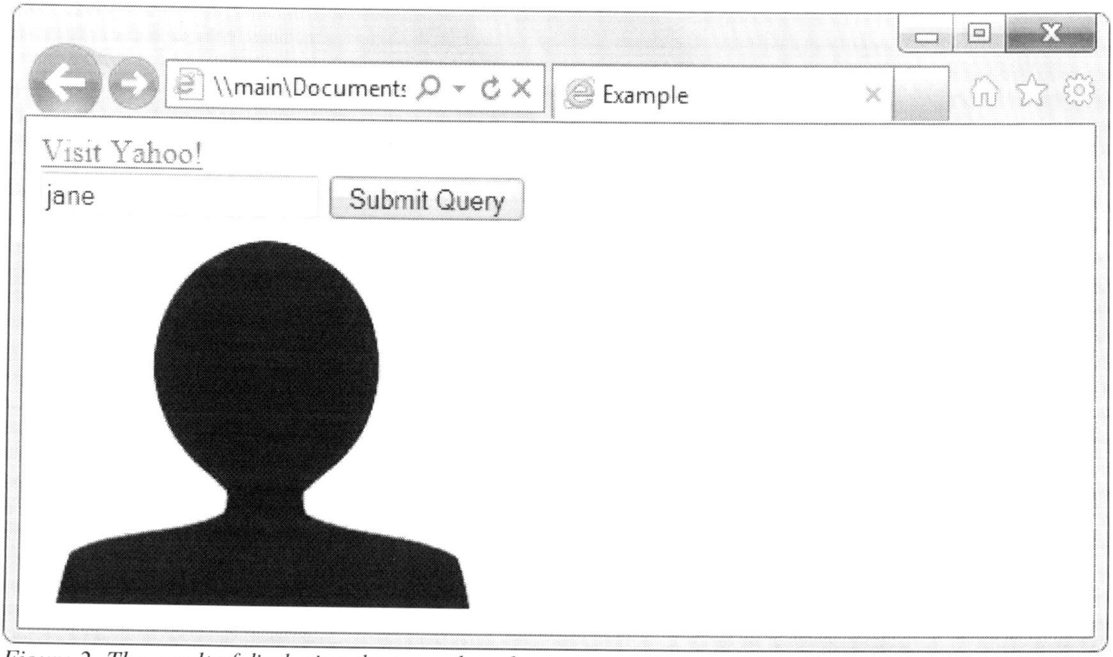

Figure 2: The result of displaying the example web page

This has the same effect as if you opened the document and went straight in and edited the title within the `<title>` and `</title>` tags yourself. See how easy JavaScript is?

Similarly the form method type of `post'` is easily changed to `get`, like this:

```
<script>
  document.forms.login.method = 'get'
</script>
```

Here the JavaScript references first the `document`, then the `forms` within that document, then the form with the `id` of `login` and its `method`, which is then modified.

Using the `getElementById()` Function

In the previous two examples I showed you how to access parts of a document by their type, but there's a far, far easier method, which is to give every element in a document a unique `id`, and then to access them from JavaScript using just those `id`s.

For example, if the `<img />` tag is given an `id` (such as `image1`) with which it can be identified, it's possible to replace the image loaded by it with another, like the following, in which the male-shaped *dad.jpg* image is replaced with *mom.jpg* to match the default name in the form field of *jane*:

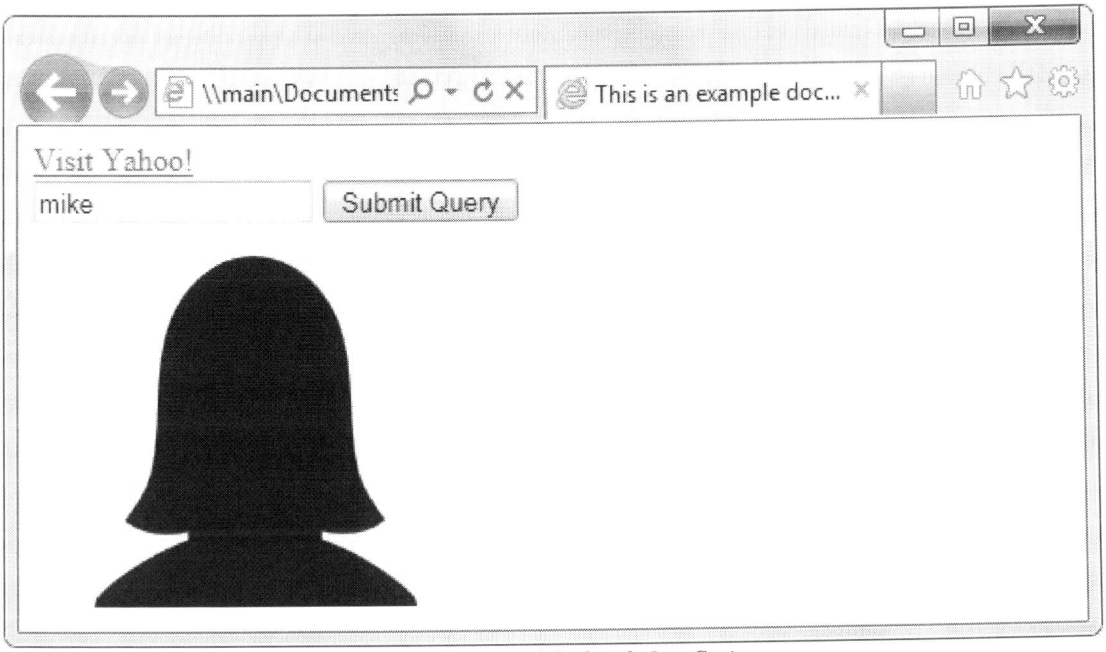

Figure 3: Three elements of the page have been modified with JavaScript

```
<img src='dad.jpg' id='image1' />

<script>
  document.getElementById('image1').src = 'mom.jpg'
</script>
```

The trick here is to use the JavaScript function `getElementById()` which will let you access any DOM element that has been given a unique `id`.

So let's look at another example by restoring the previous name and image mismatch by altering the default name value directly, rather that accessing the element via `document.forms.login`.

By giving the form field an `id` (for example of `'name'`) and using `getElementById()` we can avoid the long-windedness of the previous example and go straight to the element to change it, like this (in which I have shown only the changed `<input>` tag and not the remainder of the HTML – which remains unchanged):

```
<input name='name' type='text' value='jane' id='name' />

<script>
```

```
    document.getElementById('name').value = 'mike'
  </script>
```

See how much easier it is that having to remember whether an element is part of a form, and image or something else? All you have to do is know the name of an element and `getElementById()` will do the job of finding it for you. Figure 9-3 shows how the web page now displays after these changes. The title is different, the default input value is `'mike'` and the image shown is *mom.jpg* (yes, the gender is all confused again).

The Simpler `O()` Function

I use the `getElementById()` function so often that I always create a simple function called `O()` (with an upper case `O`) to make it quicker to type in. The function looks like this and I place it at the start of any JavaScript, right after the opening `<script>` tag, like this:

```
<script>
  function O(obj)
  { return document.getElementById(obj) }

  O('name').value = 'mike'
</script>
```

Doing this saves 22 characters of typing each time the replacement `O()` function is used instead of the longer one. One reason for the tremendous shortening is because the preceding `document.` has also been incorporated into the `O()` function, saving on typing that in too.

Note*: In JavaScript tutorials on the web and in books you may see functions referred to either by the term* function*, or using the term* method*, but they both mean the same thing: a set of instructions grouped together which can receive one or more values, and can then return a value upon completion.*

However, there's one further step I like to take that makes the function even more useful and that's to allow the passing to it of either element `id`s (which is what it does so far), or an object that has already been created as the result of having called the `O()` function.

Let me explain it like this. Instead of directly manipulating the value of the form input with the `id` of `'name'` directly, let's first create what is called an object from this element, like this:

```
newobject = O('name')
```

Now that I have this object I can access it several times without ever having to call the `O()` function again, like this (in which the value is changed on two separate occasions):

```
newobject.value = 'mike'
  // A few lines of code go here
newobject.value = 'fred'
```

However, I am a lazy programmer and once I have created a function I like to reuse it rather than write a new one, and there are times when I would also like to pass either an object to the `O()` function (as you'll see in the following section) or an `id` name.

Therefore I prefer to use the following version of the function, which supports either type of argument:

```
function O(obj) { if (typeof obj == 'object')
  return obj
  else return document.getElementById(obj) }
```

What is happening here is that the argument passed in `obj` is analyzed by the code and if it happens to already be of the type `'object'` then the object is simply returned, because it is already an object.

But if it is not of that type then it must be an `id` name, in which case it is looked up and returned as an object with a call to `getElementById()`.

Note: *If this confuses you, don't worry. You don't need to learn JavaScript, or (indeed) understand fully the workings of these snippets of code, in order to use the following examples to access the HTML5 canvas.*

The Partner `S()` Function

In a similar fashion to the savings produced by using the `O()` function, there is one other function that I employ frequently because it is also used all the time in JavaScript, and that's the new function `S()` (with an upper case `S`).

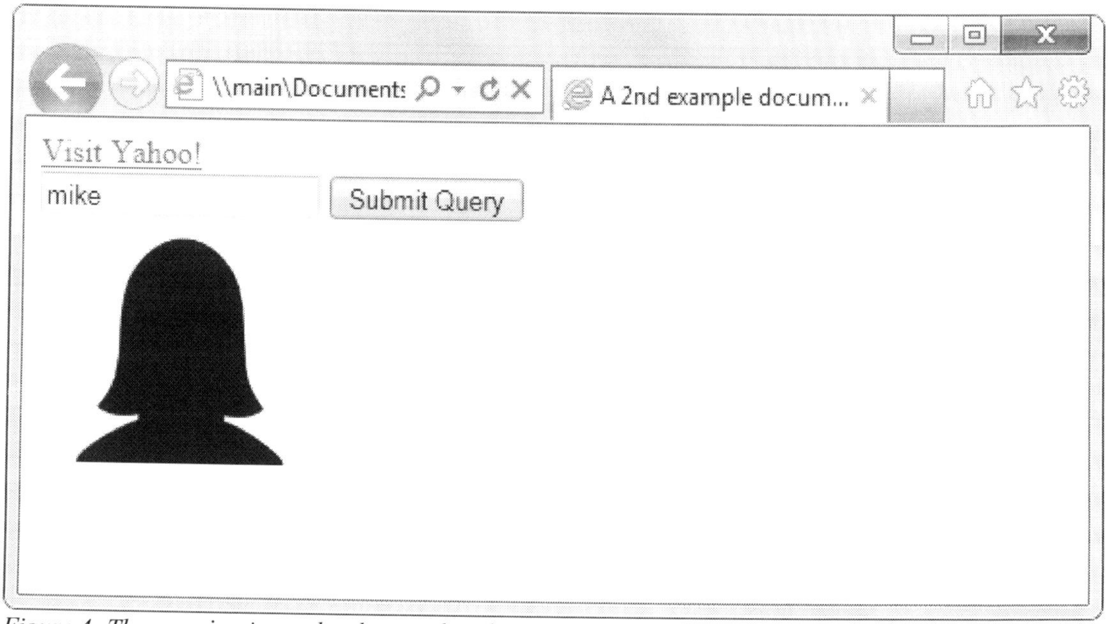

Figure 4: The mom.jpg *image has been reduced in size*

This is used to enable JavaScript to easily access any style attribute of any element.

For example, if I wish to change the width and height of the image I can do it like this (which results in Figure 9-4, when the other lines of HTML and JavaScript we've been using are included):

```
<img src='dad.jpg' id='image1' />

<script>
  function O(obj) { if (typeof obj == 'object')
    return obj
    else return document.getElementById(obj) }
  function S(obj) { return O(obj).style }

  O('image1').style.width = '150px' // Longer syntax
  S('image1').height      = '120px' // Shorter syntax
</script>
```

***Note**: The // characters create a single line comment, which I have used in the preceding example to comment each of the final two lines within the script (that the second version of syntax is shorter than the first).*

What I've done here is simply make the `S()` function place a call to the `O()` function but with an added `.style` suffix, and now I can use `O()` for accessing elements by name, and `S()` for accessing the style attributes of elements by name.

What's more, because the `O()` function allows both `id` names or objects, I can pass either type of argument to `S()` as well. So, if I have an object called `myobject` perhaps previously created from a `<div>` element using the `O()` function, I can change its width like this:

```
S(myobject).width = '100px'
```

Believe it or not, these two functions alone provide you with a huge amount of scope and power to modify any part of a document, without learning the JavaScript language. All you need to remember to do is include the following code near the start of any HTML document:

```
<script>
  function O(obj) { if (typeof obj == 'object')
    return obj;
    else return document.getElementById(obj) }
  function S(obj) { return O(obj).style }
</script>
```

Then, whenever you need to use these functions open up a new `<script>` tag and access them using code such as this:

```
<script>
  S('image1').width  = '150px'
  myobject           = O('image2')
  S(myobject).height = '120px'
</script>
```

This works because you are allowed to enter `<script>` tags as many times as you like in a document – there is no requirement to keep all your JavaScript code within a single set of `<script>` and `</script>` tags, although you may do so if you wish.

This code can be quicker as the object is only looked up once, and is therefore a more efficient way to code when an element may be accessed more than once.

By the way, the reason `myobject` does not have quotation marks around it is because it is an object, not an `id` value.

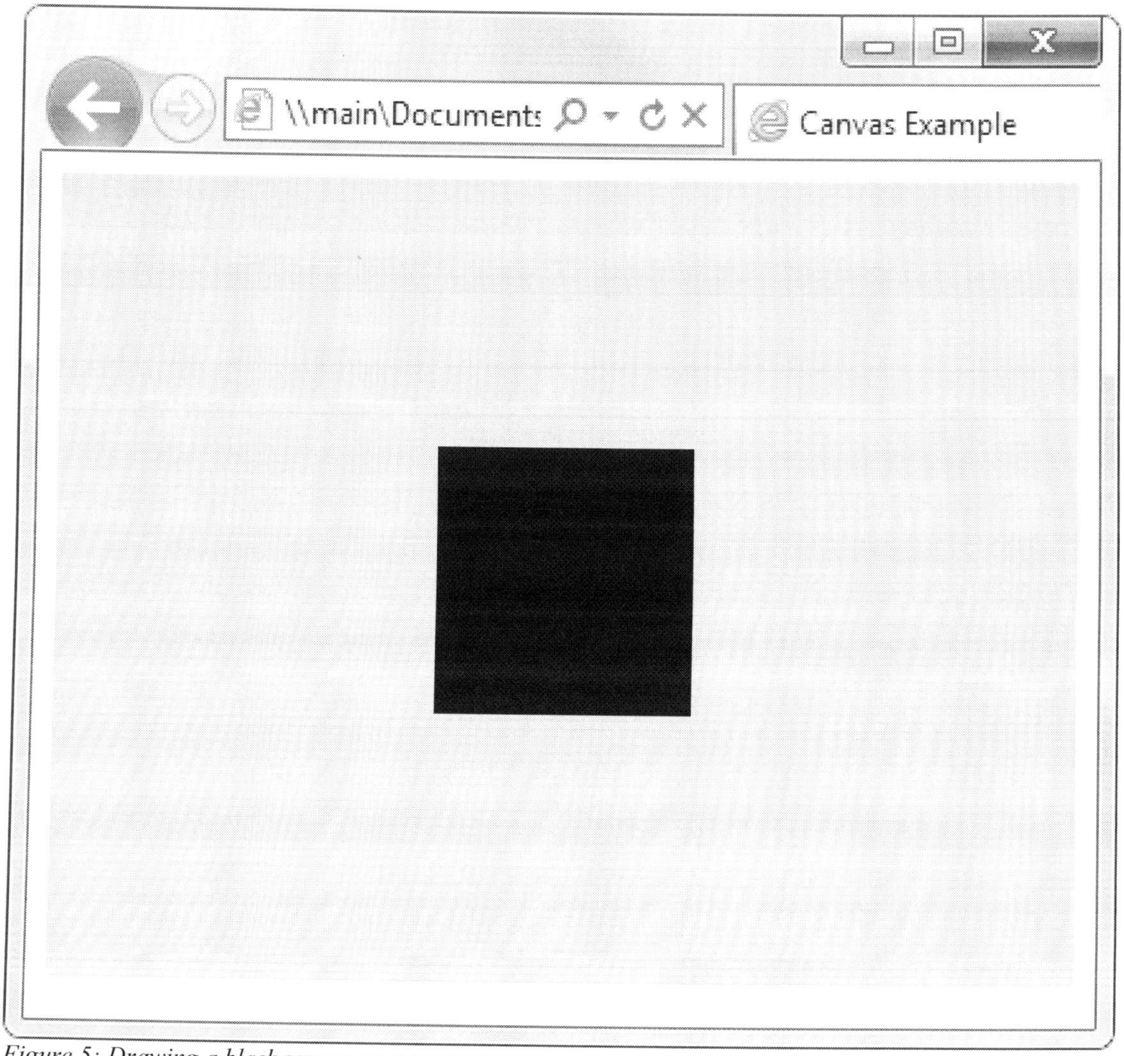

Figure 5: Drawing a black square on a gray canvas

***Note**: I use the functions `O()` and `S()` extensively throughout this course, so I recommend you get comfortable with using them by downloading the examples from the companion website (detailed at the start of this lecture), and then playing with them until you feel you have mastered their use.*

The `<canvas>` Tag

With that little (but necessary) preamble over, now we can get down to directly manipulating an HTML5 canvas.

As you may recall from Lecture 8, the following code creates a canvas and places a square in its center (resulting in Figure 9-5):

```
<canvas id='canvas1' width='400' height='300'>
  This web page uses the HTML5 canvas element, which is
  available on most modern browsers. If you wish to view
  this page at its best, please upgrade your browser to
  the most recent version.
</canvas>

<script>
  function O(obj) { if (typeof obj == 'object')
    return obj;
    else return document.getElementById(obj) }
  function S(obj) { return O(obj).style }

  canvas                = O('canvas1')
  S(canvas).background = '#DDD'
  context               = canvas.getContext('2d')
  context.fillRect(150, 100, 100, 100)
</script>
```

The `<canvas>` tag itself supports only two attributes; `width` and `height`, as used in the example. And it is important that you provide a unique identifier for each canvas you use, so that you can access them from JavaScript. In the example the `id` is given a value of `'canvas1'`.

The other thing to remember about the `<canvas>` tag is that anything between it and the closing `</canvas>` tag is ignored by all HTML5-compatible browsers, and so is displayed only by browsers that do not recognize it.

Therefore this is where you can place text and/or HTML to inform users about what they are missing and perhaps how to upgrade their browser.

Accessing The Canvas with JavaScript

Let's look closely at the code from the previous example, as follows:

```
<script>
  function O(obj) { if (typeof obj == 'object')
    return obj;
    else return document.getElementById(obj) }
  function S(obj) { return O(obj).style }

  canvas                = O('canvas1')
```

```
    S(canvas).background = '#DDD'
    context              = canvas.getContext('2d')
    context.fillRect(150, 100, 100, 100)
  </script>
```

Ignoring the opening and closing tags, the first four lines are the `O()` and `S()` functions previously described. Next the object `canvas` is created by passing the `id` of the canvas (`'canvas1'`) to the `O()` function.

Armed with this object the following line passes it to the `S()` function and then sets its `background` property to a light gray (`#DDD`) color. This is where the power of extending the `O()` function to also support objects comes in (because the `S()` function calls the `O()` function).

By virtue of this extension it has been a simple matter to pass the object created from the canvas straight to the `S()` function, allowing for far simpler and more compact coding.

Next, to be able to read from and write to the canvas a context (with the name `context`) is created with which to access it, using the JavaScript `getContext()` function, which is told to treat the canvas as a two dimensional workspace.

Then the final line uses this context to create a filled rectangle at an offset of 150 pixels horizontally from the top left corner, and 100 pixels vertically. The rectangle is given a width and height of 100 pixels, resulting in a filled, black square.

***Note**: From now onwards I will be assuming that you have placed the two functions `O()` and `S()` within `<script>` and `</script>` tags somewhere in your document, and will not be showing the code for these functions in any more examples. So please ensure that you have included them somewhere before testing any examples, or they will not work.*

Converting a Canvas to an Image

Because of the way the canvas is created it is not possible for users to right click and save a copy to the desk top, for example. Likewise you cannot directly use a canvas as an image.

But there is a way you can convert a canvas to what is known as a data URL. This displays as an image and can then be copied and/or saved.

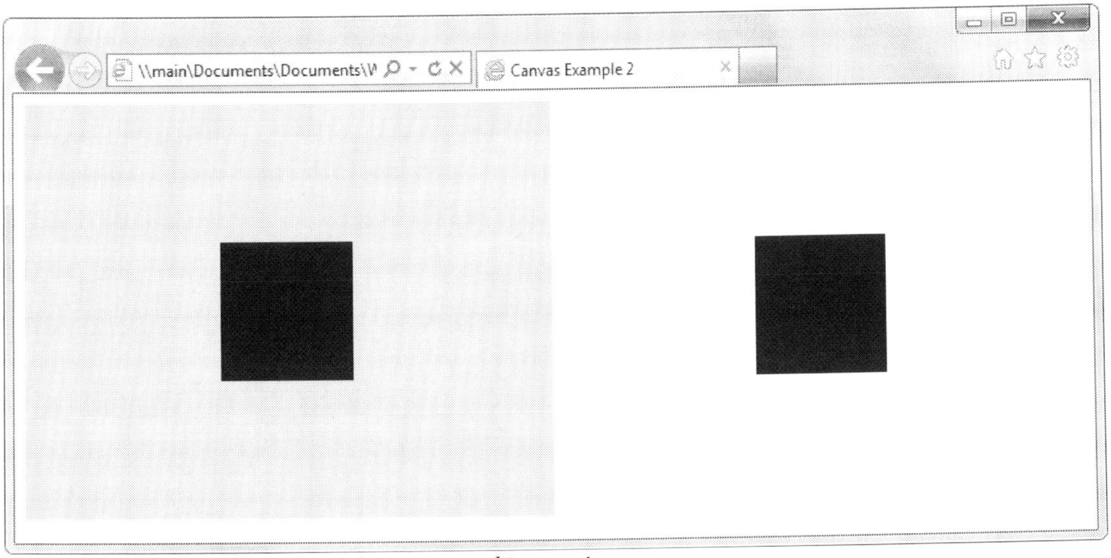

Figure 6: Displaying a canvas and a copy saved into an image

Consider the following code in which a canvas is created and the followed by an image, which does not have any `src` attribute:

```
<canvas id='canvas1' width='400' height='300'></canvas>
<img id='image' />

<script>
  canvas                 = O('canvas1')
  S(canvas).background = '#DDD'
  context                = canvas.getContext('2d')
  context.fillRect(150, 100, 100, 100)

  O('image').src = canvas.toDataURL()
</script>
```

What this code does (remember it assumes you already have the `O()` and `S()` functions listed somewhere), is identical to the previous example, but there is a new line of code at the end that accesses the image using the `O()` function and then attaches a value to its `src` attribute, which is gained by calling the `toDataURL()` function on the `canvas` object.

The `toDataURL()` function extracts the image data from the canvas referred to by the `canvas` object and returns a string of text in which the canvas has been encoded as a displayable image, which is interpreted by the browser and reconstructed into an image. When the code is loaded into a browser it displays as Figure 9-6. Notice how the background color of the canvas (which has been applied only to the canvas element and not the contents of the canvas) is ignored by the `toDataURL()` function, so that when the image data is extracted you see only the central black square.

The `imagetype` Argument

When an image is created from a canvas you can choose the type of image to use between a *.jpg* and *.png* image using the `imagetype` argument, as in the following two examples, which are identical in result since the default image type is *.png*.

```
O('image').src = canvas.toDataURL()
O('image').src = canvas.toDataURL('image/png')
```

Or, for a *.jpg* image, you can use code such as the following three examples which create a very low quality, medium quality and a very high quality image by passing an additional argument containing a value between 0 (low quality) and 1 (high quality)

```
O('image').src = canvas.toDataURL('image/jpeg', 0)
O('image').src = canvas.toDataURL('image/jpeg', 0.5)
O('image').src = canvas.toDataURL('image/jpeg', 1)
```

***Note**: Remember that the* `canvas` *object is used by the* `toDataURL()` *method not the* `context` *object. This is because the latter is for applying changes to the canvas using the context rendering assigned, while the former refers to the canvas itself.*

Uses for this feature could be online image manipulation programs that run in the browser (as opposed to on a web server somewhere far away from the browser), and which returns a transformed or newly created image ready for the user to save to their hard disk and use. This means that it is possible to use the HTML5 canvas to create a fully featured graphics program, like Photoshop, that runs within a browser and requires no interaction with a web server. Therefore it could also be turned into a web app or even a standalone app for a mobile device like a tablet or phone.

Summary

Now that you have understood the basic elements of the HTML5 canvas, and have the tools and information required to use it, in the following lectures I will explain in depth how to use each aspect of the features available for writing to a canvas, including drawing lines, rectangles and circles, changing colors, using pattern and gradient fills, writing text, changing font face, using lines, paths and curves, applying images to a canvas, adding shadows, direct pixel manipulation, compositing and transparency, and more.

LECTURE 10

RECTANGLES, FILLS, GRADIENTS AND PATTERNS

By following this lecture you will:

✓ *Be able to draw a range of different types of rectangles.*

✓ *Understand how to fill in areas with fills and gradients.*

✓ *Know how to load an external image to use as a fill pattern.*

NOW THAT YOU'VE seen how to use JavaScript to access the HTML5 canvas let's look at all the different functions available for creating different effects, including drawing lines, rectangles and circles, changing colors, and using pattern and gradient fills.

***Note**: The examples from this lecture are in the* Lecture 10 *folder of the* examples.zip *file at* tinyurlcom/html5ccexamples.

Drawing Rectangles

Other than drawing lines (which we'll get to later, since they are handled using paths), rectangles are probably the simplest type of object you can draw onto an HTML5 canvas, as you've already seen with the `fillRect()` function used in a couple of examples.

You can also fill a rectangle with a color other than black, can create unfilled (or clear) rectangles with different border widths, line styles and corners.

***Note**: Remember that in JavaScript* functions *are also often referred to as* methods, *but as the terms are interchangeable I have selected to use only the word function.*

The `fillRect(x,y,w,h)` Function

This is the function we have explored already, it takes four arguments representing the vertical and horizontal offsets of the top left hand corner of a rectangle from the top left corner of the canvas, followed by the rectangles width and height, all of which are in units of pixels, or one screen dot.

The syntax of the function is as follows, which (in this instance) creates a 50 pixels wide and 70 pixels high filled rectangle, at an offset of 20 pixels in from the left edge of the (410 by 170 pixels) canvas, and 30 pixels down from its top:

```
<canvas id='example' width='410' height='170'></canvas>

<script>
  // The O() and S() functions go here,
  // or in an earlier script section

  canvas                   = O('example')
  S(canvas).background = '#DDD'

  context.fillRect(20, 30, 50, 70)
</script>
```

This example shows all the bits and pieces needed to set up everything ready to make the call to `fillRect()`, but for simplicity in the rest of this lecture I will show only the relevant calls required for the function or functions being explained, like this:

```
context.fillRect(20, 30, 50, 70)
```

***Note**: If you are trying out these examples, you must ensure that you have first created a suitable canvas using the `<canvas>` and `</canvas>` tags and specified a reasonable width and height for it (with enough room to display whatever is written to the canvas). You must also have entered the `O()` and `S()` functions within any pair of `<script>` and `</script>` tags preceding (or including) the current pair, and have created a context for accessing the canvas called `context`.*

The default color of a filled rectangle is black but you will learn how to change this in the next section, or even how to use a gradient or a pattern to fill it later in this lecture.

The `fillStyle` Property

Using this property you can set the type of fill color to use, using either short (three digit) or long (six digit) hexadecimal colors. For example, to choose red you can pass the value `#F00` or `#FF0000`, like this:

```
context.fillStyle = '#F00'
```

You may also use any of the HTML color names (listed in Lecture 4) such as `red`, `steelblue` and so on, like this:

```
context.fillStyle = 'red'
```

Once selected the color will apply to all fill operations until it is changed. For example, the following pair of lines will create a red rectangle, rather than a (default) black one:

```
context.fillStyle = 'red'
context.fillRect(20, 30, 50, 70)
```

For more information on using colors please refer to *Lecture 4*.

The `clearRect(x,y,w,h)` Function

If you want to draw a clear rectangle, in which all the RGBA (Red, Green Blue and Alpha transparency) values of a pixel are set to zero you can use this function, as follows:

```
context.clearRect(20, 30, 50, 70)
```

The `clearRect()` function uses the same arguments as `fillRect()`, namely the horizontal and vertical offset of the top left hand corner of the rectangle from the top left corner of the canvas, followed by the width and height of the rectangle to clear.

The cleared area will be stripped of all color, leaving only any underlying background color that may have been applied to the `<canvas>` tag (and which therefore is not part of the canvas, but is actually underneath it).

The `strokeRect(x,y,w,h)` Function

With the `strokeRect()` function you can create a rectangle that uses the current `strokeStyle`, `lineWidth`, `lineJoin`, and `miterLimit` properties to draw the border lines and corners (as detailed in the *Drawing Lines* section later on), and is used like this:

```
context.strokeRect(20, 30, 50, 70)
```

The function takes the same arguments as `fillRect()`, namely the horizontal and vertical offset of the top left hand corner of the rectangle from the top left corner of the canvas, followed by the width and height of the rectangle to draw.

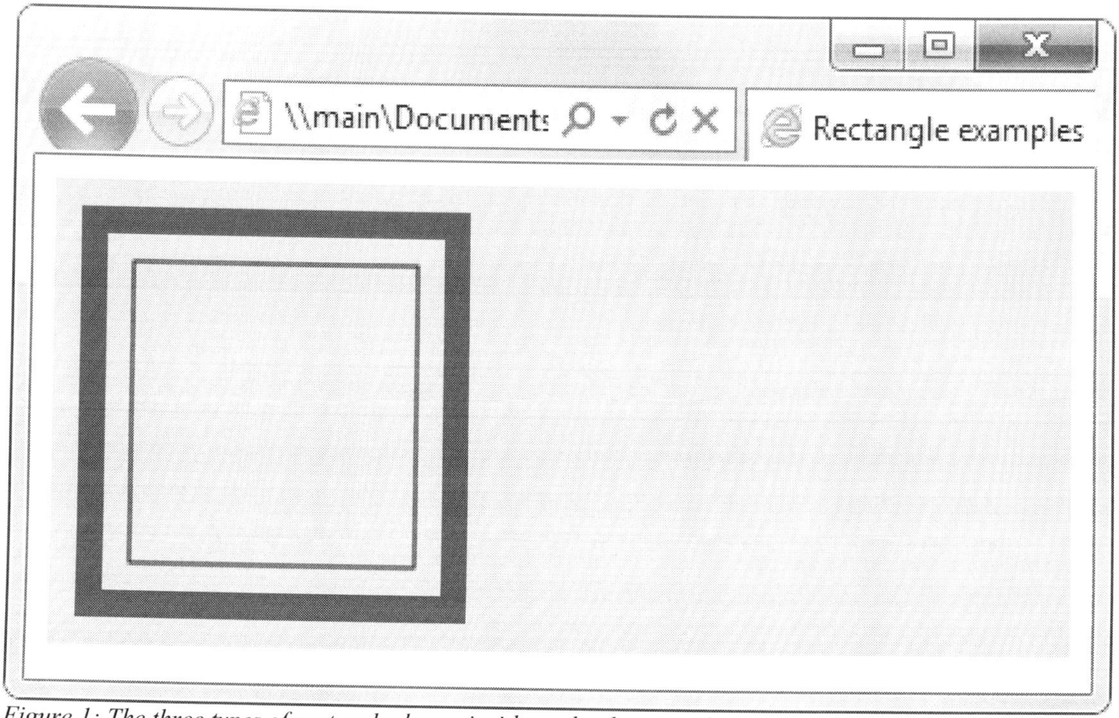

Figure 1: The three types of rectangle drawn inside each other in red

It is possible to apply these effects on their own or in combination with others, so the following code (in which I have lined up the columns of arguments for ease of comparison) is valid and results in Figure 10-1.

In the figure red outer square created using `fillRect()` has a clear one drawn over it using `clearRect()`, and within the clear square is another created using the `strokeRect()` function. the inner square has slightly rounded corners due to the default stroke style:

```
context.fillStyle = 'red'
context.fillRect(  10, 10, 150, 150)
context.clearRect( 20, 20, 130, 130)
context.strokeRect(30, 30, 110, 110)
```

***Note**: I have covered rectangles before lines because they are simpler to draw. As you will see later, lines must be drawn by creating paths of locations that you connect up. Therefore the properties that are associated with lines and paths are explained in that section, rather than here.*

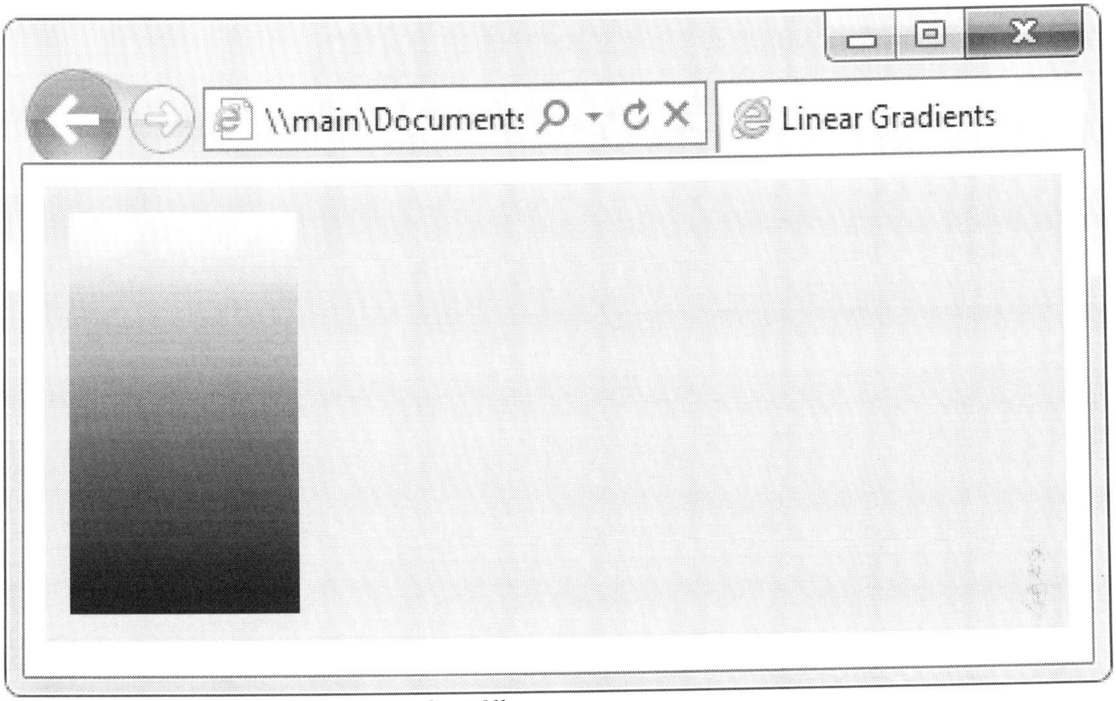

Figure 2: A vertically aligned linear gradient fill

Creating Gradients

You saw how to create a simple, filled rectangle in the previous section, but it's also easy to apply a variety of different types of gradient to both the `fillRect()` function as already seen, and the `fill()` function which is introduced later on.

The `createLinearGradient(x1,y1,x2,y2)` Function

The simplest type of gradient available with the HTML5 canvas is a default linear gradient. To create a linear gradient you need to specify the colors to use and the positions at which they should change. For example, in the following statement the object `gradient` is set to start at the location `55,10` and end at `55,160`, using the `createLinearGradient()` function:

```
gradient = context.createLinearGradient(55, 10, 55, 160)
```

Why these coordinates? Well, you must specify the start and end relative to the entire canvas, not to the object being filled. Therefore, seeing as I will be drawing a 90 by 150

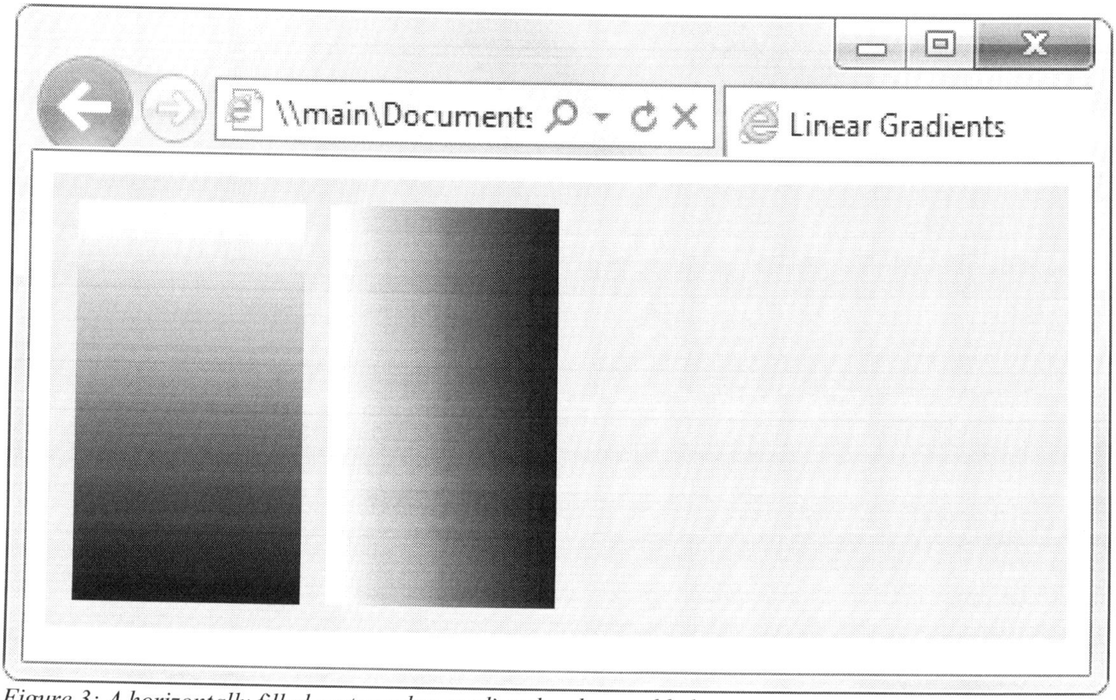

Figure 3: A horizontally filled rectangular gradient has been added

pixel rectangle with its top left corner at location `10,10`, then I choose a start point of `55,10`, which is halfway along the top of the rectangle, and an end point of `55,160`, which is halfway along the rectangle's bottom edge.

***Note**: The reason that the gradient start and end locations are relative to the canvas and not to objects being filled is to allow you greater subtlety and the ability to create a gradient that covers the entire canvas (or as much or little as you like), and of which only that part existent underneath an object being filled is revealed. This, for example, would enable you to create a gradient that represents a sunset and then draw the inside of a car and use the gradient fill on the windows to reveal the correct parts of the outside gradient behind the windows.*

Now that the linear gradient object is created it is necessary to choose the start and end colors, as with the following two lines, which set a start stop position (as it is known) of the color `#FFF` (white), and an end of `#000` (black).

This is achieved using the `addColorStop()` function, which is fully explained a little further on, as follows

```
gradient.addColorStop(0, '#FFF')
gradient.addColorStop(1, '#000')
```

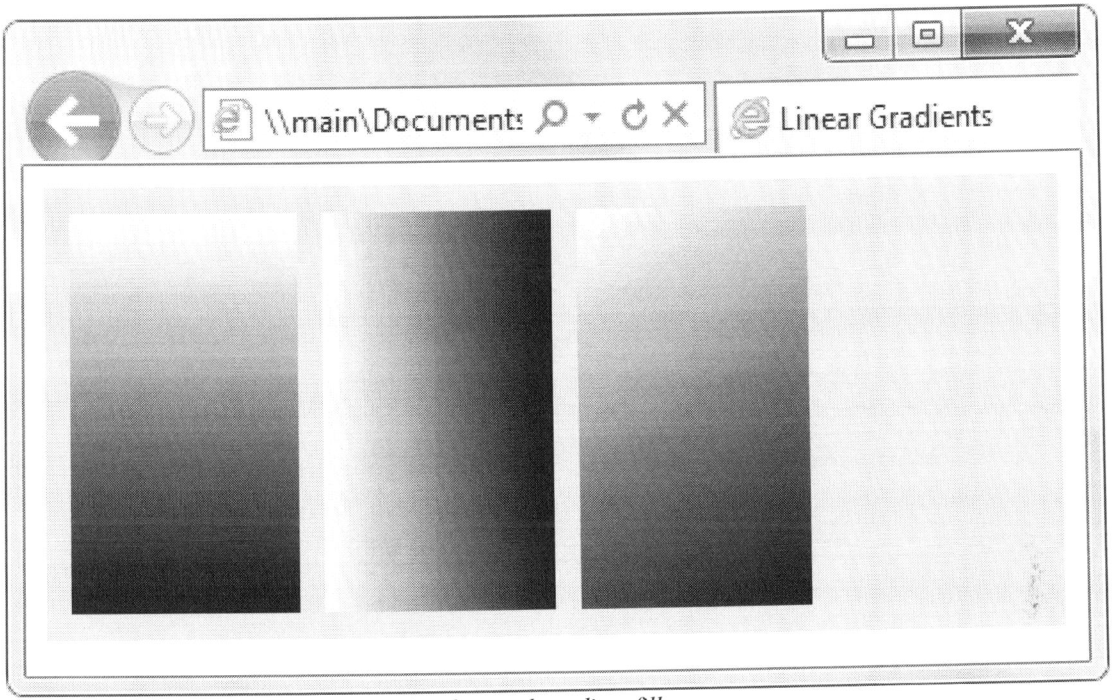

Figure 4: A new rectangle is added with a diagonal gradient fill

What these two calls do is specify with the first argument to each the position at which the color is to be applied (in these case they are `0` and `1` for the start and end), and the second argument sets the color to apply at each of these positions.

This gradient is then applied to the current context using the `fillStyle` property, and then a 90 by 150 pixels rectangle is drawn using these fill values:

```
context.fillStyle = gradient
context.fillRect(10, 10, 90, 150)
```

The result of these commands looks like Figure 10-2, in which you can see the fill fade linearly from white to black starting at the top and ending at the bottom of the rectangle.

You can change the start and end coordinates for the fill to any other locations. For example, in Figure 10-2 a second rectangle has been filled from left to right by choosing the following values for the call to `createLinearGradient()`:

```
gradient = context.createLinearGradient(110, 85, 200, 85)
```

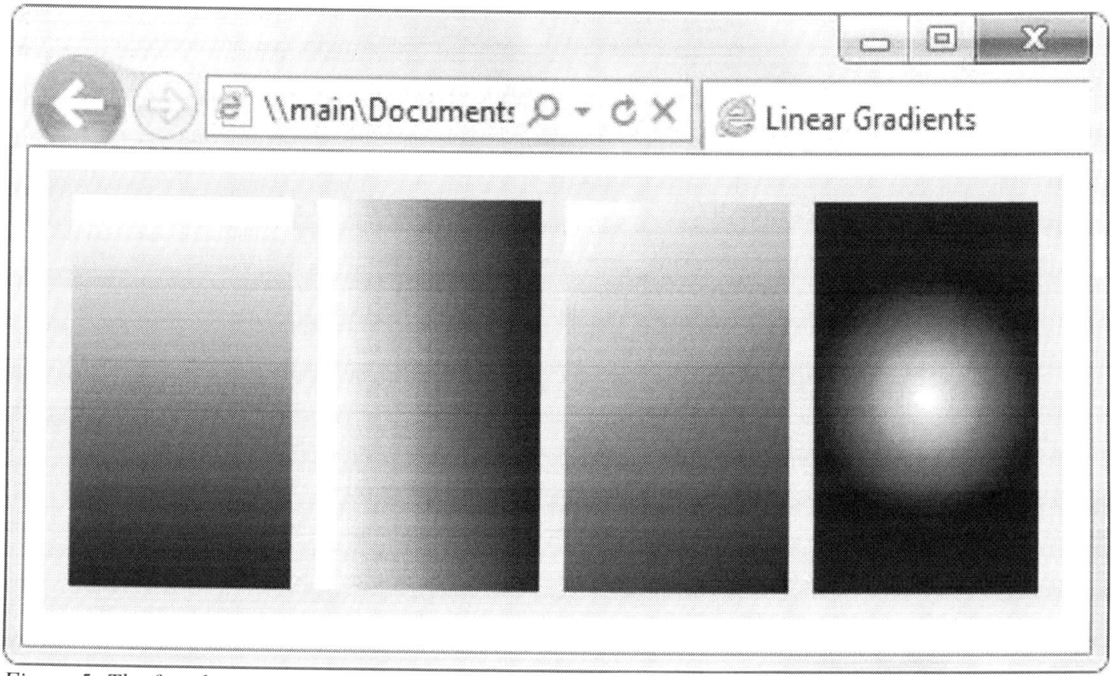

Figure 5: The fourth rectangle features a radial gradient

These coordinates specify a start point halfway down the rectangle's left edge, and an end that is halfway down its right edge, as used by this `fillRect()` call:

```
context.fillRect(110, 85, 200, 85)
```

In fact you can choose any start and end location (within or without the area to be filled) as, for example, with this code, which creates a diagonal gradient from top left (`210,60`) to bottom right (`300,160`), as shown in Figure 10-4:

```
gradient = context.createLinearGradient(210, 10, 300, 160)
context.fillRect(210, 10, 90, 150)
```

The `createRadialGradient(x1,y1,r1,x2,y2,r2)` Function

You can also create a gradient that expands radially. That is, it starts at a point and has a certain radius, and then ends focused around another point, with a different (or the same) radius. For example, the following call to `createRadialGradient()` specifies an initial location at the center of a rectangle and a width of 0 pixels. The second pair of coordinates remains the same, but with a radius of 45 pixels, so that the gradient starts in the center and

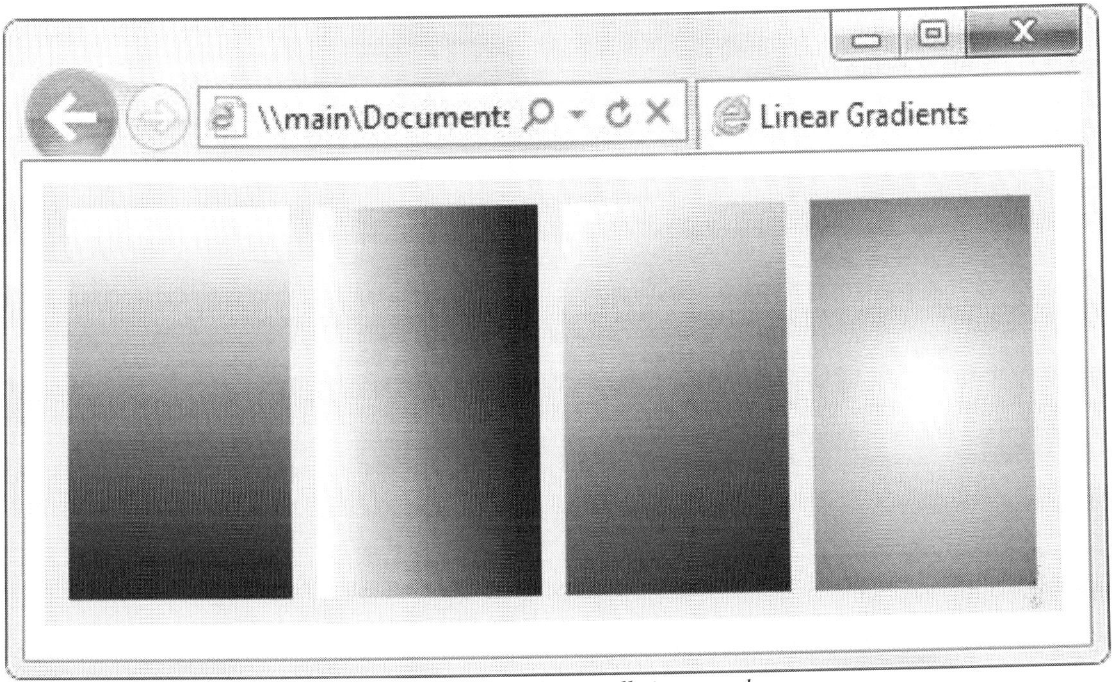

Figure 6: The radius of the gradient fill has been substantially increased

continues to the left and right edges. As you can see in Figure 10-5, The top and bottom of the rectangle are outside the radius and so are provided with the color applied to the final stop, which is black:

```
gradient =
  context.createRadialGradient(355, 85, 0, 355, 85, 45)
context.fillRect(310, 10, 90, 150)
```

So that you can see the effect of using start and/or end coordinates that are outside the area being filled, I have increased the radius of the second part of the gradient in Figure 10-6 to 150 pixels, so that it extends past all the rectangle's edges, like this (as shown in Figure 10-6):

```
gradient = context.createRadialGradient(355, 85, 0, 355, 85, 150)
```

***Note**: The second radius value of 150 pixels creates a circle of diameter 300 pixels. But note how although this circle extends beyond the area being filled and well into the previous rectangle, the other rectangle is not affected. This is because the gradient applies only to future fills, and not to any pre-existing fills.*

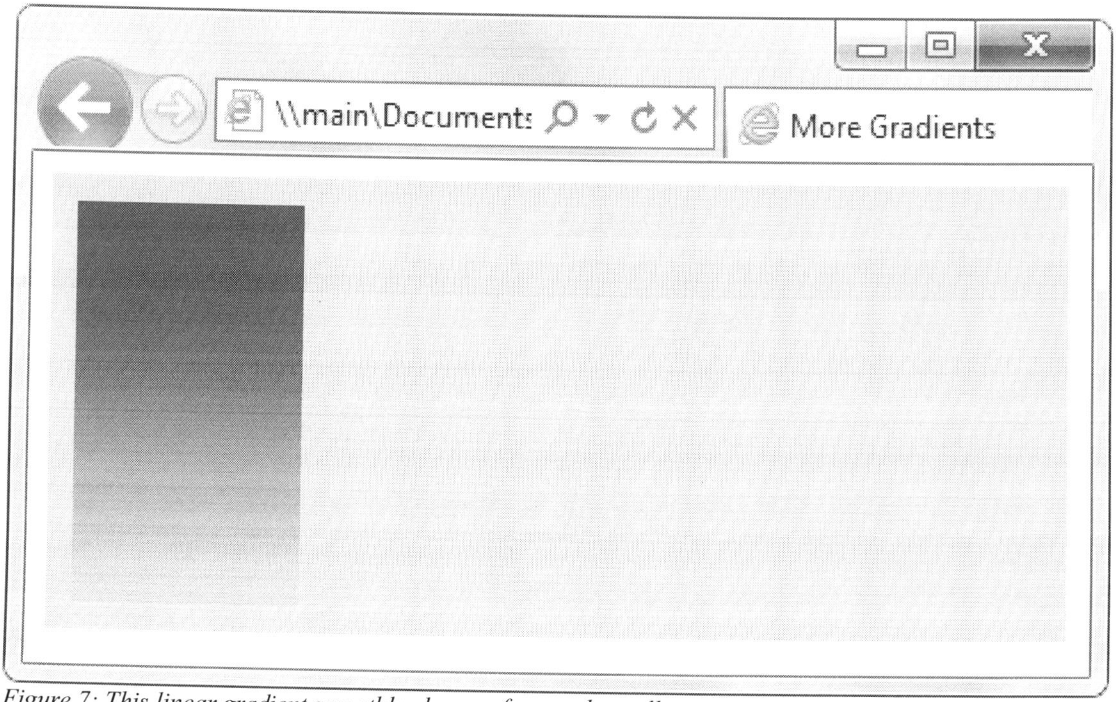

Figure 7: This linear gradient smoothly changes from red to yellow

The `addColorStop(p, c)` Function

Now that you've seen how to create two different types of gradient fills, let's look at how to modify these to stretch areas of a color and provide non-linear fills, and to also incorporate colors.

The way to do this is to modify the values passed to the `addColorStop()` function, and to add more of them to create in-between steps. For example, here's the code that created the first rectangle in Figures 10-2 to 10-6:

```
gradient = context.createLinearGradient(55, 10, 55, 160)
gradient.addColorStop(0, '#FFF')
gradient.addColorStop(1, '#000')
context.fillStyle = gradient
context.fillRect(10, 10, 90, 150)
```

The two lines of importance are the second and third in which the position is either 0 or 1 (for the start and the end) and the two colors of `#FFF` (for white) and `#000` (for black), which I will now change as follows, to create the rectangle shown in Figure 10-7:

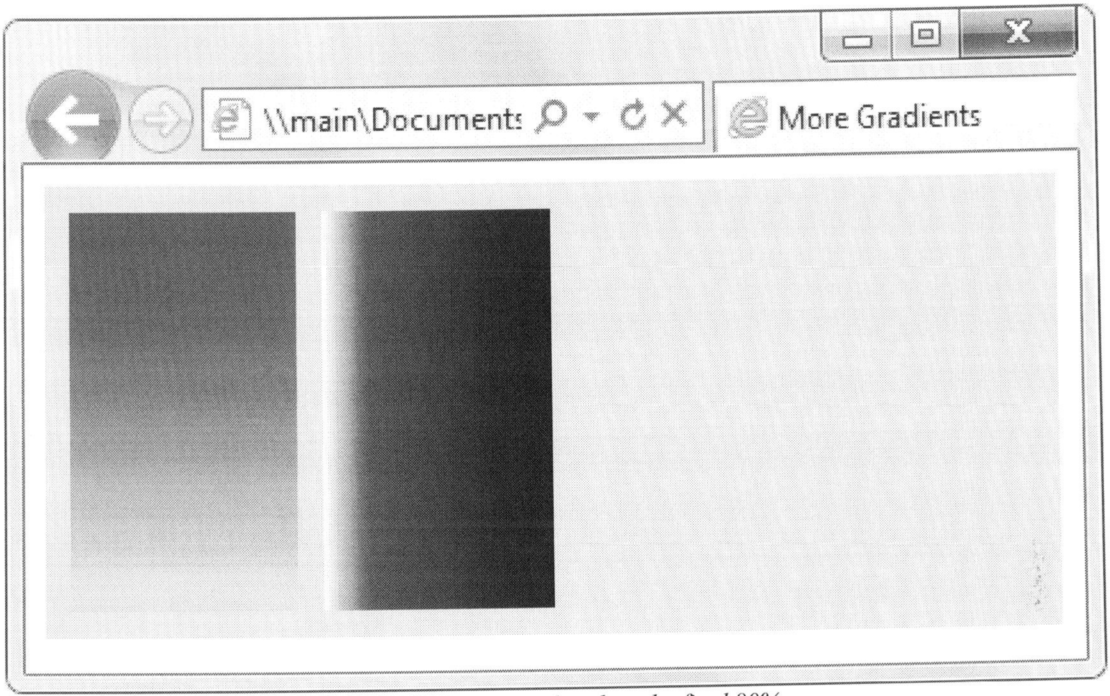

Figure 8: The first 20% of the gradient fades far quicker than the final 80%

```
gradient.addColorStop(0, '#f00')
gradient.addColorStop(1, 'yellow')
```

***Note**: I used both types of color values supported by the* `addColorStop()` *function; a hexadecimal string (in this instance 3 digits, but it could have been 6), and a color name (in this case* `yellow`*).*

Now let's modify the gradient applied to the second rectangle used in the previous examples, by keeping it grayscale, but adding an additional stop point and color value:

```
gradient.addColorStop(0.0, '#FFF')
gradient.addColorStop(0.2, '#555')
gradient.addColorStop(1.0, '#000')
```

Here, in the second line, a very dark gray color with the value `#555` has been applied at position `0.2`, which is only 20 percent into the gradient. This forces the left 20 percent to

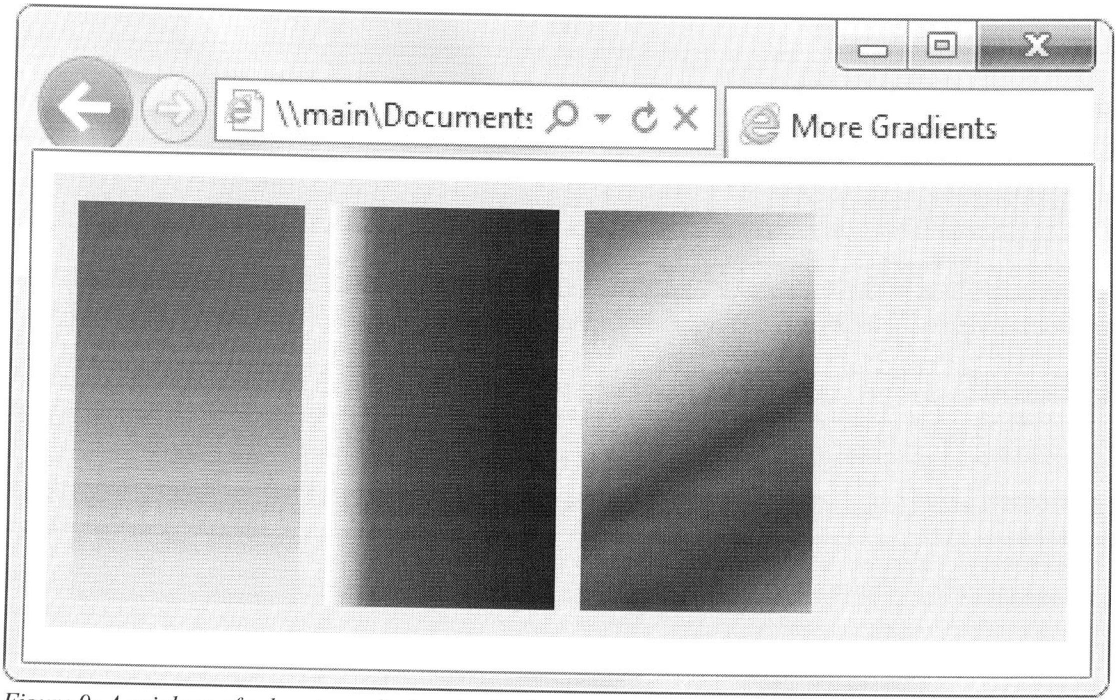

Figure 9: A rainbow of colors is applied to the third rectangle's gradient fill

quickly fade from `#FFF` to `#555`, and then the remaining 80 percent fades more slowly from `#555` to `#000`, as shown in Figure 10-8.

You can include more stops if you like, and they can be any colors you like.

So I have chosen to use a rainbow of colors for rectangle three, like this, with the result being Figure 10-9:

```
gradient.addColorStop(0.00, 'red')
gradient.addColorStop(0.16, 'orange')
gradient.addColorStop(0.33, 'yellow')
gradient.addColorStop(0.50, 'green')
gradient.addColorStop(0.66, 'blue')
gradient.addColorStop(0.83, 'indigo')
gradient.addColorStop(1.00, 'violet')
```

And remember that all these fills apply equally well to radial gradient fills, so I have chosen to reapply the same rainbow gradient used in the third rectangle to the fill in the final rectangle. But this circle has a radius of 75 pixels to allow the circle to touch the top and bottom edges – and show more of the fill, with the result shown in Figure 10-10.

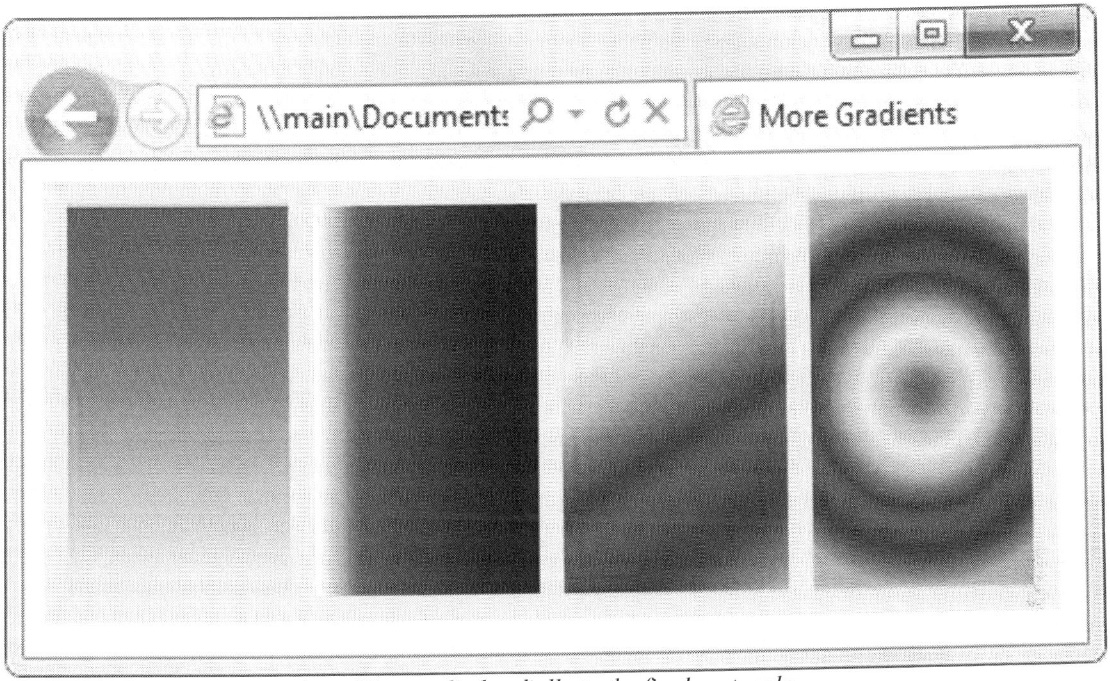

Figure 10: The rainbow gradient fill is applied radially to the final rectangle

Using Patterns

In the final part of this lecture I'll show you how to use patterns on an HTML5 canvas, which you can apply instead of a plain or gradient fill by simply modifying the details you pass to the `fillStyle` property, and using the same `fillRect()` or other fill functions.

The `createPattern(i,r)` Function

To create a pattern you need to supply a pre-existing image such as a *jpg*, *png* or *gif* file, and the type of repetition to use when applying the fill, out of the following:

- **`repeat`** Repeat the image both vertically and horizontally
- **`repeat-x`** Repeat the image horizontally
- **`repeat-y`** Repeat the image vertically
- **`no-repeat`** Do not repeat the image

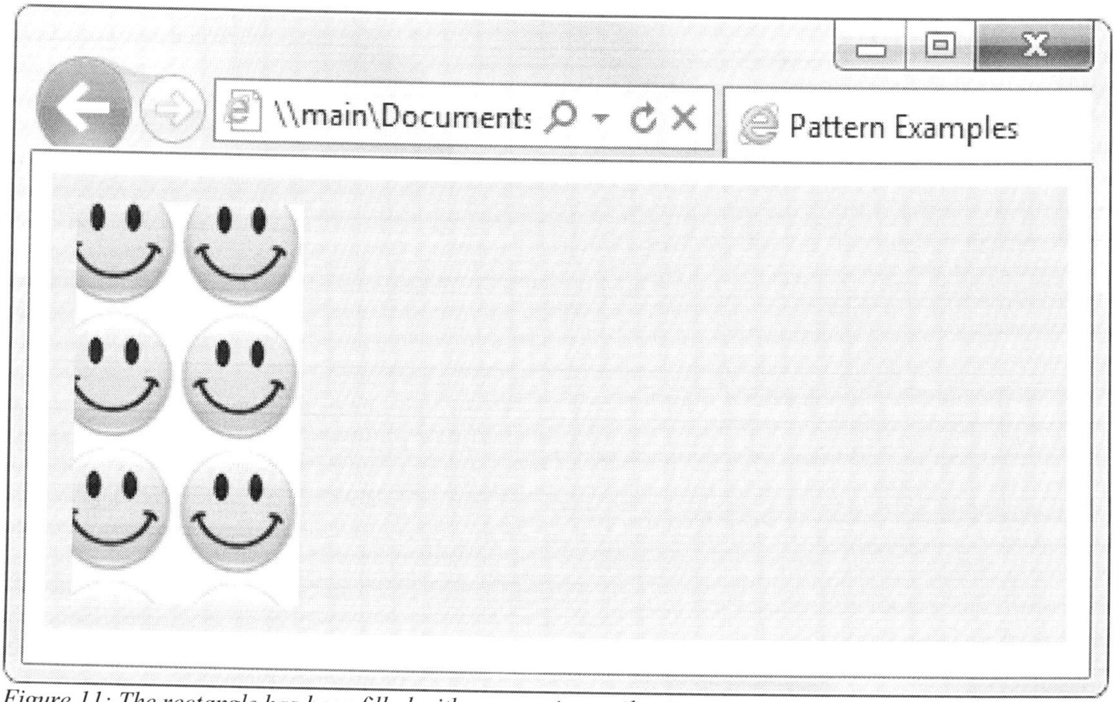

Figure 11: The rectangle has been filled with a repeating smiley image

For example, the following code loads in the image *smiley-50.png* and then uses it as a fill for the first rectangle, using the `createPattern()` function:

```
image      = new Image()
image.src = 'smiley-50.png'

image.onload = function()
{
   pattern = context.createPattern(image, 'repeat')
   context.fillStyle = pattern
   context.fillRect(10, 10, 90, 150)
}
```

This code requires some explaining (especially if you are new to JavaScript). What is happening is that in the first line a new object called `image` is created using the JavaScript `Image()` function and the keyword `new`. This new object then has the value of its `src` attribute set to `'smiley-50.png'`, which is a file already saved into the same folder.

Then the `onload` event of the image has a function attached to it. But what does this mean? Well, the `image` object has various attributes such as its width and height, the source from where it is loaded and, in this instance, `onload`. However, the `onload`

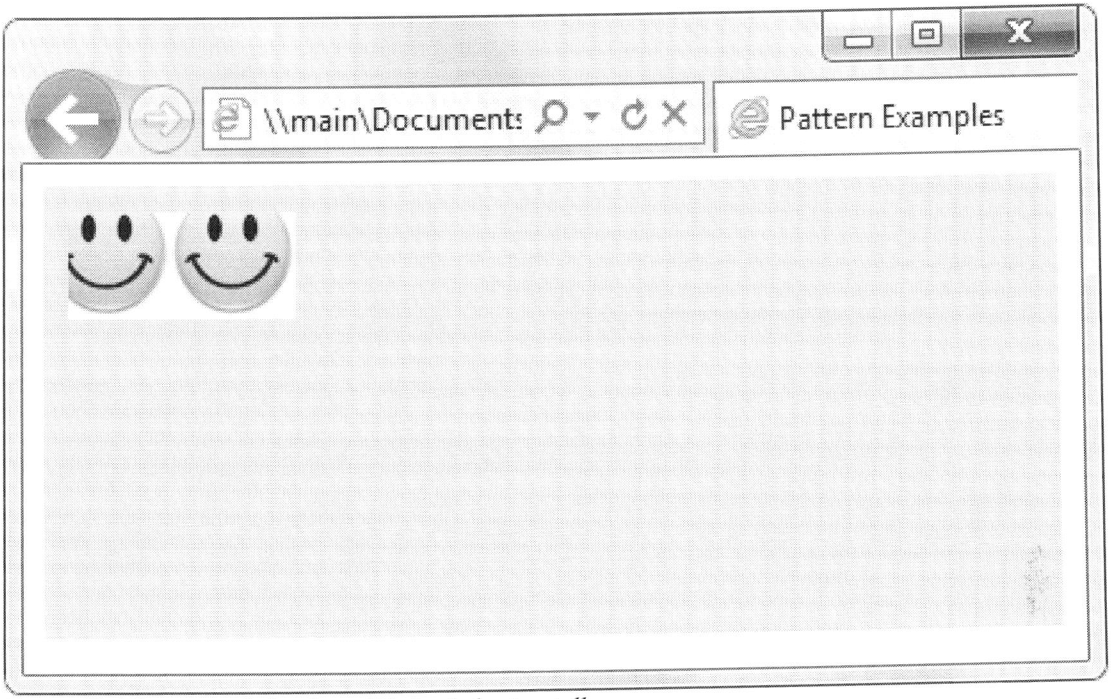

Figure 12: The rectangle has been filled only horizontally

attribute is known as an *event* because it is handled in a special manner such that only when the image has been fully loaded from its source is the event called.

To handle the event when it is called, a function is attached which will access the canvas and do the pattern filling. Within the function (inside its curly braces) there are three lines of code, and here you should be back on familiar territory, because the first function call made is simply a call to `createPattern()` specifying the `image` object and a value of `repeat`, indicating how the image should be used, the result of which is placed in the new object called `pattern`.

The final two lines simply apply this `pattern` object to the `fillStyle` property and then call the `fillRect()` function to use that fill on a rectangle whose top left corner is at `10,0`, and with a width of 90 and height of 150 pixels. The result is shown in Figure 10-11.

***Note**: If the function is not attached to the image's `onload` event, and the code is simply called from outside of the function, then you run the risk that the image may not be fully loaded when you make the fill command, and therefore the call may fail. This is a standard issue with JavaScript and external images that you must always consider, and so*

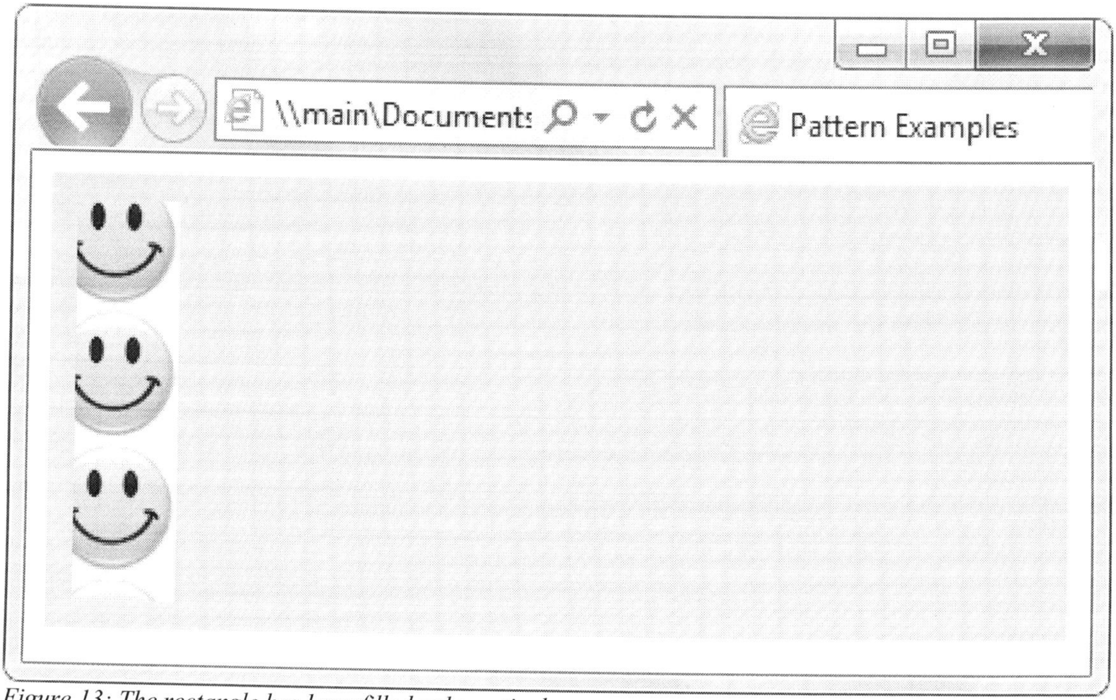

Figure 13: The rectangle has been filled only vertical

wherever such an image is loaded in you are recommended to attach the code that will use it to the `onload` *event of the image.*

In the Figure you can see that the first smiley image is not fully within the rectangle. This is because the fill area is considered to be the entire canvas, and therefore the fill commences at the top left of the canvas (location `0,0`), but is only revealed within the constraints of the fill area.

Using the value of `repeat-x` for the repetition results in Figure 10-12, `repeat-y` results in Figure 10-13, and `no-repeat` results in Figure 10-14.

Summary

At this point you already have substantial ability to work with the HTML5 canvas, and will be able to draw on these concepts in the following lecture which moves onto writing text (including using gradients and pattern fills), drawing lines and curves, drawing with images and more.

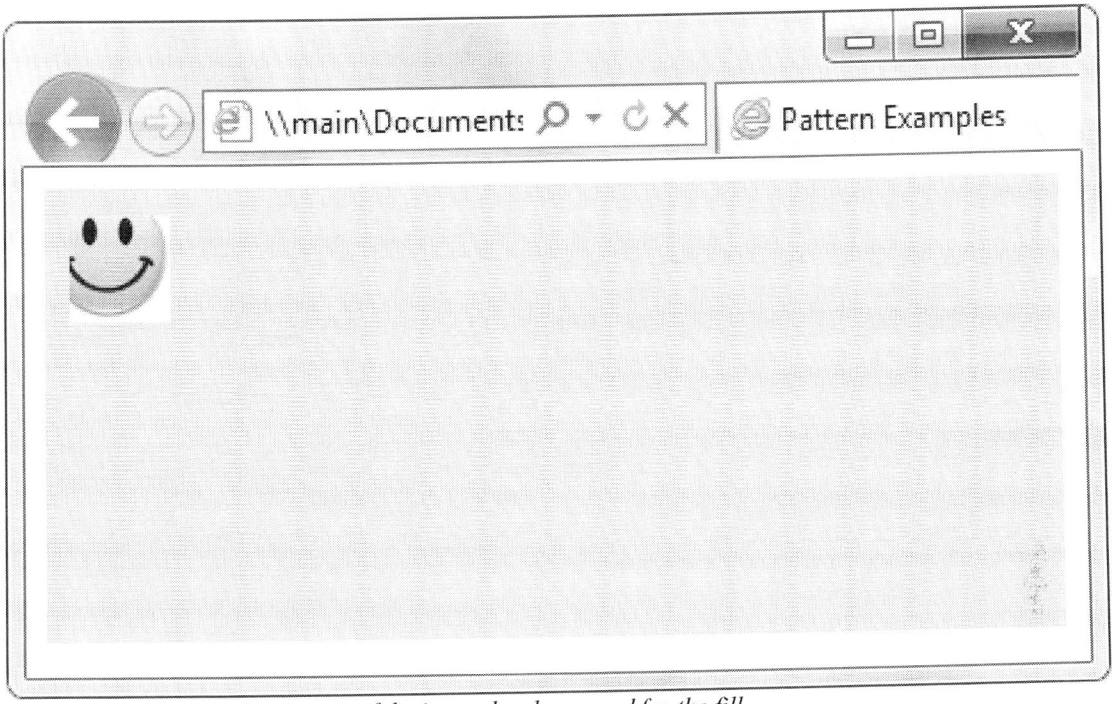

Figure 14: Only a single instance of the image has been used for the fill

LECTURE 11

WRITING TEXT TO THE CANVAS

By following this lecture you will:

- ✓ *Be able to use various different fonts for writing text to the canvas.*
- ✓ *Understand how to add colors, fills and patterns to text.*
- ✓ *Learn how to control the vertical and horizontal text offsets.*

THIS LECTURE CONTINUES our exploration of the HTML5 canvas by looking at how you can write text to it, including using a variety of fonts and styles, as well as incorporating the various fill styles covered in the previous lecture.

Many of these examples draw on those in Lecture 10, so you may wish to refer back to that from time to time as you work your way through this one.

Note*: The examples from this lecture are in the* Lecture 11 *folder of the* examples.zip *file at* tinyurlcom/html5ccexamples.

Writing Text

HTML 4.01 provides some handy tags for setting font sizes, colors and faces, and CSS gives you even more control over how these are applied, including using effects such as shadowing. But when you want absolutely precise control over how your text should display the canvas has what you need.

Also, although you can use CSS to overlay text on top of a canvas, you can't use it to layer text into a canvas, or to apply the gradient and pattern fill effects that the canvas supports.

The `font` Property

Let's look at the `font` property first, and see how to select the font face to use. As ever I am assuming that if you follow these examples yourself you have also included the `O()` and `S()` functions and the code to create a `2d` context onto the canvas in an object with the name `context`. To recap, your code should look something like this:

```
<canvas id='example' width='410' height='170'></canvas>

<script>

  // The O() and S() functions go here,
  // or in an earlier script section

   canvas                = O('example')
   S(canvas).background = '#DDD'

  // Enter the examples from this lecture
  // so that they replace these comments

</script>
```

You must place the `O() and S()` functions where the first two commented lines appear, and example lines that I provide in this lecture should replace the second pair of commented lines. The width and height of 410 by 170 pixels shown will be suitable for all the examples, and this code will create a light gray background behind the canvas so that its position and dimensions are clearly visible. So, let's choose a font face, like this:

```
context.font = '72pt Arial'
```

And that's it - when you write the text to the canvas it will be in size 72 point Arial.

Font Size Measurements

You can also use other measurements for your font sizes, which can be either relative or fixed. The full list of supported relative font measures is:

- **em** Ems: Based on the default preference set in the browser.
- **ex** X-height: Based on the height of the lowercase x character.
- **px** Pixels: Based on the resolution of the screen.
- `%` Percentage (similar to `em`): Based on the default preference of the browser.

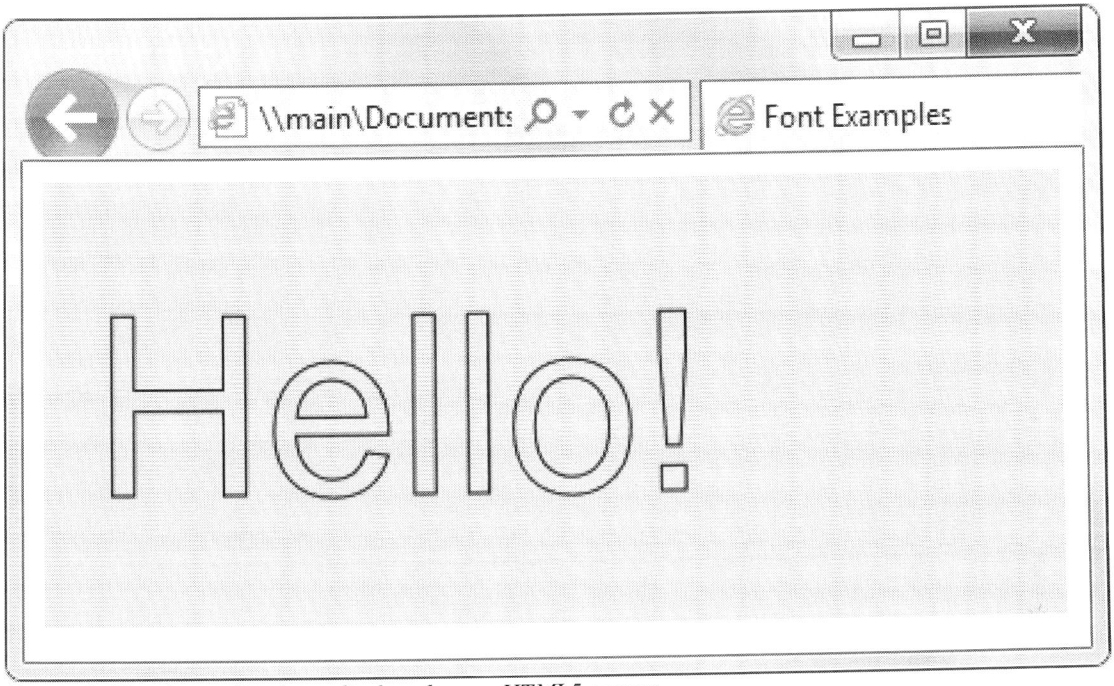

Figure 1: 72 point outlined text displayed on an HTML5 canvas

And the fixed measures available are:

- `in` Inches: Imperial measurement.
- `cm` Centimeters: Metric measurement equivalent to 100th of a meter.
- `mm` Millimeters: Metric measurement equivalent to 10th of a centimeter.
- `pt` Points: A print unit.
- `pc` Picas: Another print unit.

Therefore the following examples are all valid:

```
context.font = '3em Helvetica'
context.font = '16px Impact'
context.font = '150% Courier'
context.font = '10mm Times'
context.font = '72pt Arial'
```

Figure 2: The text is centered using the textAlign property

The `strokeText(t,x,y)` Function

Of course, you now need a way to write text in the newly selected font to the canvas, and you can do that using the `strokeText()` function, like this (which results in Figure 11-1):

```
context.strokeText('Hello!', 20, 120)
```

And that's how easy it is to get text onto a canvas. Simply set the font property to the font and size to use and then (for an outlined font) call `strokeText()`, passing the text to display and the location where the bottom left corner of the text should appear by default, although you will see next how you can choose a different horizontal alignment with the `textAlign` property, and use the `textBaseline` property to specify the offset of the text relative to the vertical coordinate supplied.

The `textAlign` Property

But there's more to writing text to a canvas than that because there are three properties you can pass values to that will further customize the way text appears.

Figure 3: The border outline has been thickened to 5 pixels wide

For example, using the `textAlign` property you can specify the alignment of the text out of the values start, end, left, right and center. So, to center some text you could set the property like this:

```
context.textAlign = 'center'
context.strokeText('Hello!', 205, 120)
```

As you may have noticed, in order to properly center the text, the call to `strokeText()` needed its horizontal offset changed from 20 in the previous example to 205, because that is half the width of the canvas (which is 410 pixels wide), and the result is shown in Figure 11-2.

Incidentally, with the `lineWidth` property you can also change the width of any line drawn using any of the line drawing functions (more of which in Lecture 12), and this also includes `strokeText()`.

The following line of code increases the width to 5 pixels, as seen in Figure 11-3, where the previous example has been modified to create a very thick border.

Figure 4: The text has been vertically aligned using the textBaseline property

```
context.lineWidth = 5
context.strokeText('Hello!', 205, 120)
```

The `textBaseline` Property

Using the `textBaseline` property you can choose the horizontal line about which the text will be based out of the following:

- **`top`** Aligns to the top of the text.
- **`middle`** Aligns to the middle of the text.
- **`alphabetic`** Aligns to the alphabetic baseline of the text.
- **`bottom`** Aligns to the bottom of the font.

Figure 11-4 illustrates using a value of `middle` for this property as in the following line of code. As you can see instead of the bottom of the text aligning with the vertical coordinate specified, the text has been vertically centered at that location.

```
context.textBaseline = 'middle'
context.strokeText('Hello!', 205, 120)
```

Figure 5: A 116 point font filled in with the color black

The `fillText(s,x,y)` Function

In the same way that you can use `strokeText()` in a similar fashion to `strokeRect()` (as detailed in the previous lecture), you can also use `fillText()` to create solid, gradient and pattern filled text, just as you can provide those types of fills to rectangles with the `fillRect()` function.

To show how this works, here's some code to write the word HTML5 in a big and bold black color, since no fill color has been specified (and so the default of black is used), as shown in Figure 11-5:

```
context.font = '116pt Impact'
context.fillText('HTML5', 0, 150)
```

Now let's look at applying different colors, gradient fills and patterns, starting by simply changing the text to blue, like this:

```
context.fillStyle = 'blue'
```

Figure 6: The solid fill has been replaced with a gradient

By now you should be so used to simple color changes that there's no need to show the result of this in a figure. Instead let's see how a simple vertical gradient works with the font (as shown in Figure 11-6), like this:

```
gradient = context.createLinearGradient(205,25, 205, 150)
gradient.addColorStop(0, '#FFF')
gradient.addColorStop(1, '#000')
context.fillStyle = gradient
context.fillText('HTML5', 0, 150)
```

***Note**: As explained in the previous lecture, you can set the start and end point of the gradient to any locations within (or even outside of) the canvas, allowing you to create a wider variety of effects than if they were limited to simply applying it under the object being drawn.*

Using the rainbow color gradient from the previous lecture but applying it creatively as a radial gradient allows the effect of a real rainbow to be applied as the fill effect, like this, which displays as Figure 11-7:

```
gradient = context.createRadialGradient(205, 230, 120, 205, 230, 240)
gradient.addColorStop(0.00, 'red')
gradient.addColorStop(0.16, 'orange')
```

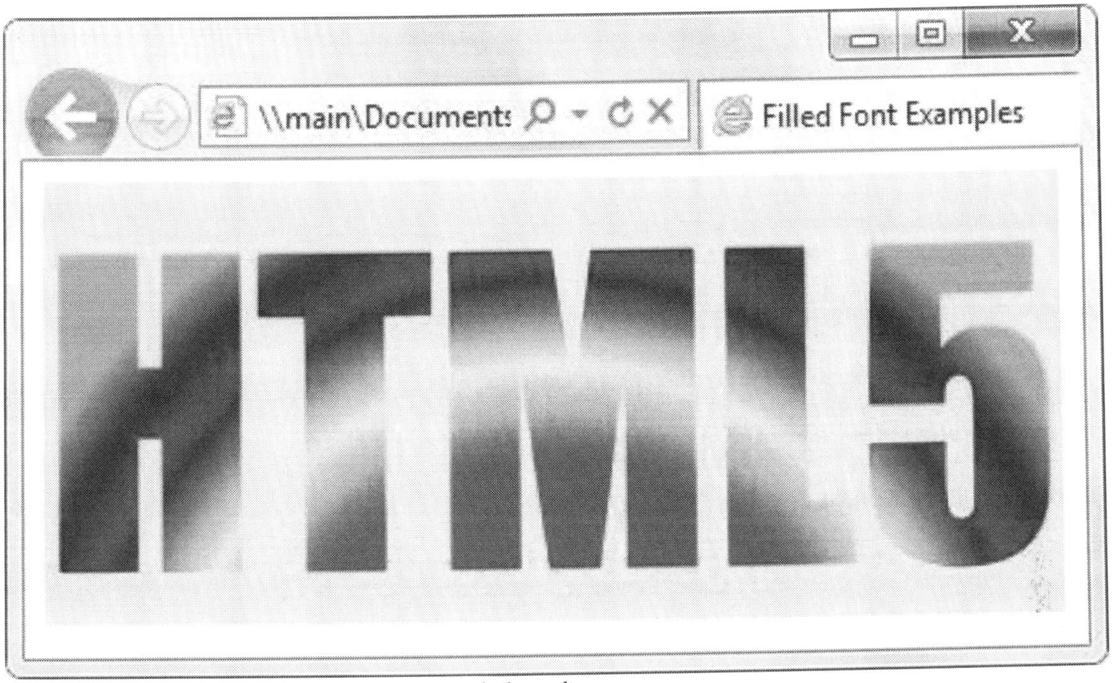

Figure 7: Creating a rainbow effect with a radial gradient

```
gradient.addColorStop(0.33, 'yellow')
gradient.addColorStop(0.50, 'green')
gradient.addColorStop(0.66, 'blue')
gradient.addColorStop(0.83, 'indigo')

gradient.addColorStop(1.00, 'violet')
context.fillStyle = gradient
context.fillText('HTML5', 0, 150)
```

In this example, a vertical offset of 230 pixels from the top of the canvas was selected. This places the center of the radial gradients at a location 60 pixels below the bottom of the canvas.

This allows only a top portion of the rainbow to be used for the fill. By selecting radius values of 120 pixels for the inner gradient and 240 for the outer one, the rainbow is 120 pixels wide. However, due to the way the fill works, the areas inside and outside of this section are set to the initial and final color values, so that he inside is red and the outside is violet.

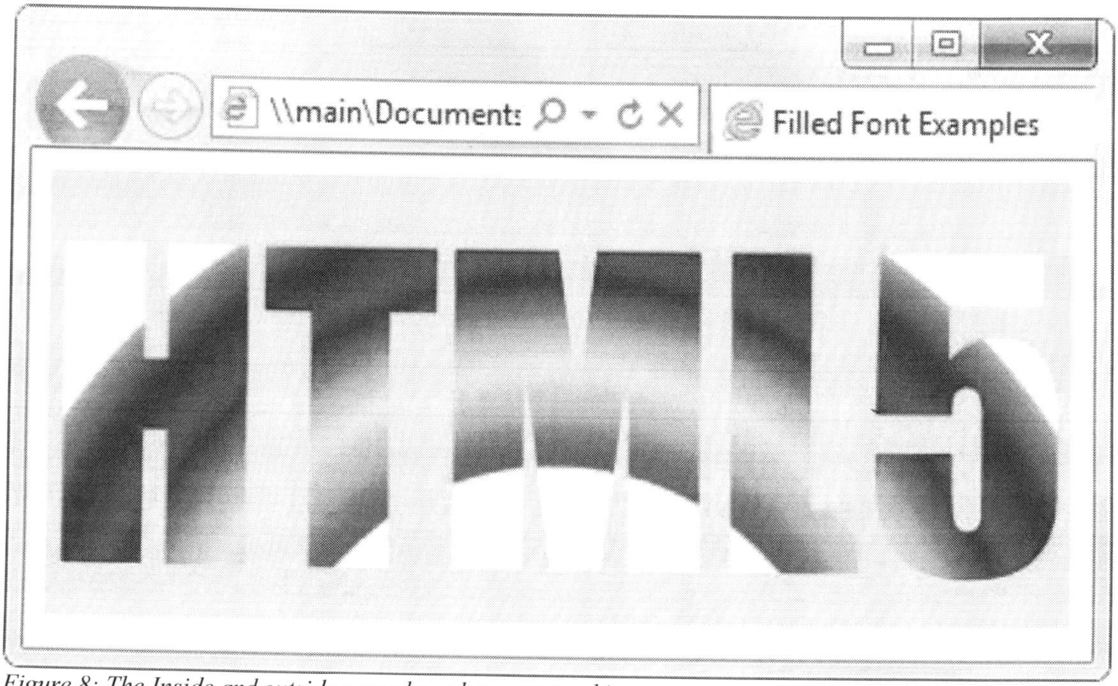

Figure 8: The Inside and outside areas have been set to white

If this is not the effect required it is a simple matter to add a preceding initial and following final color of white (or whichever colors you prefer), like this:

```
gradient.addColorStop(0.00, 'white')
// Original gradient colors
gradient.addColorStop(1.00, 'white')
```

As shown in Figure 11-8, this results in only the rainbow itself being displayed. You can also use patterns with the `fillText()` function, as with the following code, which attaches a function to the `onload` event of an image object called `image` that uses a marble pattern from the file *marble.jpg* – using the event ensures that the code runs only once the image has fully loaded:

```
context.font = '116pt Impact'
image        = new Image()
image.src    = 'marble.jpg'

image.onload = function()
{
  pattern = context.createPattern(image, 'no-repeat')
  context.fillStyle = pattern
  context.fillText('HTML5', 0, 150)
}
```

Figure 9: The text has now been filled with a pattern

The image is then processed using the `createPattern()` function with a setting of `no-repeat`, and passed to a new object called `pattern`. In turn pattern is used as the value for the `fillStyle` property, which is then used to fill the text using the `fillText()` function. The result of this can be seen in Figure 11-9.

In this instance the image used for the fill pattern is larger than the canvas, so there is no need to repeat (or tile) it.

But if you have a smaller image that will tile well you can repeat it horizontally, vertically, or in both directions. See Lecture 10 for more details on how to create and use patterns.

Determining Text Width

Sometimes you need to know how wide some text will be in order to best position it.

To find out this value, set all the properties as you would before writing the text and then issue statements such as the following, which creates an object called metrics into which information about the text is stored.

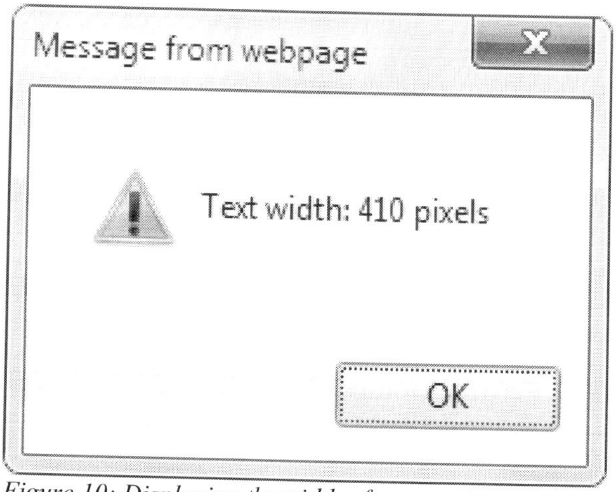

Figure 10: Displaying the width of some text

The `width` property of `metrics` then holds the width of the text in pixels, which is displayed by the JavaScript `alert()` function (which pops up a small window containing the details within the brackets following the `alert` function name, namely some text surrounding the `width` property):

```
metrics = context.measureText('HTML5')
alert('Text width: ' + metrics.width + ' pixels')
```

The object returned by the `measureText()` function currently only supports the `width` property. This value can then be used in JavaScript calculations to help determine the right place to write the text.

Summary

With creating text now in your toolkit, in the following lecture we will return to looking at some of the drawing tools, this time ones that use paths to create lines, so that you have fine control over all the straight lines, shapes and curves you could want.

LECTURE 12

LINES, PATHS & CURVES

By following this lecture you will:

- ✓ *Learn how to construct all manner of line types.*
- ✓ *Use paths to create complex drawings.*
- ✓ *Discover how to create a wide variety of different curves.*

IN THIS LECTURE I'll be showing you how you can customize all the functions that draw using lines such as `strokeRect()` and `strokeText()` (which you've already seen), as well the line drawing functions, and how to use paths to create complicated patterns and curves.

Note*: The examples from this lecture are in the* Lecture 12 *folder of the* examples.zip *file at* tinyurlcom/html5ccexamples.

Drawing Lines

The HTML5 canvas supports line drawing using many different styles because you can precisely specify the width of lines with the `lineWidth` property (as you have previously seen), and can also set properties such as `lineCap`, `lineJoin` and `miterLimit`.

The `lineWidth` Property

You previously encountered this in Lecture 11 where it was used to thicken the line width used in a call to the `strokeText()` function. What this property does is change the line width for future operations that use line drawing, including `strokeText()` and `stroke()` (detailed a little later).

For example, the following command sets the `lineWidth` property to 10 pixels, as seen in the horizontal and angled lines in Figure 12-1:

```
context.lineWidth = 10
```

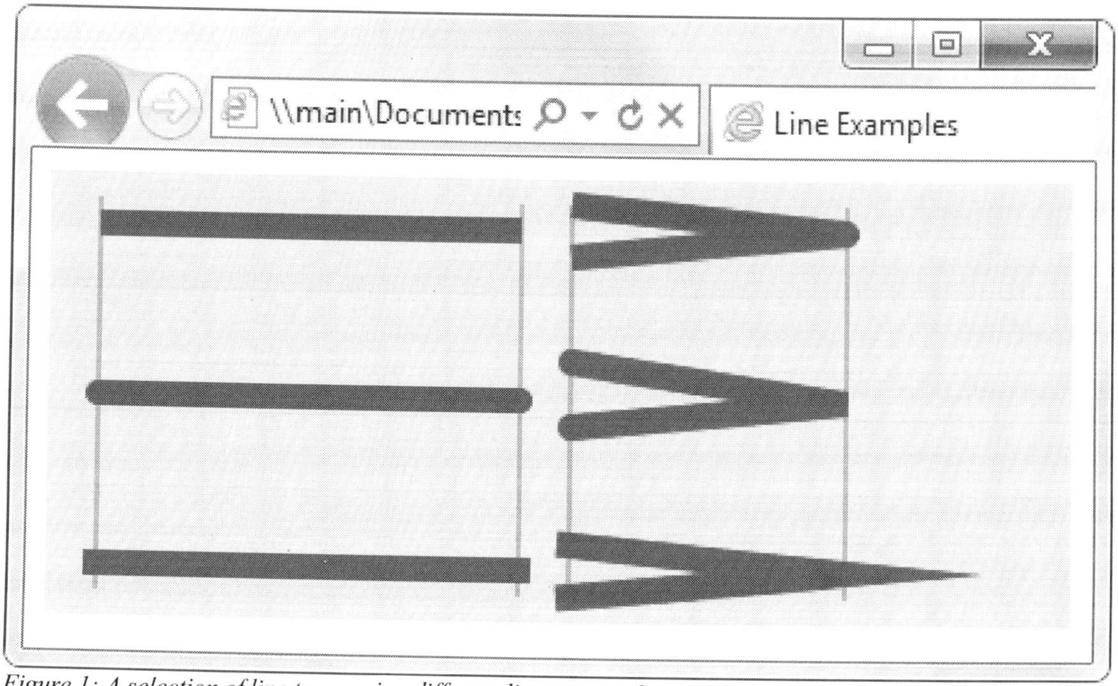

Figure 1: A selection of line types using different line caps and joins

For comparison the thin, vertical lines in the figure are 1 pixel wide.

The `lineCap` Property

Using this property you can choose the way the start and ends of lines are displayed. This is known as their line cap, and hence the `lineCap` property name, which can be any value out of `butt`, `round` and `square`, as shown in the left half of Figure 12-1, and used like these examples:

```
context.lineCap = 'butt'
context.lineCap = 'round'
context.lineCap = 'square'
```

The top line on the left of the figure uses the `lineCap` value of `butt` in which the ends but up exactly against the vertical lines I have drawn (for comparing the line cap types), indicating the start points and end points of each line. If no value is given to the `lineCap` property it assumes a default value of `butt`.

The middle line uses a `lineCap` property of `round` and, as you can see, it therefore extends past the left and right edges, with the center point of the rounded cap being the end points of the line.

The bottom line uses the value `square` for the `lineCap` property, which is almost the same as `round`, in that the centers of the squares are the end points of the line.

The `lineJoin` Property

The `lineJoin` property is similar to the `lineCap` property, but it applies only at the points at which lines are joined. It supports the values of `round`, `bevel` and `miter`, as you can see by looking at the joins of the three right-hand pairs of lines in Figure 12-1, in which the end caps are the same as the lines on the left. Following are examples of setting this property:

```
context.lineJoin = 'round'
context.lineJoin = 'bevel'
context.lineJoin = 'miter'
```

However the top pair of angled lines uses the value `round` for the `lineJoin` property, the middle pair uses the value `bevel`, and the bottom one uses the value `'miter'`.

The `miterLimit` Property

In order to achieve the sharp miter in the bottom right pair of lines in Figure 12-1, it was necessary to use the `miterLimit` property, giving it a value of 12, in order to allow the quite sharp angle to extend far enough. Here is how you would set this property:

```
context.miterLimit = '12'
```

Note: *If* `miterLimit` *is not set to a sufficiently large enough value for a miter then mitered joins will simply use the* `'bevel'` *value instead, so if you are having trouble with your pointed miters simply increase the value you supply for* `miterLimit` *until the miter displays.*

Drawing With Paths

Figure 12-1 was created using a combination of line properties (as described in the previous section), along with a combination of path handling functions. Using them it is easy to move an imaginary pen to a start location, define a path it must follow, and then tell it to draw along that path using the properties already set up for it such as width, caps, joins and color, as described next.

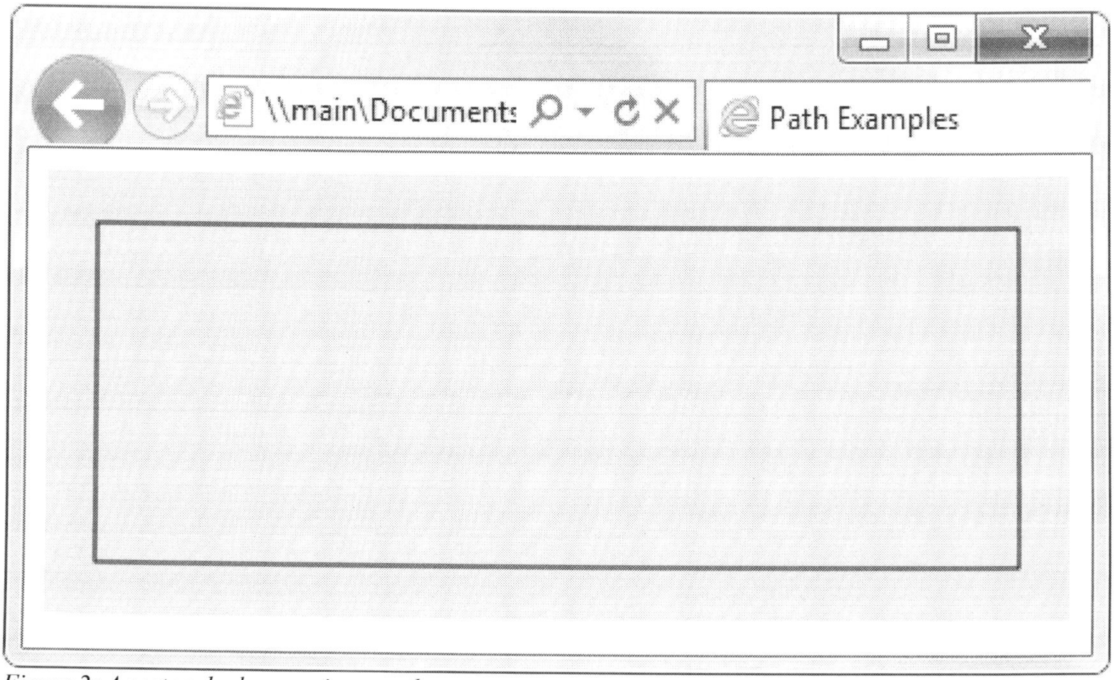

Figure 2: A rectangle drawn using a path

The `beginPath()` & `closePath()` Functions

Every path created for an HTML5 canvas must start with a call to `beginPath()`, and end with a call to `closePath()`, like this:

```
context.beginPath()
// Path instructions go here
context.closePath()
```

Think of them as being similar to the opening and closing `<html>` and `</html>` or `<script>` and `</script>` tags.

Once a path is created you can make it display, but first let's look at how to create one.

The `moveTo(x, y)` & `LineTo(x, y)` Functions

The first step in a path is generally to move to a location on the canvas so, for example, to move to the location `20,20` you would issue this `moveTo()` command:

```
context.moveTo(20, 20)
```

To then specify that a line should be drawn (once the path is completed) you can then issue a command such as the following, `lineTo()` call, which will specify that the next part of the path is top draw a line from the current location (`20,20`) to `390,20`:

```
context.lineTo(390, 20)
```

Let's look at the path used to draw a rectangle, including the opening and closing path function calls:

```
context.beginPath()
context.moveTo( 20,  20)

context.lineTo(390,  20)
context.lineTo(390, 150)

context.lineTo( 20, 150)
context.lineTo( 20,  20)
context.closePath()
```

The `stroke()` Function

Once you have a path created you can draw in onto the canvas using the `stroke()` function like this, which in the case of the current example displays as Figure 12-2:

```
context.stroke()
```

And there you have it. The path has been processed by the `stroke()` function and all the parts in the path are now drawn.

The `rect(x,y,w,h)` Function

If all you wanted to draw in the first instance was a rectangle, then there's a quicker way to do this than defining an entire path. Instead you can use the `rect()` function with a path, like this:

```
context.beginPath()
context.rect(40, 40, 330, 90)
```

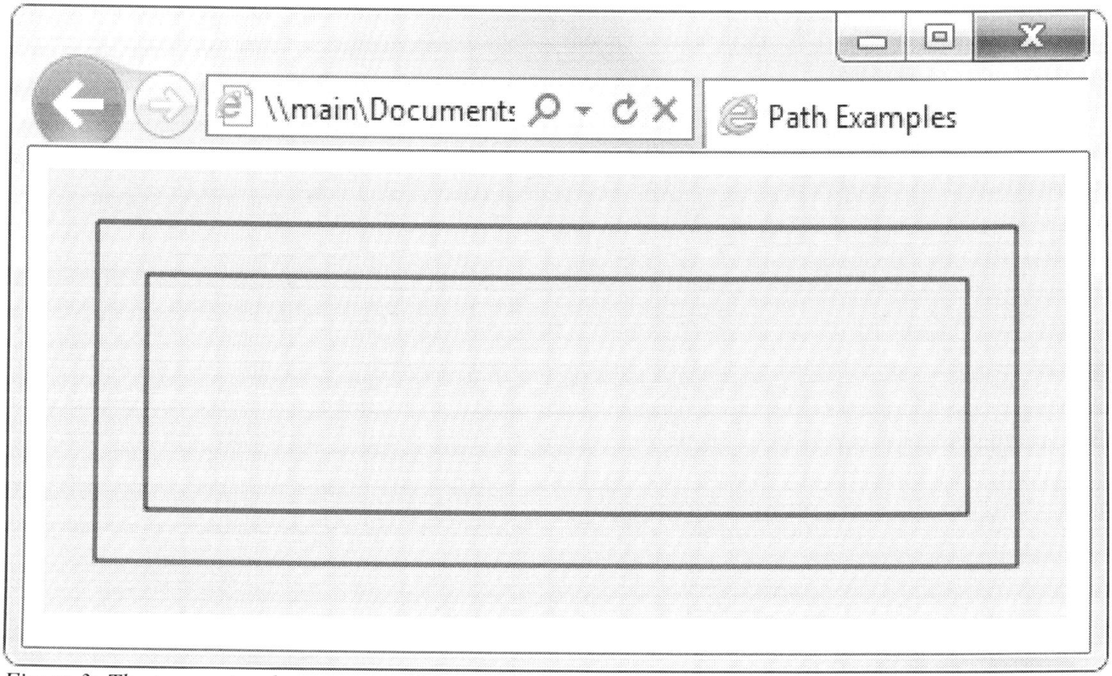

Figure 3: The two rectangles are created from a single path

```
context.closePath()
context.stroke()
```

The top left hand corner of the rectangle is specified by the first two arguments in the function call, and the second two contain the width and height of the rectangle. The end result is shown in Figure 12-3, in which both rectangles (from the previous and current examples) have been combined and created within the same path, as follows:

```
context.beginPath()
context.moveTo( 20,  20)
context.lineTo(390,  20)
context.lineTo(390, 150)
context.lineTo( 20, 150)
context.lineTo( 20,  20)
context.rect(40, 40, 330, 90)
context.closePath()
context.stroke()
```

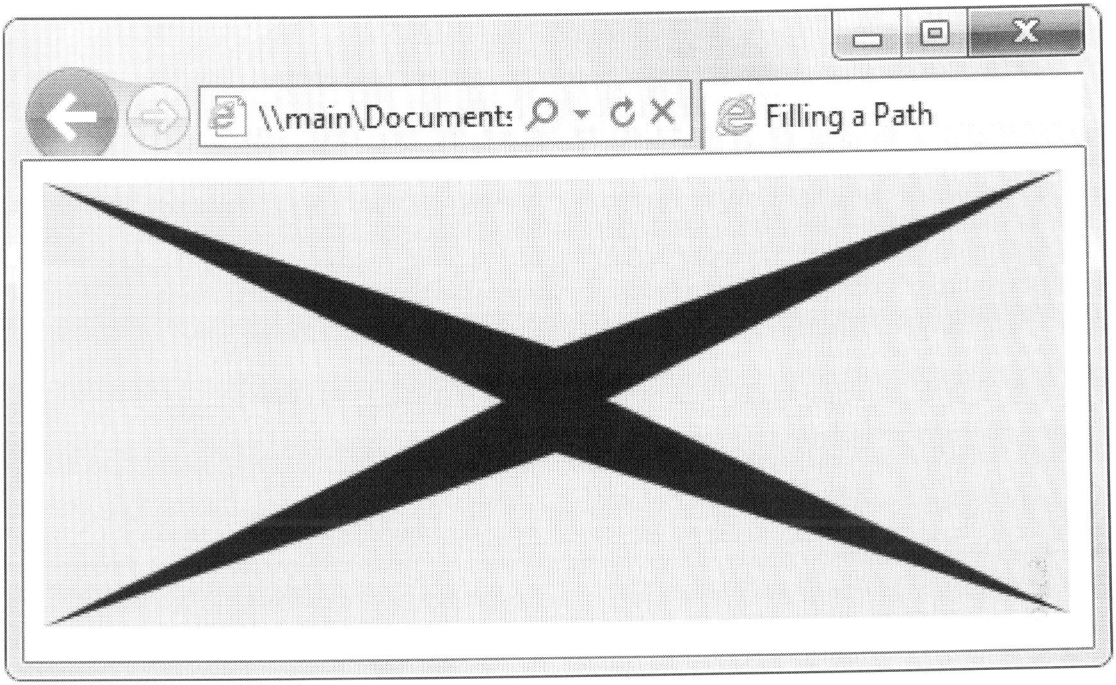

Figure 4: Filling in a four pointed star

The `fill()` Function

Using the `fill()` function you can fill in any area bounded by a path. For example, the following code creates a four pointed star, which is then filled in, as shown in Figure 12-4:

```
context.beginPath()
context.moveTo(0,     0)
context.lineTo(205,  65)
context.lineTo(410,   0)
context.lineTo(225,  85)
context.lineTo(410, 170)
context.lineTo(205, 105)
context.lineTo(0,   170)
context.lineTo(185,  85)
context.lineTo(0,     0)
context.closePath()
context.fill()
```

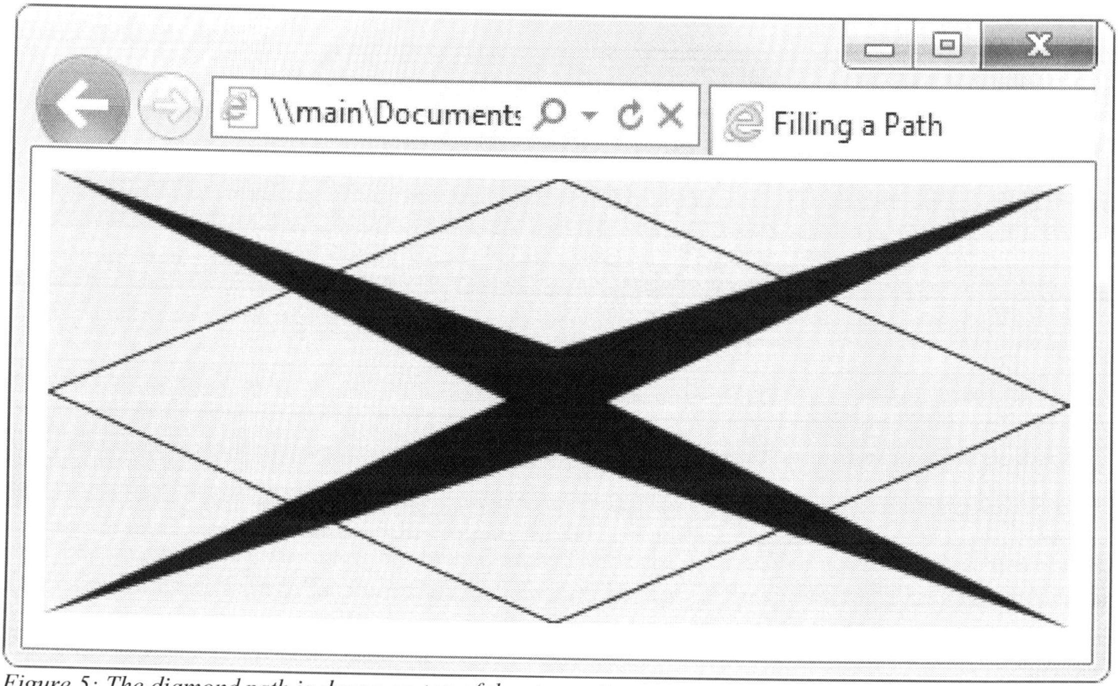

Figure 5: The diamond path is drawn on top of the star pattern

If you don't fully enclose the shape by drawing a line back to the start point the function still does a very good attempt at filling only the shape by making that final link for you before performing the fill.

The `clip()` Function

When creating a path you can choose to constrain the drawing area using the `clip()` function to select any area of the canvas, so that any part that would be drawn outside of this area will be ignored, and only parts of the path that fall inside the clipped area will be used.

The `clip()` function works on a path in the same way as the `stroke()` or `fill()` functions. For example, the following code creates a diamond shaped path, which is then revealed with a simple call to `stroke()`, as shown in Figure 12-5, in which the diamond has been drawn over the star shape:

```
context.beginPath()
context.moveTo(0,     85)
context.lineTo(205,    0)
context.lineTo(410,   85)
```

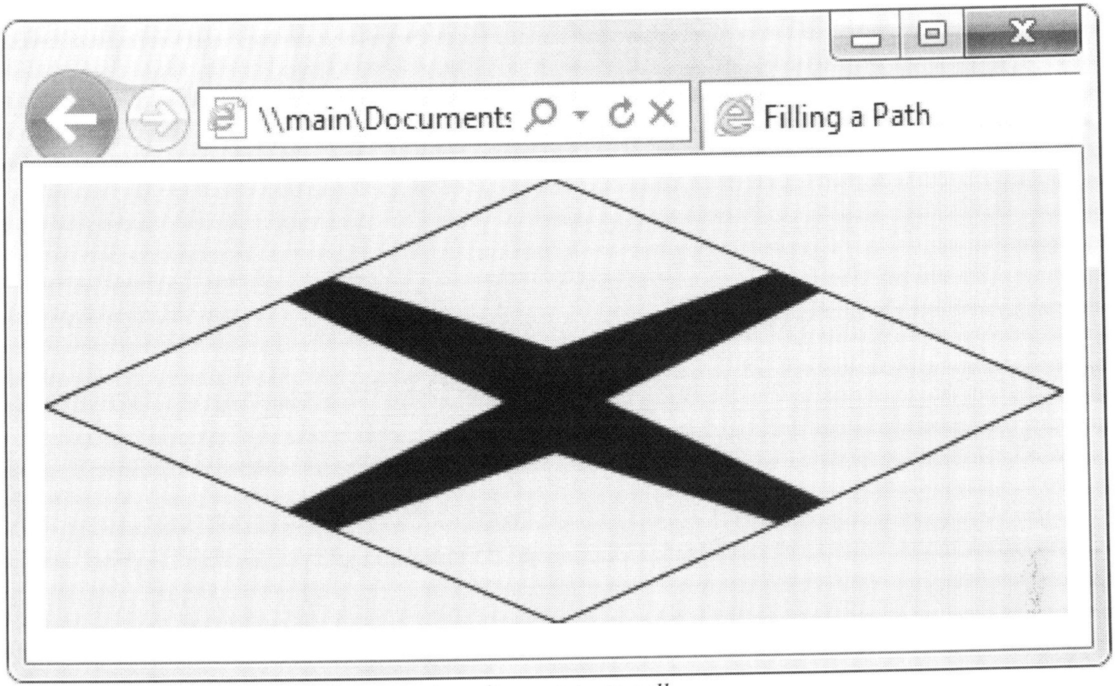

Figure 6: The diamond is both drawn and used in a `clip()` call

```
context.lineTo(205, 170)
context.lineTo(0,    85)

context.closePath()
context.stroke()
```

However, by placing the diamond path before the star shape is drawn, and using the `clip()` function on it after the `stroke()` function, this path becomes a bounded area, outside of which future path-related functions cannot draw, as with the following code (the result of which is shown in Figure 12-6):

```
context.beginPath()
context.moveTo(0,    85)
context.lineTo(205,   0)
context.lineTo(410,  85)

context.lineTo(205, 170)
context.lineTo(0,    85)
context.closePath()
context.stroke()
context.clip()
```

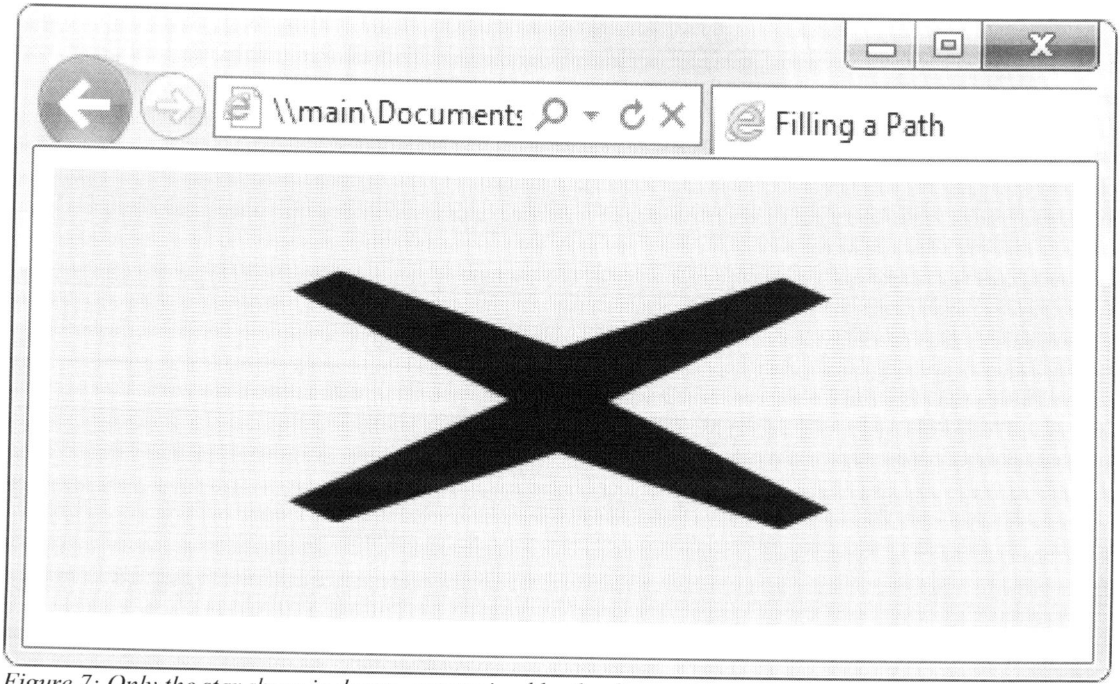

Figure 7: Only the star shape is drawn, constrained by the diamond area

```
context.beginPath()
context.moveTo(0,      0)
context.lineTo(205,   65)

context.lineTo(410,    0)
context.lineTo(225,   85)
context.lineTo(410,  170)
context.lineTo(205,  105)
context.lineTo(0,    170)

context.lineTo(185,   85)
context.lineTo(0,      0)

context.closePath()
context.fill()
```

If you want to use a path for constraint only, and not actually draw it, simply omit the call to stroke from the previous example, and the result is Figure 12-7.

Or, perhaps you simply may wish to fill the diamond shape with one color, and the area of the star within that shape in another, which is easily achieved by placing the relevant `fillStyle` assignments before the drawing commands, as shown in Figure 12-8.

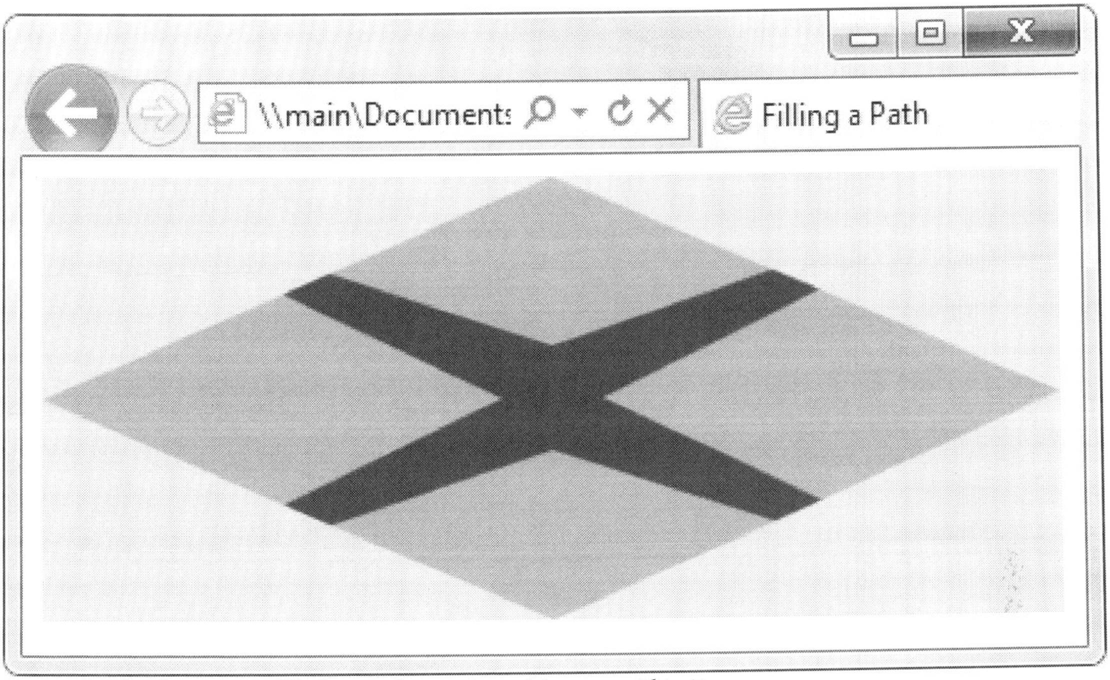

Figure 8: The diamond is filled, as is the portion of the star within it

I'll leave it up to you to work out how to achieve this effect – it's very simple (or you can view the commented code in the accompanying example files, downloadable using the link at the start of this lecture).

***Note**: You may, of course use any types of fill on a path as well as the solid color fills, including linear and radial gradients and patterns. Simply assign the relevant value to the* `fillStyle` *property before making a fill.*

The `isPointInPath(x,y)` Function

Sometimes you need to know whether a particular point lies in a path you have constructed.

However, you will normally only want to use this function if you are quite proficient with JavaScript. You will generally call it as part of a conditional `isPointInPath()` statement, like this:

```
if (isPointInPath(100, 123))
{
   // Do something here
}
```

If the location specified lies along any of the points in the path the function returns the value `true` and the contents of the `if()` statement are executed.

Otherwise the value `false` is returned and the contents of the `if()` do not get executed. Possible uses for this include hit detection for shooting games, and so on.

Creating Curves

I leapt a little ahead of myself by demonstrating how to fill in and clip paths, but I wanted to show you some of the fun you could have with them and couldn't resist. So now (slightly out of order) here are some more path functions you can use, this time for creating arcs, circles and complex curves.

As with the previous examples, all of these can be filled in with plain colors, gradient or radial fills and patterns, or you can draw curves using stroke functions and their associated properties such as `lineWidth`, `lineCap` and `lineJoin`.

The `arc(x,y,r,s,e,d)` Function

Probably the simplest form of curve is the arc, which is simply a segment of the perimeter of a circle. To create an arc you include a call to `arc()` within a path with the start of the curve connected to the final point on the path previous to it, and the curve's end connected to the next point in the path after it.

Note: *It is possible to create an arc without using the path functions, but a path will be assumed based on the previous and future drawing points, and these will connect up to it. So for precise control I recommend always using it inside a path.*

You must provide six arguments to the function: A pair of coordinates representing the center of the circle upon which the arc is based, the radius required, the radian offset value for the start of the arc, a radian offset value for the end of the arc, and then a value indicating whether to draw the arc clockwise or counterclockwise. Let's look at these in turn.

- **X & Y coordinates** The coordinates for an arc are simply the horizontal and vertical offset from the top left corner of the canvas for the center of the circle, such as `205,85`, which is 205 pixels in from the left, and 85 pixels down from the top of the canvas.
- **Radius** This is a value in pixels representing the distance from the center of the circle to its perimeter (or circumference). This is the location at which the arc will

be drawn. For example the value `75` states that the arc will be drawn at a distance of 75 pixels from the center of the circle.

- **Radian offsets** These specify the start and end position on the circle's perimeter between which the arc should be created. A value of 0 radians specifies the 3 O'clock position directly to the right of the circle's center. The value of a radian is `180 / π` (or about 57.2958 degrees). Therefore there are about `π * 2` radians in a complete circle. This means that to draw a quarter circle from the 3 O'clock to 6 O'clock positions you would use an initial value of `0` radians, and a second value of `π / 2` radians. For a semi-circle the second value would be π radians, and for a circle it would be `π * 2` radians. Remember that π is the number of times the diameter of a circle fits into its circumference.
- **Direction** To create a clockwise arc the final argument must have a value of `false`. For a counterclockwise arc it should be `true`.

So, for example, the following code draws four segments of a pie, with the final one filled in using the `fill()` function, rather than drawn using the `stroke()` function, as shown in Figure 12-9:

```
context.beginPath()
context.moveTo(55, 85)
context.arc(55,  85, 45, 0, Math.PI / 2, false)
context.closePath()
context.stroke()

context.beginPath()
context.moveTo(155, 85)
context.arc(155, 85, 45, 0, Math.PI, false)
context.closePath()
context.stroke()

context.beginPath()
context.moveTo(255, 85)
context.arc(255, 85, 45, 0, Math.PI / 2 * 3, false)

context.closePath()
context.stroke()

context.beginPath()
```

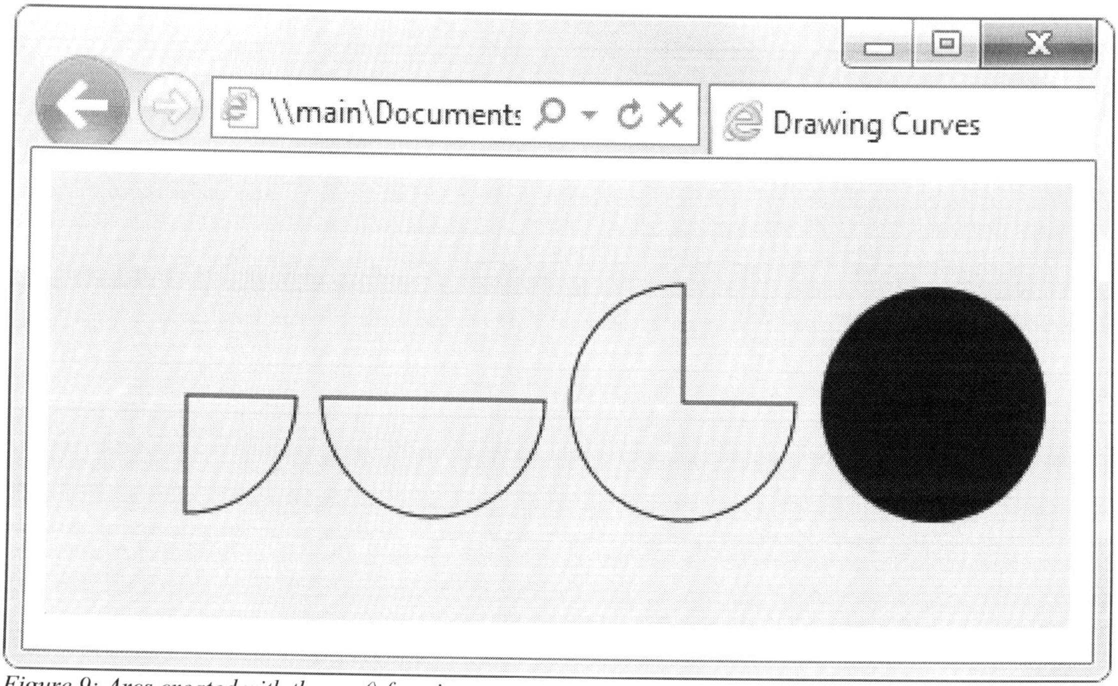

Figure 9: Arcs created with the arc() function

```
context.moveTo(355, 85)
context.arc(355, 85, 45, 0, Math.PI * 2, false)
context.closePath()
context.fill()
```

The first image in the figure uses radian values of `0` and π `/ 2`, the second uses `0` and π, the third uses `0` and π `/ 2 * 3`, and the fourth uses π `* 2`. In each case a call to `moveTo()` moves the path starting point to the center of the circle, then the next point in the path is the start of the arc, followed by the arc's end, and then the initial starting point again. By doing this a

slice of the circle is created to clearly show the arcs. In the final image the `fill()` function was used to illustrate how you can use that instead of `stroke()` if you wish, as well as the linear, gradient and pattern fills.

If you wish to draw the only arc portion of the images in Figure 12-9 then you need to close the path *after* issuing the call to the `stroke()` function, and you do not need to first move the path start to the center of each circle. So you could use code such as this (which results in Figure 12-10):

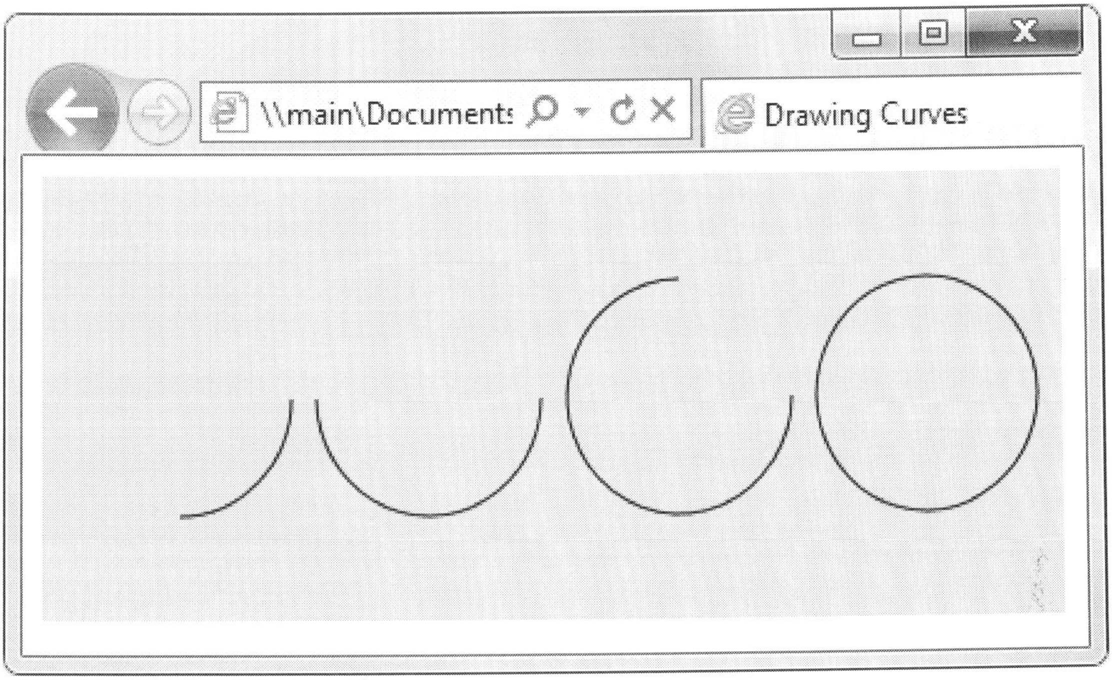

Figure 10: Only the arcs are now drawn

```
context.beginPath()
context.arc(55,  85, 45, 0, Math.PI / 2, false)
context.stroke()
context.closePath()

context.beginPath()
context.arc(155, 85, 45, 0, Math.PI, false)
context.stroke()
context.closePath()

context.beginPath()
context.arc(255, 85, 45, 0, Math.PI / 2 * 3, false)
context.stroke()
context.closePath()

context.beginPath()
context.arc(355, 85, 45, 0, Math.PI * 2, false)
context.stroke()
context.closePath()
```

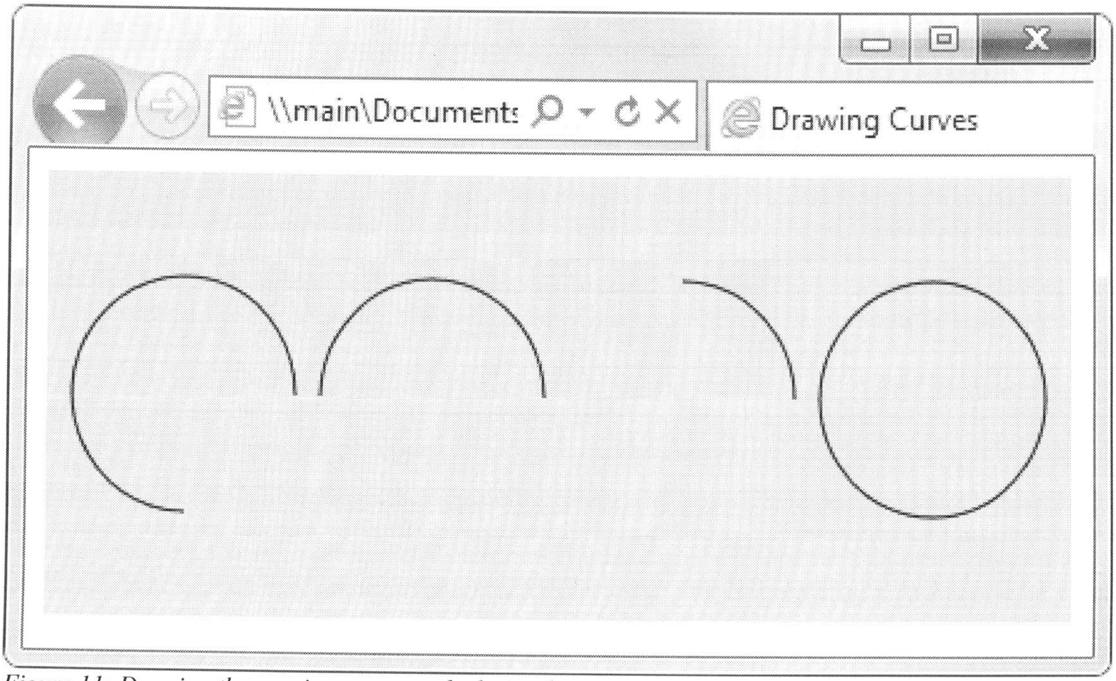

Figure 11: Drawing the arcs in a counter-clockwise direction

For this example, I chose not to fill in the final circle so you can see how to draw a complete, outlined circle.

Remember too that you can change the stroke width and other properties by assigning the relevant values to the `strokeStyle` property. If you wish to draw the arcs in a counterclockwise direction you can change the final argument in the call to `arc()` to `true`, and this will result in Figure 12-11, in which you will note that you always get a full circle for image four, regardless of the direction of drawing.

The `arcTo(x1,y1,x2,y2,r)` Function

There's another way you can draw an arc, which is to use the `arcTo()` function, which draws a curve based on the current location the path has reached, and arguments that you supply to it representing a pair of imaginary tangent lines touching the circles perimeter.

For example, let's assume that the current path position has been achieved using a `moveTo()` call, like this, which places the start position of the path at the bottom left corner of the canvas:

```
context.beginPath()
context.moveTo(0, 170)
```

Now a curve can be created with its start point at the above location and an end point at location `0,90`, like this:

```
context.arcTo(0, 0, 170, 0, 170)
```

So, we have the start point of `0,170` from the `moveTo()` call, and end point of `0,90` being the third and fourth arguments to `arcTo()`, but what about the first two and final arguments in the `arcTo()` call?

Well, the first two arguments of `0, 0` in the `arcTo()` call represent the end point of an imaginary tangent line starting at `0,170` and ending at `0,0`. Then the third and fourth arguments (as well as being the end point for the arc) represent the end of a tangent line drawn from `0, 0` to `170,0`.

Where these two tangents meet the circle's circumference are the arc's start and end points and, because a tangent must always be at a right angle to the radius of a circle, the arc to create can now be calculated.

Let's see how this works by first drawing the imaginary lines, with the following code, as shown in Figure 12-12:

```
context.strokeStyle = 'green'
context.beginPath()
context.moveTo(0, 170)
context.lineTo(0,   0)
context.lineTo(170, 0)
context.stroke()
context.closePath()
```

The first line sets a green color to differentiate form the arc that will be drawn in a moment.

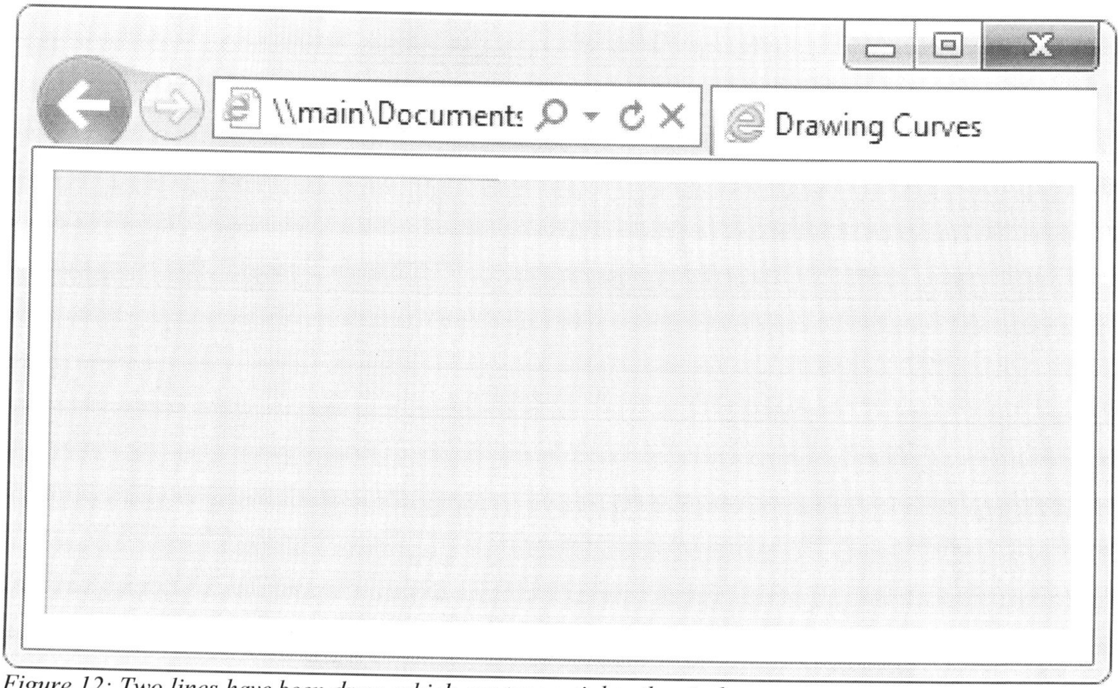

Figure 12: Two lines have been draw, which are tangential to the circle

Then a simple path is created to draw the two lines, which are simply to show where the imaginary tangents would be if they were displayed, so the preceding code is only for illustrative purposes.

The `arcTo()` code is as follows, and results in Figure 12-13:

```
context.strokeStyle = 'blue'
context.beginPath()
context.moveTo(0, 170)

context.arcTo(0, 0, 170, 0, 170)
context.stroke()
context.closePath()
```

Figure 12-13 also serves to demonstrate the purpose of the final argument to the `arcTo()` function, which is the radius of the circle on which the arc is based.

In this example the two tangents are sides of a square (at 90 degrees to each other), and the arc is a quarter circle with a radius of 170 pixels (whose origin – or center - is therefore at location `90,170`).

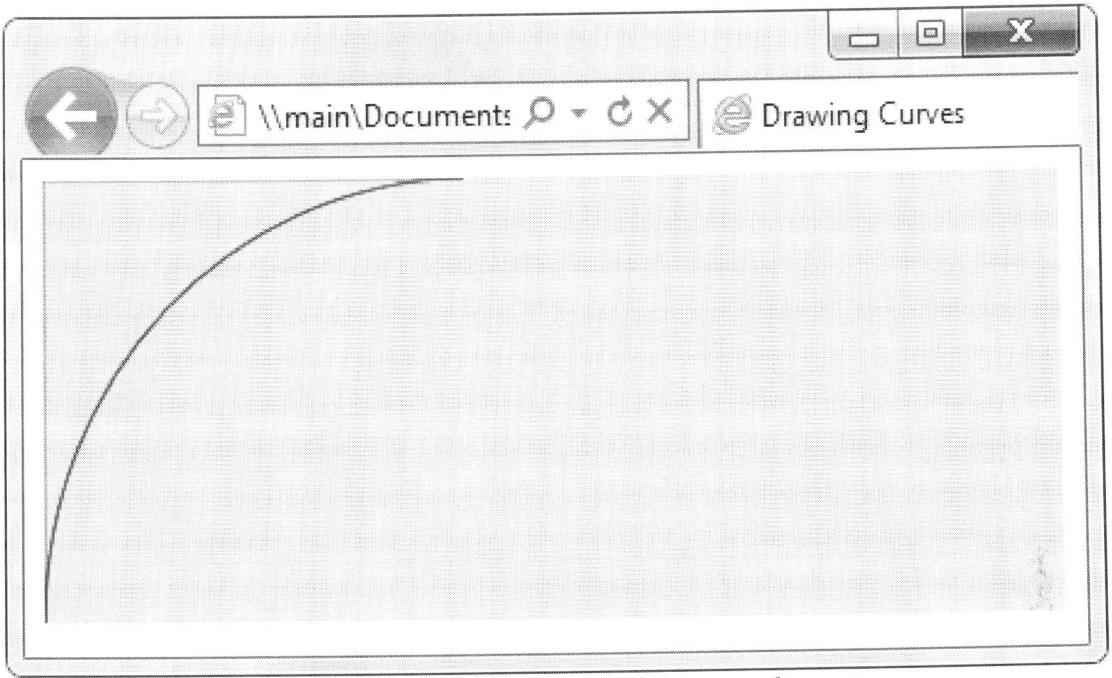

Figure 13: The arc has been drawn connecting the end points of the pair of tangents

***Note**: If this function baffles you try playing with the examples on the companion website and you'll soon get to grips with how these tangents work.*

The `quadraticCurveTo(x1,y1,x2,y2)` Function

As well as arcs you can even create the most fancy of curves using the function `quadraticCurveTo()`, which employs an imaginary attractor object that pulls the curve towards it.

For example, let's draw a line between the left and right side of the canvas using a simple `stroke()` call, like this (as shown in Figure 12-14):

```
context.strokeStyle = 'green'
context.beginPath()
context.moveTo(0,   85)
context.lineTo(410, 85)
context.stroke()
context.closePath()
```

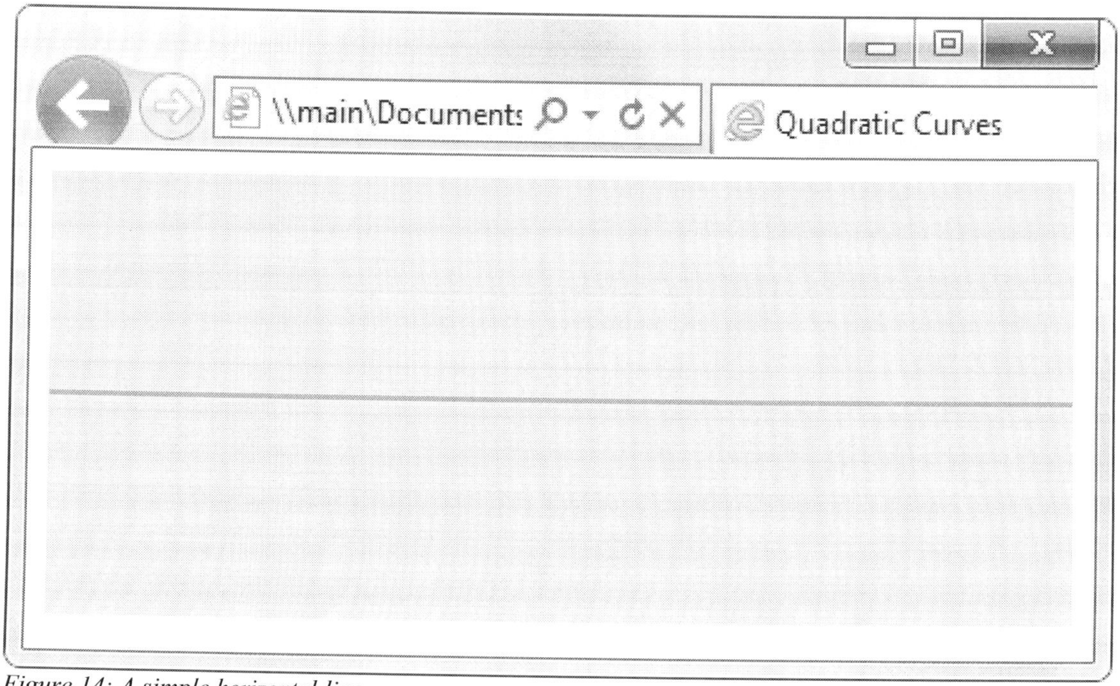

Figure 14: A simple horizontal line

Now let's draw a curved line between these positions, but with an imaginary attractor up in the top left hand corner, at location `0,0`, like this (and shown in Figure 12-15):

```
context.strokeStyle = 'blue'
context.beginPath()
context.moveTo(0, 85)
context.quadraticCurveTo(0, 0, 410, 85)
context.stroke()
context.closePath()
```

As you can see from the figure the whole curve has been pulled towards the attraction point as if the curve were made of an elasticated magnetic material being attracted towards a magnet.

The further up the attractor is placed the higher the curve will be pulled. Similarly, if the attractor is moved to the left or right, then the attraction will also move in that direction.

***Note**: Sometimes it takes a little trial and error to get just the curve you need, but you should soon get the hang of this function.*

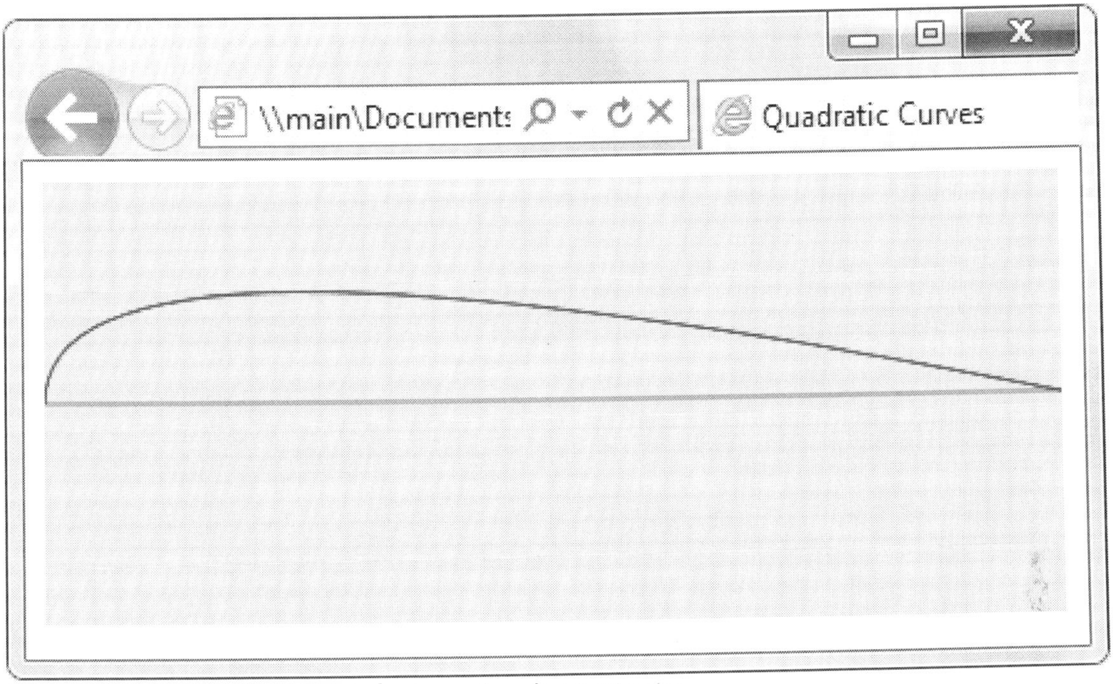

Figure 15: A curve has been created using an imaginary attractor

The `bezierCurveTo(x1,y1,x2,y2,x3,y3)` Function

If you thought quadratic curves were funky then wait till you check out Bézier curves. These are similar but support the use of two imaginary attractors, which can be placed anywhere on (or off) the canvas.

For example, let's adapt the previous example, to add a second attractor at the bottom right corner of the canvas by replacing the call to `quadraticCurveTo()` with one to `bezierCurveTo()`, like this (resulting in Figure 12-16):

```
context.strokeStyle = 'blue'
context.beginPath()
context.moveTo(0, 85)
context.bezierCurveTo(0, 0, 410, 170, 410, 85)
context.stroke()
context.closePath()
```

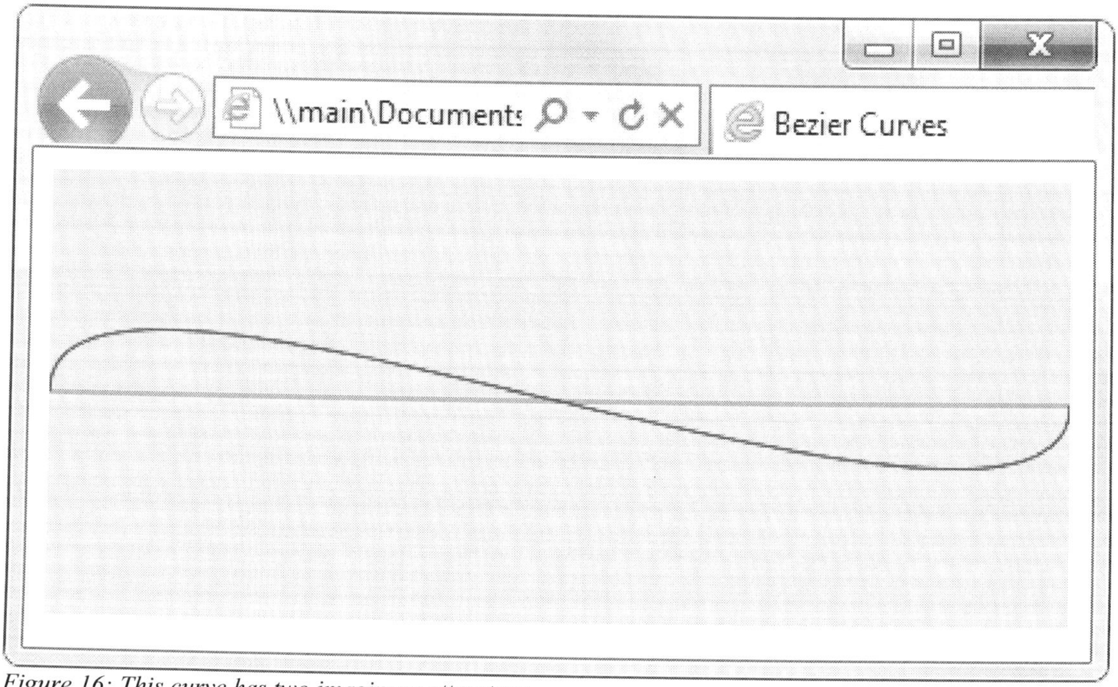

Figure 16: This curve has two imaginary attractors

***Note**: Since you can place the pair of attractors anywhere you like (not necessarily at opposite sides of the curve), you can create any curve that is possible to draw using Bézier curves, although trial and error may again be required.*

Summary

You now have all the line, curve and path tools added to your toolkit. Remember that you may create as complicated and lengthy paths as you like, and are not limited to the small snippets of examples I have shown you in this lecture. Properly implemented you can create sketches and logos, or use the functions as part of a design program you can write in JavaScript.

In the following lecture I'll continue our journey into the vast resource that is the HTML5 canvas by showing you how to write onto the canvas using images, how to apply shadows and even the use of direct pixel manipulation.

LECTURE 13

IMAGES, SHADOWS & PIXELS

By following this lecture you will:

- ✓ *Discover how to draw using external images as brushes.*
- ✓ *Learn how to add an assortment of different shadow styles.*
- ✓ *See how to directly manipulate the pixels of a canvas.*

IN THIS LECTURE I'll begin to look into the more advanced aspects of the HTML5 canvas, including drawing uses images, adding shadows and even directly manipulating the pixels (individual dots) of the canvas by their constituent primary colors of red, blue and green, and their transparency too.

***Note**: The examples from this lecture are in the* Lecture 13 *folder of the* examples.zip *file at* tinyurlcom/html5ccexamples.

Using Images

On top of all the other drawing functions available to you for manipulating the HTML5 canvas, you have also seen how you can import an image to use as a fill pattern. However, you can also use images to draw directly onto the canvas.

The `drawImage(various)` Function

Using the `drawImage()` function you can load in an image such as a *jpg*, *gif* or *png*, and draw it directly onto the canvas, like this code which draws it with its top left corner at location `10,10`, as displayed in Figure 13-1:

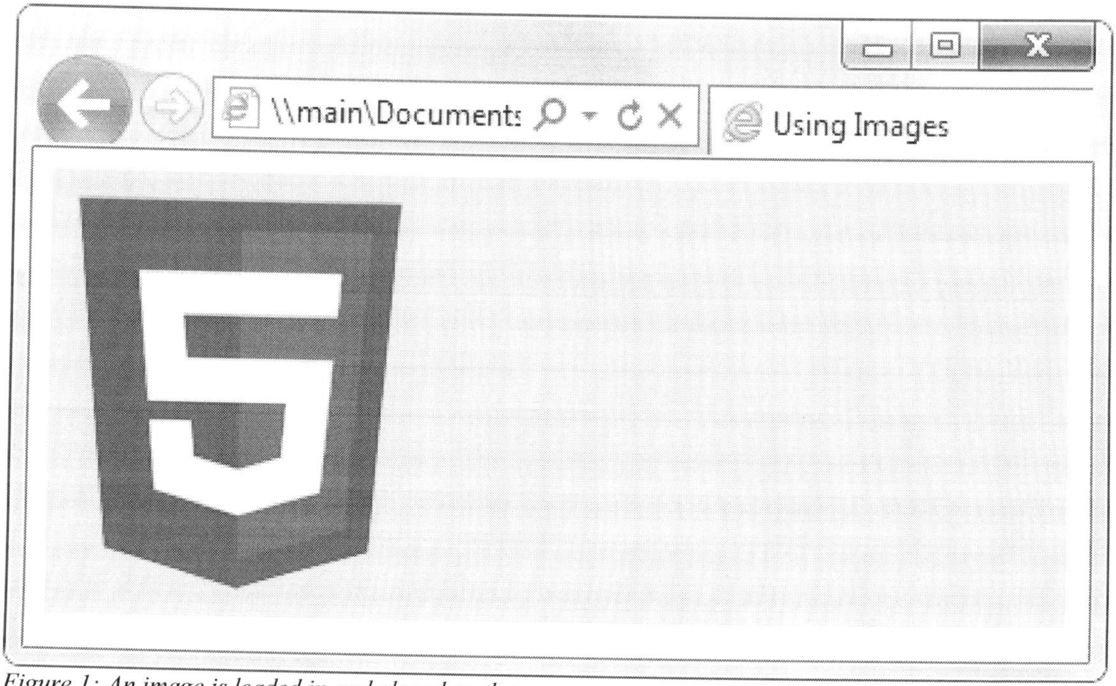

Figure 1: An image is loaded in and placed on the canvas

```
image      = new Image()
image.src = 'html5.png'

image.onload = function()
{
  context.drawImage(image, 10, 10)
}
```

As you will recall from previous lectures, the `onload` event of the `image` object is attached to with a function, whose code is executed only once the image has been fully loaded. If this were not the case the image might not display.

In this instance only the first three parameters the function accepts have been used. These are the image to use and the horizontal and vertical location at which it should be displayed, so the image is displayed full size.

However, it is also possible to resize the image before it is placed on the canvas by passing additional arguments, as with these two examples, the result of which is shown in Figure 13-2:

```
context.drawImage(image, 152, 10, 62, 70)
context.drawImage(image, 152, 90, 62, 70)
```

Figure 2: Two copies of the reduced image have been added

Here the image has been reduced to just under a quarter of its original size by more than halving its dimensions, and then two copies have been placed alongside the original, one above the other. This version of the function call takes arguments in this order: the image to display, the horizontal and vertical location to display it, and the width and height to use for displaying it.

***Note**: When using rescaling on an image you may not always get the sharpest anti-aliased results you could otherwise achieve by first resizing them in a graphic program. However the results are fast, and if you understand writing loops in JavaScript you can even use them for animation.*

But, as they say in the infomercials, there's more. Not only can you resize an image down, you can resize it up too. You can also choose which area of the image to use when doing so, and you are therefore not restricted to using the entire image.

For example, the original *html5.png* image used in these examples has dimensions of 132 by 150 pixels. Using the following line of code a rectangular subsection of this image has been selected, enlarged, and placed to the right of the two smaller images, as shown in Figure 13-3:

Figure 3: The image has been cropped and enlarged before use

```
context.drawImage(image, 23, 26, 86, 98, 224, 10, 118, 150)
```

You must be wary when using this version of the function call because, rather than adding parameters onto the existing ones in the previous calls to the function, four new arguments are inserted between the image argument and those in the previous examples. For example, in this instance the first four numeric arguments of 23, 26, 86 and 98 are two pairs, the first of which is the location of the top left corner of the part of the image to crop, and the second pair are the width and height for the crop.

These values result in clipping out the number 5 from the image. Then the remaining four values are the same as in the previous examples. They are the horizontal and vertical location at which to place the cropped image, and the width and height to use for displaying it.

Using The Canvas As a Source Image

You are not restricted to using only external images within a canvas because you can copy sections of the canvas itself and write them back to it, even after cropping and/or reducing or enlarging them.

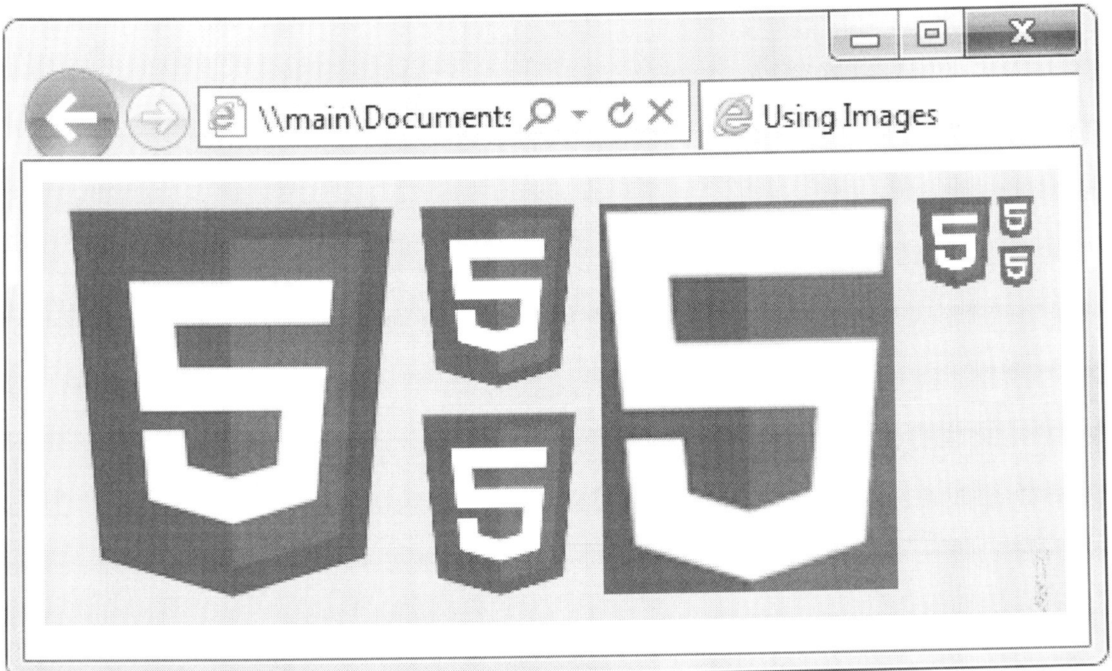

Figure 4: A portion of the image has been grabbed and reused

For example, in the following code the left half of the canvas is captured, reduced in size and copied to the top right of the canvas, as shown in Figure 13-4:

```
context.drawImage(canvas, 10, 10, 205, 150,
  352, 10, 48, 35)
```

This code works by referring to the canvas object in the first argument, rather than an object of an external image.

As you can see the reduced images are looking quite jagged now, so it's probably worth doing your own resizing in an editor for major changes like this although, as I previously mentioned, as part of an animation or transition effect this function works just great.

Note*: The HTML5 specifications also call for being able to use an HTML video element for drawing onto a canvas, but this doesn't seem to work with any of the browsers I have tested it with. Hopefully this feature will be operational soon as it would be really useful. In the meantime, if you are skilled with JavaScript, there are other (more complicated) ways you can Google to find out how to place video on a canvas.*

Adding Shadows

The HTML canvas supports the addition of a shadow to any element that you draw onto it. This feature requires the use of a group of four properties you can set to specify a vertical and horizontal offset, the shadow blur and its color, as follows:

- **shadowOffsetX** The horizontal offset in pixels that the shadow should be shifted to the right by (or to the left if the value is negative).
- **shadowOffsetY** The vertical offset in pixels that the shadow should be shifted down by (or up if the value is negative).
- **shadowBlur** The number of pixels over which to blur the shadow's outline.
- **shadowColor** The base color to use for the shadow. If a blur is in use this color will blend with the background in the blurred area.

For example, in the following (somewhat longer than usual) example code four elements are drawn on the canvas using slightly different shadow properties, as shown in Figure 13-5.

```
image1 = new Image()
image2 = new Image()
image3 = new Image()
image4 = new Image()

image1.src = 'html5.png'
image2.src = 'smiley-50.png'
image3.src = 'mom.jpg'
image4.src = 'dad.jpg'

image1.onload = function() // HTML5 logo
{
  context.shadowOffsetX = 8
  context.shadowOffsetY = 8
  context.shadowBlur    = 8
  context.shadowColor   = '#000'
  context.drawImage(image1,  10, 10)
}

image2.onload = function() // Smiley image
{
  context.shadowOffsetX = 6
  context.shadowOffsetY = 6
  context.shadowBlur    = 6
  context.shadowColor   = '#333'
```

```
    context.drawImage(image2,  152, 10)
  }
  image3.onload = function() // Mom image
  {
    context.shadowOffsetX = 4
    context.shadowOffsetY = 4
    context.shadowBlur    = 4
    context.shadowColor   = '#666'
    context.drawImage(image3,  212, 10, 90, 73)
  }

  image4.onload = function() // Dad image
  {
    context.shadowOffsetX = 2
    context.shadowOffsetY = 2
    context.shadowBlur    = 2
    context.shadowColor   = '#999'
    context.drawImage(image4,  312, 10, 90, 73)
  }

  context.shadowOffsetX = 3  // "Hello" text
  context.shadowOffsetY = 3
  context.shadowBlur    = 5
  context.shadowColor   = '#444'
  context.font          = '38pt Arial'
  context.fillStyle     = 'blue'
  context.fillText('Hello', 152, 135)

  context.shadowOffsetX = 0  // Outlined rectangle
  context.shadowOffsetY = 0
  context.shadowBlur    = 6
  context.shadowColor   = '#000'
  context.strokeStyle   = 'red'
  context.lineWidth     = 3
  context.strokeRect(280, 95, 120, 65)
```

I used a variety of elements in this example as they illustrate a number of different points. So let's look at them in turn, starting with the HTML5 logo.

The first thing you may notice with this image is that, unlike the other external images, this one doesn't have a colored background but, instead, features a transparent one, and therefore the shadow properties make use of this and draws the shadow only around the non-transparent areas. This image also has the largest shadow set, with vertical and

Figure 5: A variety of different elements using different shadow properties

horizontal offsets and a blur area of 8 pixels, and the background color used for the shadow is black (`#000`).

The following three external images all have white backgrounds and so the shadow forms around the rectangular outside edges of each image. In turn these images use shadow offsets and blur areas of 6, 4 and 2 pixels respectively. At the same time the background color for the shadows uses increasingly lighter shades of gray (`#333`, `#666` and `#999`).

Next the word "Hello" is drawn in blue, 38 point Arial text, has a vertical and horizontal offset of 3 pixels, and a blur area of 5 pixels. See how the shadow lifts it from the background.

Finally, the rectangle uses a line width of 3 pixels and is drawn in red. The shadow offsets are both 0 but the blur area is 6 pixels and black (`#000`) has been used for the shadow background color. This makes the shadow appear both inside and outside the rectangle.

Note*: The rectangle at the bottom right of Figure 13-5 illustrates how you can create inner shadows, which aren't directly supported by the HTML5 canvas. Simply draw an object and specify a shadow that will appear inside that shape. Then draw another shape to cover over the outside shadows in the places where you don't want them. Alternatively,*

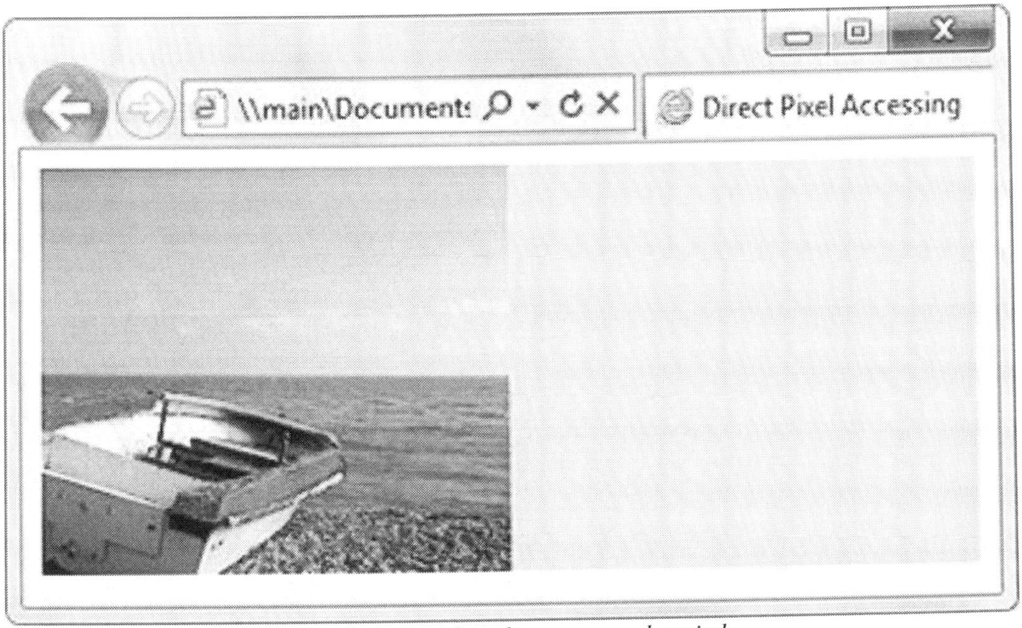

Figure 6: An image has been loaded, placed on the canvas and copied

it may be easier to simply create a clipped area using the `clip()` function, to prevent any drawing (such as the shadows) from being made outside of this area. If you do so, remember to reset the clipped area back to the entire canvas once done.

Pixel Editing

We've now covered just about every conceivable drawing tool you could want for getting creative with the HTML5 canvas, but there's one more trick remaining in the hat, and that's direct pixel editing.

Using the `getImageData()`, `putImageData()` and `createImageData()` functions, in conjunction with the `data[]` array you can directly manipulate the canvas at pixel level, even down to the red, green, blue and transparency constituents of a pixel.

The `getImageData(x,y,w,h)` Function

Let's start by creating an image on a canvas (as shown in Figure 13-6) and then grabbing a portion of it with `getImageData()`, like this:

```
image     = new Image()
image.src = 'boat.png'

image.onload = function()
{
  context.drawImage(image, 0, 0)
  imagedata = context.getImageData(0, 0, 205, 170)
}
```

This code uses the usual technique of loading in an image and then attaching a function to its `onload` event so that the code in the function is called only once the image is fully loaded. Within the function the image is then drawn onto the canvas so that it takes up its left half. The final line then creates an object called `imagedata` by grabbing information from the canvas starting at location `0,0` and with a width of 205 and height of 170 pixels.

At this point the image data that constitutes the left half of the canvas is now loaded into the `imagedata` array and it can be accessed from JavaScript to read or write its pixel data. This is done using the `data[]` array, which is a property of `imagedata`.

The `data[]` Array

The canvas element support millions of colors (as well as transparency) for each pixel, and these are managed by allocating four locations per pixel for its red, green, blue and alpha (transparency) components, each accepting a value of between 0 and 255. These locations are stored contiguously in the `data[]` array so that the pixel at the top left of the canvas (at location `0,0`) can be accessed as follows:

```
imagedata.data[0] // The red portion of:   0,0
imagedata.data[1] // The green portion of: 0,0
imagedata.data[2] // The blue portion of:  0,0
imagedata.data[3] // The alpha portion of: 0,0
```

Therefore the pixel one to the right of this at location `1,0` can be accessed like this:

```
imagedata.data[4] // The red portion of:   1,0
imagedata.data[5] // The green portion of: 1,0
imagedata.data[6] // The blue portion of:  1,0
imagedata.data[7] // The alpha portion of: 1,0
```

This continues until the end of the first row of pixels is reached, when the array continues with the next line. So, for a 205 pixel wide section (such as the one grabbed in this example), there are 4 * 205 locations (or 820) on each row. Therefore the pixels at location `204,0` are accessed like this:

```
imagedata.data[816] // The red portion of:   204,0
imagedata.data[817] // The green portion of: 204,0
imagedata.data[818] // The blue portion of:  204,0
imagedata.data[819] // The alpha portion of: 204,0
```

And the pixels at location `0,1` are accessed as follows:

```
imagedata.data[820] // The red portion of:   0,1
imagedata.data[821] // The green portion of: 0,1
imagedata.data[822] // The blue portion of:  0,1
imagedata.data[823] // The alpha portion of: 0,1
```

Or, if you don't mind using JavaScript expressions, you can address the array with code such as the following, where the JavaScript variables `x` and `y` contain the pixel to reference, and `w` is the width of the area:

```
imagedata.data[x * 4 + y * w    ] // Red
imagedata.data[x * 4 + y * w + 1] // Green
imagedata.data[x * 4 + y * w + 2] // Blue
imagedata.data[x * 4 + y * w + 3] // Alpha
```

The `putImageData(i,x,y)` Function

Let's use the previous information to convert the image data grabbed from the left half of the canvas into grayscale, by averaging all the color values and setting them to the same value in each pixel. For example, if a pixel displays as yellow, which is a combination of red and green (color string `#FFFF00`) then we add up the `FF` the `FF` and the `00` to get a value of `1FE` in hexadecimal (or 510 decimal, since `FF` hexadecimal is 255 in decimal, and twice that is 510).

Next that value is divided by 3 (the number of different component colors) to return the value `AA` (or 170 in decimal), which is then assigned to all components of the pixel as the hexadecimal color `#AAAAAA`. Therefore the average brightness value of the color yellow (`#FFFF00` in hexadecimal) is a gray tone with the value `#AAAAAA`, in which each color component has a value of `AA` in hexadecimal, or 170 in decimal.

Let's look at some code to do this for the pixel at location `0,0`:

```
average = (imagedata.data[0] +
           imagedata.data[1]
           imagedata.data[2]) / 3
```

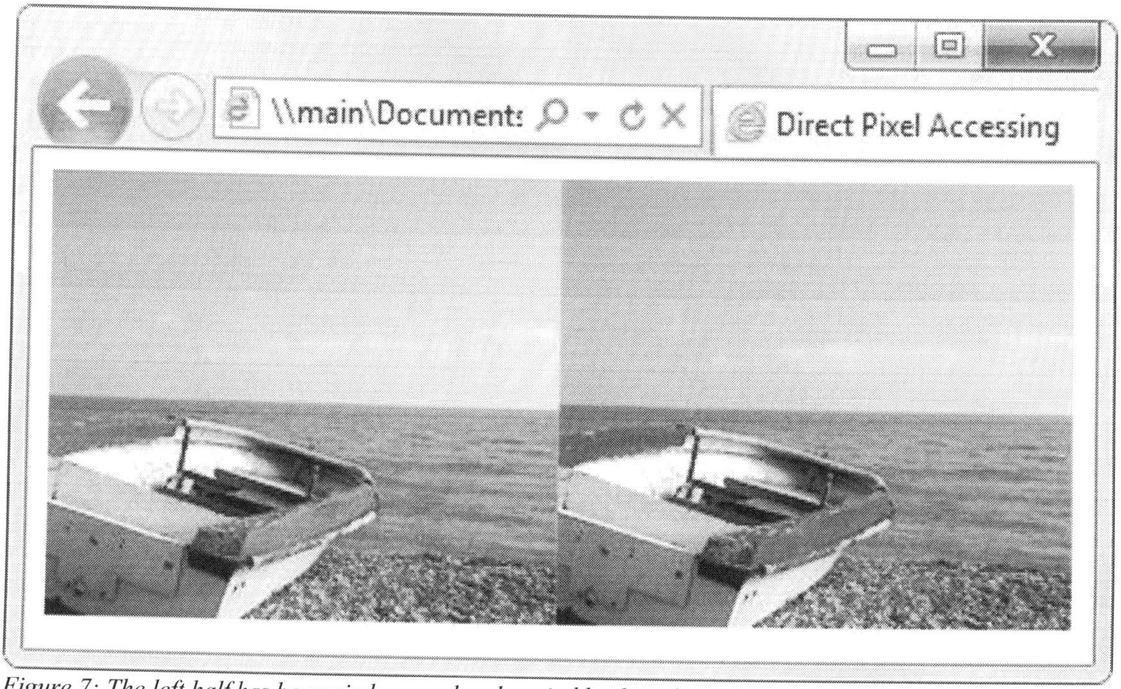

Figure 7: The left half has be copied, grayed and copied back to the right

The variable `average` now contains the average value of the red, green and blue components of the pixel's color. In this instance the fourth constituent of the pixel (which is the transparency) is being ignored.

Assuming that all the pixels in the `imagedata` object's `data[]` array have been averaged in this manner, the updated image data can now be written back to the canvas like this, as shown in Figure 13-7:

```
context.putImageData(imagedata, 205, 0)
```

Following is the code that was used to perform this transformation. Be warned, though, that you may find it a little complicated, and use of techniques such as this are recommended only if you have a good understanding of JavaScript programming:

```
image     = new Image()
image.src = 'boat.png'

image.onload = function()
{
  context.drawImage(image, 0, 0)
  imagedata = context.getImageData(0, 0, 205, 170)
  width     = 205
  height    = 170
```

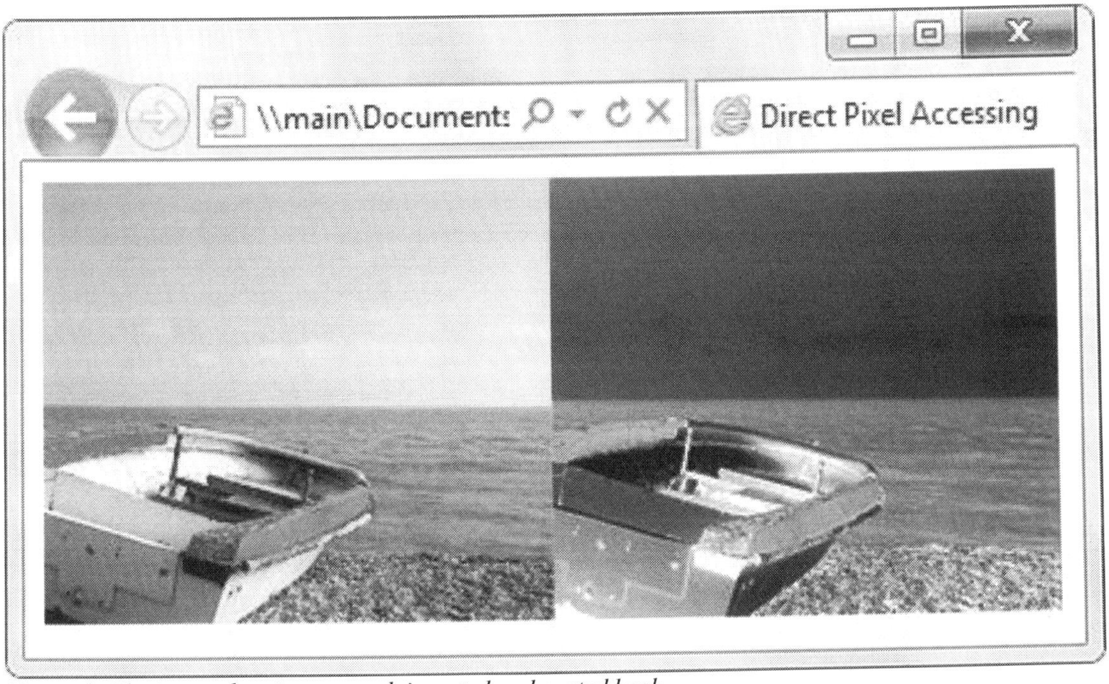

Figure 8: The image data is averaged, inverted and pasted back

```
    for (y = 0 ; y < height ; ++y)
    {
      pos = y * width * 4

      for (x = 0 ; x < width ; ++x)
      {
        average = (imagedata.data[pos    ] +
                   imagedata.data[pos + 1] +
                   imagedata.data[pos + 2]) / 3

        // Uncomment below for more effects
        //   average = 0xFF - average
        //   average += 0x50
        for (j = 0 ; j < 3 ; ++j)
          imagedata.data[pos + j] = average

        pos += 4
      }
    }
    context.putImageData(imagedata, 205, 0)
  }
```

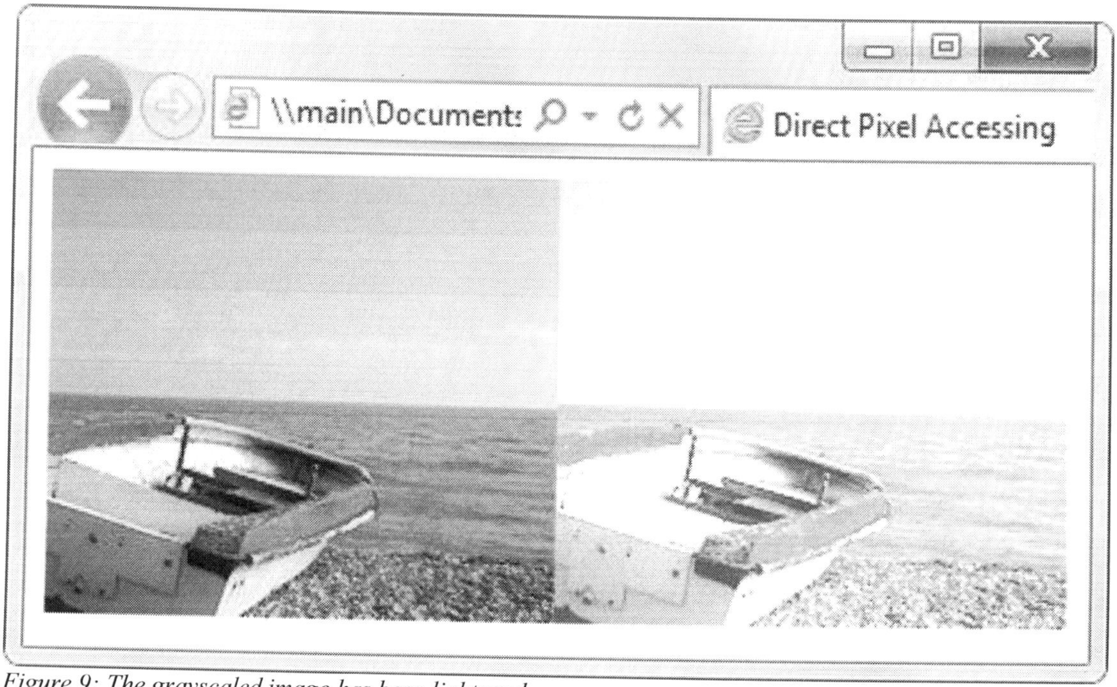

Figure 9: The grayscaled image has been lightened

By simply adding an extra line after the three lines of code that calculate the average, you can change the transformation to create a negative grayscale image.

This is achieved by subtracting the value in average from the hexadecimal value `FF` (255 in decimal), like this:

```
average = 0xFF - average
```

What this does is change the value 1 to 254, 17 to 238, 255 to 0, and so forth, inverting the image, as shown in Figure 13-8.

You can do other things too such as changing the overall brightness of the image instead of inverting it, by using this line (for example) instead, which adds hexadecimal 50 (80 in decimal) to each color component, as displayed as Figure 13-9:

```
average + = 0x50
```

As you can see, once you have access to this data in the `data[]` array of the `imagedata` object you can perform all manner of transformations on it.

For example you can mirror or flip the image, use matrixes (and advanced programming concept) to sharpen or blur the image and so on. In fact, with a little ingenuity, you can do all the things a professional graphic editing program like Photoshop can do.

The `createImageData(w,h)` Function

You don't have to create an `imagedata` object directly from a canvas and can simply create a new one with blank data by calling the `createImageData()` function, like the following, which creates an object with a width of 320 and height of 240 pixels:

```
imagedata = createImageData(320, 240)
```

Alternatively, you can create a new object from an existing object, like this:

```
newimagedataobject = createImageData(imagedata)
```

It's then up to you what you do with these objects to add pixel data to them, and how you paste them onto the canvas or create other objects from them.

Summary

You now have all the basic HTML5 canvas skills in your toolkit, but there are a few more advanced features yet to come, all of which are covered in the final lecture of this part of the course on the HTML5 canvas. In it you'll learn about compositing, transparency and transformations, which you can use to create just the professional touch you need in your canvases.

LECTURE 14

COMPOSITING, TRANSPARENCY & TRANSFORMATIONS

By following this lecture you will:

✓ *Discover how to add elements under, over or merge them with others.*

✓ *Learn how to apply transparency to a drawing element.*

✓ *See how you can warp elements using transformations.*

IN THIS FINAL lecture on the HTML5 canvas I show you how to use the remaining advanced graphical features not yet introduced, including compositing, transparency and transformations, as well as how to save and restore context between operations.

***Note**: The examples from this lecture are in the* Lecture 14 *folder of the* examples.zip *file at* tinyurlcom/html5ccexamples.

Compositing & Transparency

Compositing is the method used for placing an element onto the canvas, and there are 12 different available types which have the effect of placing new elements in front or behind existing ones, only on top of an existing element, never over an existing element, and so forth.

This is achieved using a property called `globalCompositeOperation`, providing it with the required value for the compositing you require.

The `globalCompositeOperation` Property

This property drastically affects the way new elements are added to the canvas. It supports 12 different values such as `source-over`, which is the default, and is applied like this:

```
context.globalCompositeOperationProperty = 'source-over'
```

Following is a breakdown of all 12 types and the way they work. You should read them in conjunction with looking at Figure 14-1, which displays an example of each type:

- **`source-over`** The default. The source image is copied over the destination image.
- **`source-in`** Only parts of the source image that will appear within the destination are shown, and the destination image is removed. Any alpha transparency in the source image causes the destination under it to be removed.
- **`source-out`** Only parts of the source image that do not appear within the destination are shown, and the destination image is removed. Any alpha transparency in the source image causes the destination under it to be removed.
- **`source-atop`** The source image is displayed where it overlays the destination. The destination image is displayed where the destination image is opaque and the source image is transparent. Other regions are transparent.
- **`destination-over`** The source image is drawn under the destination image.
- **`destination-in`** The destination image displays where the source and destination image overlap, but not in any areas of source image transparency. The source image does not display.
- **`destination-out`** Only those parts of the destination outside of the source image's non transparent sections are shown. The source image does not display.
- **`destination-atop`** The source image displays where the destination is not displayed. Where the destination and source overlap the destination image is displayed. Any transparency in the source image prevents that area of the destination image being shown.
- **`lighter`** The sum of the source and destination is applied such that where they do not overlap they display as normal, but where they overlap the sum of both images is shown, but lightened.
- **`darker`** The sum of the source and destination is applied such that where they do not overlap they display as normal, but where they overlap the sum of both images is shown, but darkened.
- **`copy`** The source image is copied over the destination. Any transparent area of the source causes any destination that it overlaps to not display.
- **`xor`** Where the source and destination images do not overlap they display as normal. Where they overlap their color values are exclusive-ored.

Compositing can be really tricky to get right so my advice is to use trial and error and you may prefer to choose a compositing type based on the examples shown in Figure 14-1, rather than on the descriptions given previously, as it's a lot easier to understand the images.

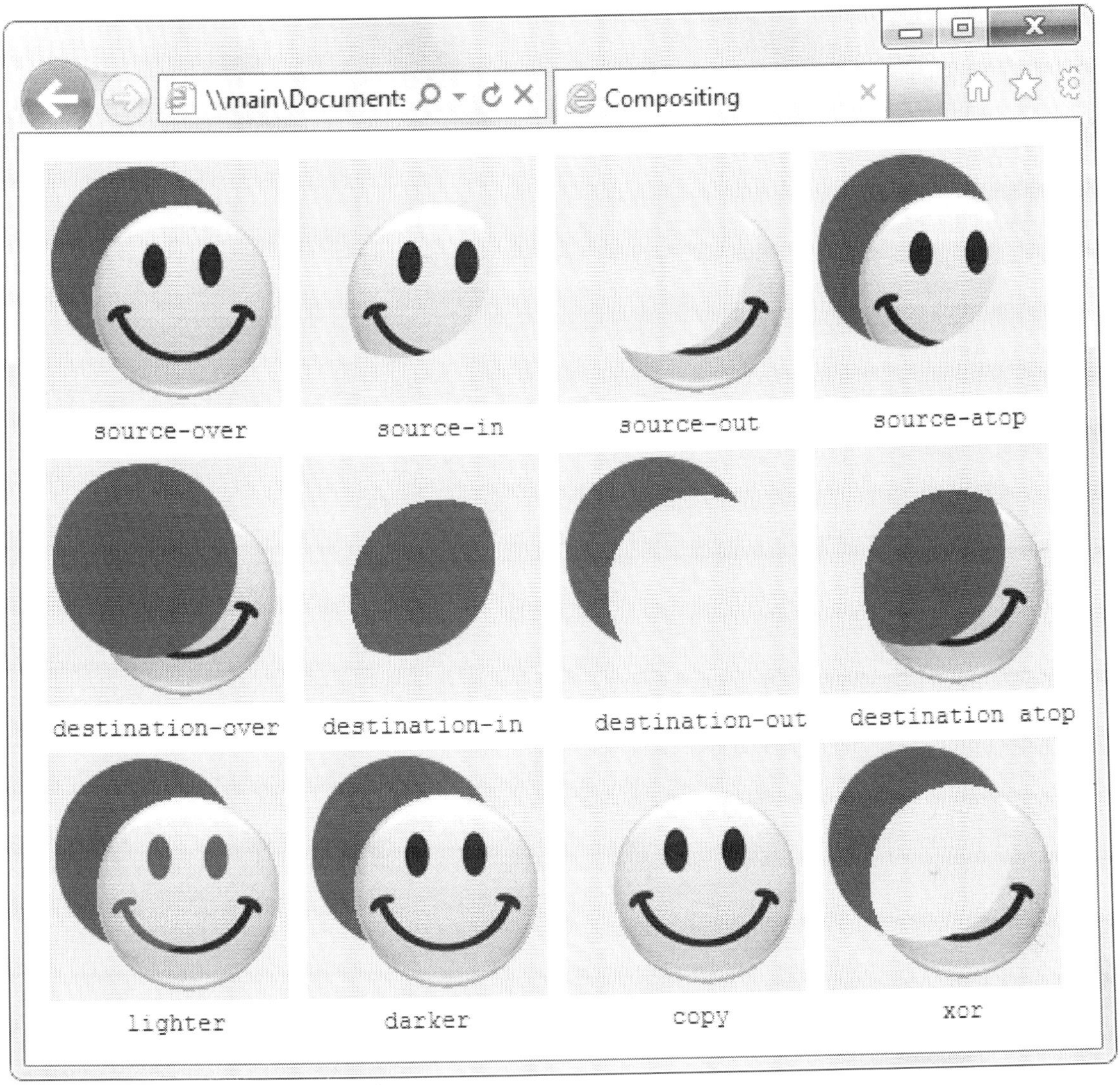

Figure 1: The 12 different compositing types

The `globalAlpha` Property

When drawing an element to the canvas you can choose how much transparency to give it by providing a fractional value to the `globalAlpha` property of between 0.00 and 1.00 inclusive, with 0.00 (or simply 0) signifying no transparency, 1.00 being totally transparent, and 0.50 being half transparent, and so on, like this:

```
context.globalAlpha = 0.5
```

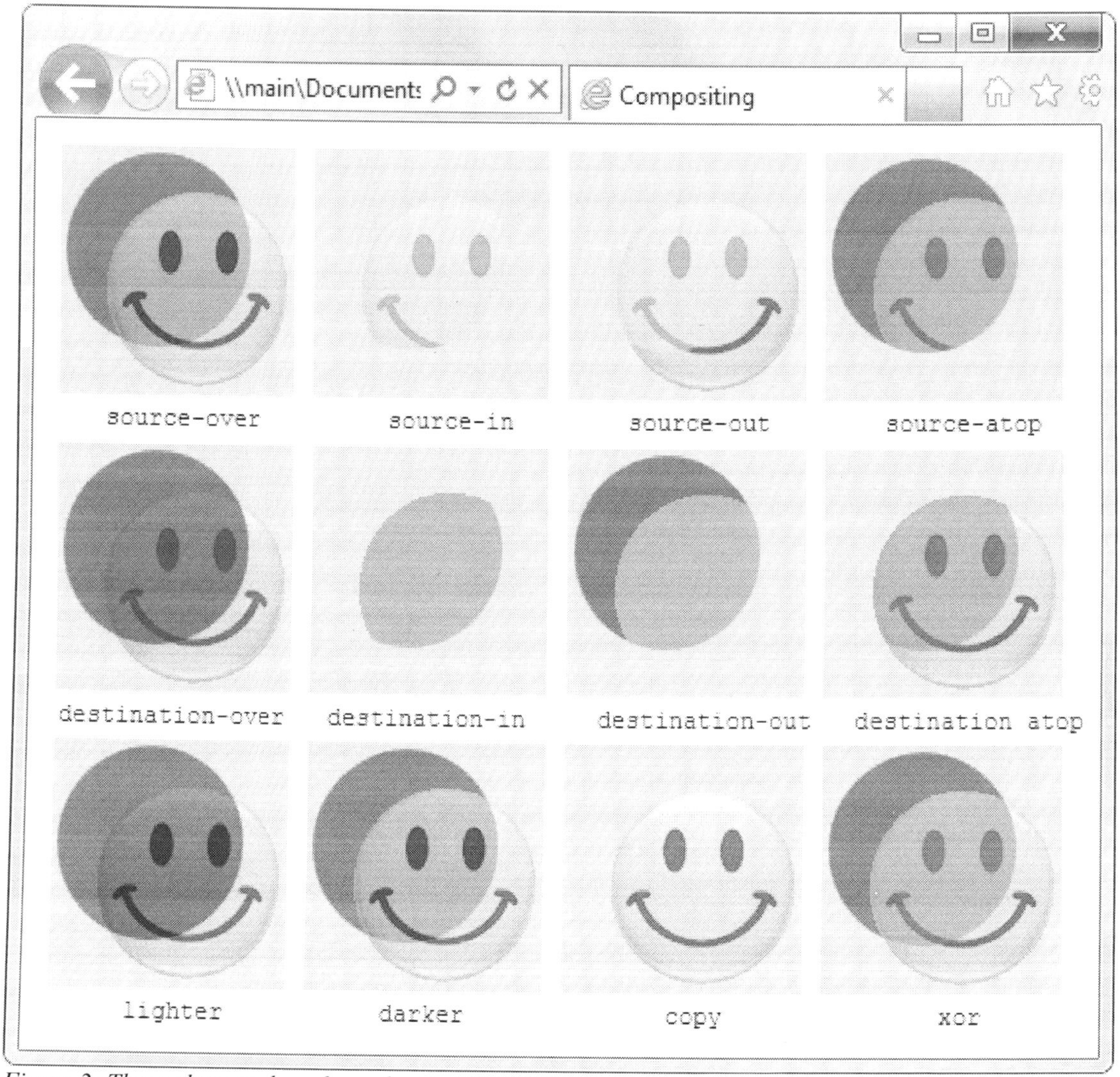

Figure 2: These elements have been drawn using 50% transparency

For example, In Figure 14-2 a value of 0.5 has been applied to the `globalAlpha` property of the previous compositing example by adding the preceding line of code.

Using Transformations

There are four functions available for applying transformations to elements when drawing them to the HTML5 canvas. They are: `scale()`, `rotate()`, `translate()` and `transform()`, and with them, if your element is not quite at the right angle, the correct size or at the right perspective you can tweak it until you get it just right.

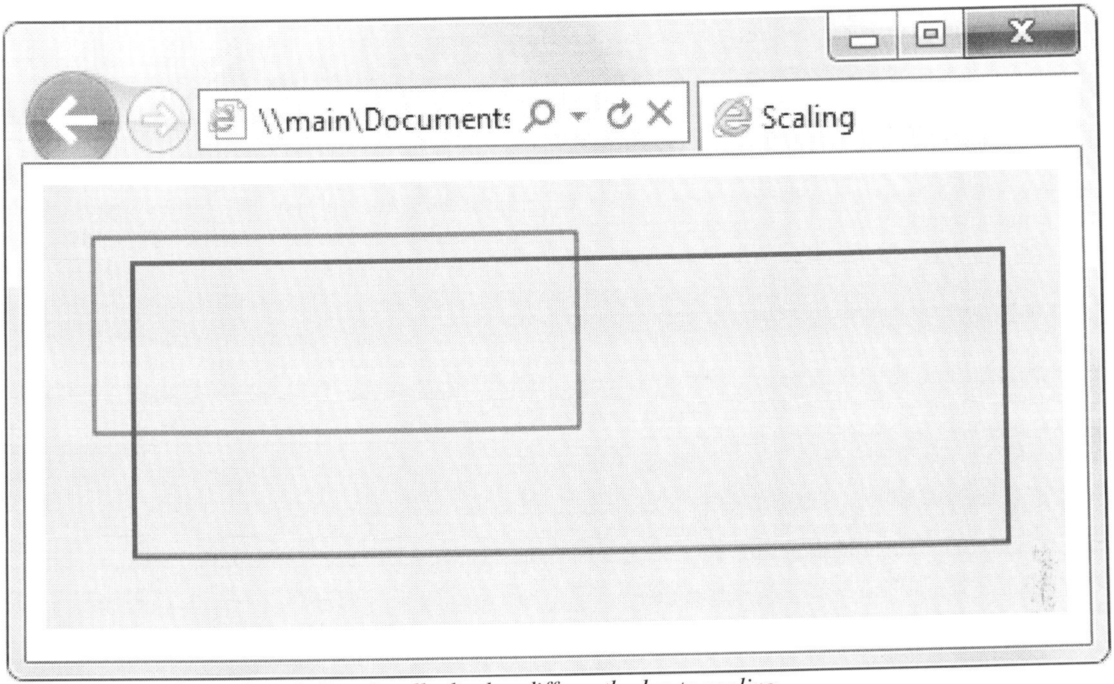

Figure 3: Two identical strokeRect() calls display differently due to scaling

The `scale(h, v)` Function

As you've already seen there are various ways you can scale different objects, such as by specifying the width and height at which to draw them on the canvas. But you can also use the `scale()` function to apply a global scaling factor to all future elements drawn on the canvas, like the following, which sets the scaling of horizontal dimensions to 1.8 times and vertical to 1.5 times the original size:

```
context.scale(1.8, 1.5)
```

Let's look at this in practice with the following code which draws a rectangle, increases the scaling factors, and then redraws the rectangle, as shown in Figure 14-3:

```
context.strokeStyle = 'red'
context.strokeRect(20, 20, 195, 75)

context.scale(1.8, 1.5)

context.strokeStyle = 'blue'
context.strokeRect(20, 20, 195, 75)
```

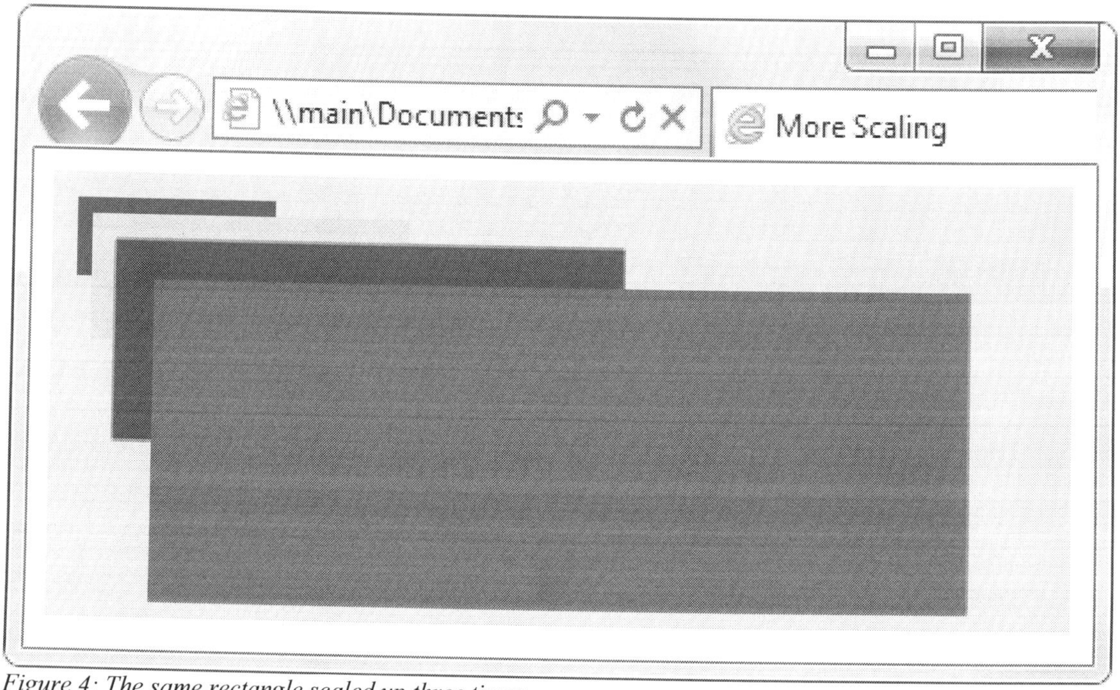

Figure 4: The same rectangle scaled up three times

To help show the difference between the rectangles, the original (smaller) one is displayed in green, and the second (larger) one in blue. The arguments used in the parameters to the calls for drawing the rectangles are identical to each other, but the `scale()` call between the two ensures that the second rectangle is 1.8 times wider and 1.5 times deeper.

As well as modifying the dimensions, this scaling is applied to the origin of the rectangles (their top left corners) and so the larger one is offset to a location 1.8 times the original rectangle's horizontal offset of 20 pixels (to a new coordinate of 36), and 1.5 times the original vertical offset of 20 pixels (to a new coordinate of 30).

This the new origin for the larger square is at location `36,30`, rather than `20,20`.

Here's an example of using the `scale()` function more than once on the same rectangle (but changing the colors so you can see the difference), as shown in Figure 14-4:

```
context.fillStyle = 'red'
context.fillRect(10, 10, 80, 30)

context.scale(1.6, 1.6)
context.fillStyle = 'yellow'
context.fillRect(10, 10, 80, 30)
```

```
context.scale(1.6, 1.6)
context.fillStyle = 'blue'
context.fillRect(10, 10, 80, 30)

context.scale(1.6, 1.6)
context.fillStyle = 'green'
context.fillRect(10, 10, 80, 30)
```

The `save()` & `restore()` Functions

After drawing elements using a changed scaling, if you then wish to draw some using their original dimensions you'll need to issue the correct `scale()` call with negative values to get the scaling back down to a ratio of 1:1. But in the preceding example where the scaling ratio was increased upwards three times, you would have to reduce the scaling ratio back three times by using values lower than 1 that achieve the same amount of reduction, like this (where 0.625 is the inverse of 1.6):

```
context.scale(0.625, 0.625)
context.scale(0.625, 0.625)
context.scale(0.625, 0.625)
```

Obviously this is somewhat fiddly in that it involves calculating the inverse value, and also repeating a function call unnecessarily. Or, you could calculate the full inverse value for a single call to `scale()`, which happens to be 0.24414 (arrived at by multiplying 0.625 by itself three times), like this:

```
context.scale(0.24414, 0.24414)
```

But there's a much simpler method for returning the scale back to the default (along with many other properties too), and that's to issue a call to `save()` before making any changes to properties or calling functions such as `scale()`, and then call `restore()` afterwards to reset all the properties to the way they were, like this code which uses the functions to restore the scaling before drawing a final rectangle in orange on top of the very first red one, as shown in Figure 14-5:

```
context.save()

context.fillStyle = 'red'
context.fillRect(10, 10, 80, 30)
context.scale(1.6, 1.6)
context.fillStyle = 'yellow'
context.fillRect(10, 10, 80, 30)
context.scale(1.6, 1.6)
```

```
context.fillStyle = 'blue'
context.fillRect(10, 10, 80, 30)
context.scale(1.6, 1.6)
context.fillStyle = 'green'
context.fillRect(10, 10, 80, 30)

context.restore()

context.fillStyle = 'orange'
context.fillRect(10, 10, 80, 30)
```

As well as the scaling ratio, several other properties are saved and restored by these functions, as follows:

- `fillStyle`
- `font`
- `globalAlpha`
- `globalCompositeOperation`
- `lineCap`
- `lineJoin`
- `lineWidth`
- `miterLimit`
- `shadowBlur`
- `shadowColor`
- `shadowOffsetX`
- `shadowOffsetY`
- `strokeStyle`
- `textAlign`
- `textBaseline`
- `scale()` properties
- `rotate()` properties
- `translate()` properties
- `transform()` properties

This process of using `save()` and `restore()` is known as saving and restoring the drawing context. You can call the `save()` method as often as you like and each time the current context will be saved.

For each call to save you can issue a matching `restore()` call to return the context to the previous state. This enables you to save the state as you perform more steps and then 'unwind' the state backwards as each step completes.

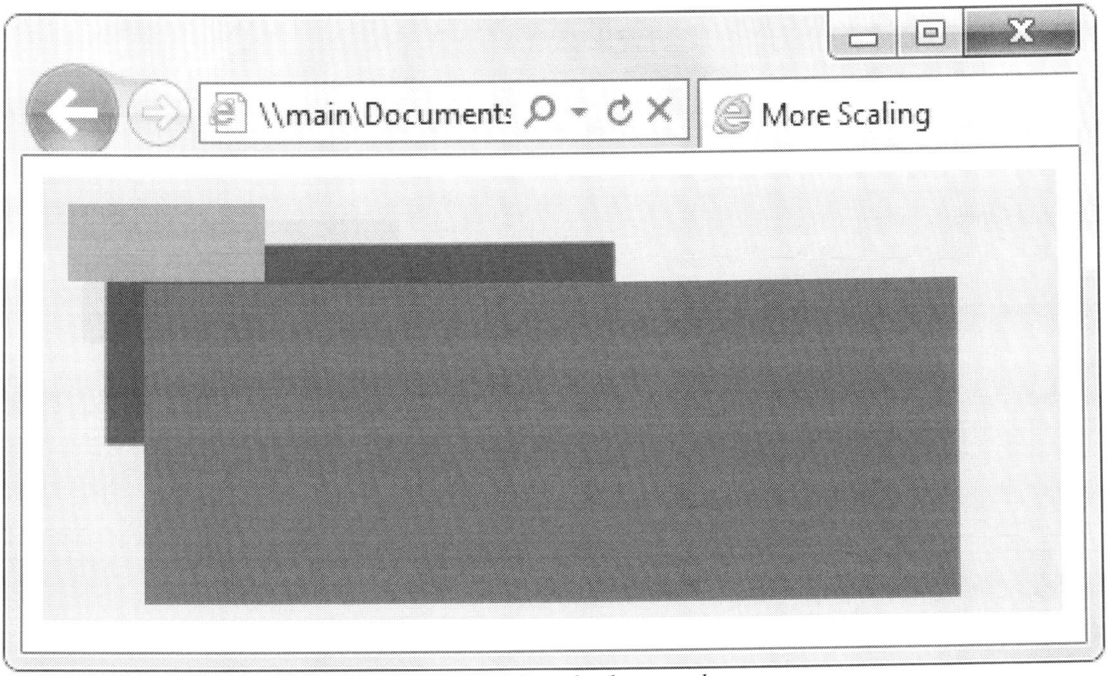

Figure 5: The scaling is saved, and then restored for a final rectangle

The `rotate(a)` Function

Before applying an element to a canvas you can also rotate it to just the right angle with a call to `rotate()`, like this:

```
context.rotate(Math.PI / 2)
```

The value passed to the function is in radians, each of which has a value of `180 / π` (or about 57.2958 degrees). Therefore there are about `π * 2` radians in a complete circle. Radians are a sensible unit of measurement because `π / 2` radians is a quarter of a circle, `π / 2` radians is a half circle, `π / 3 * 2` radians is three-quarters of a circle, and `π * 2` radians is a full circle. I leave it to you to calculate other values you might need, but generally you will need to only use fractions and multiples of π, whose value you can get by using the JavaScript property of `Math.PI`.

Therefore the previous example line will rotate all future elements placed on the canvas by a quarter turn (or 90 degrees). Here's an example in action, as seen in Figure 14-6, in which a square has been rotated 9 times:

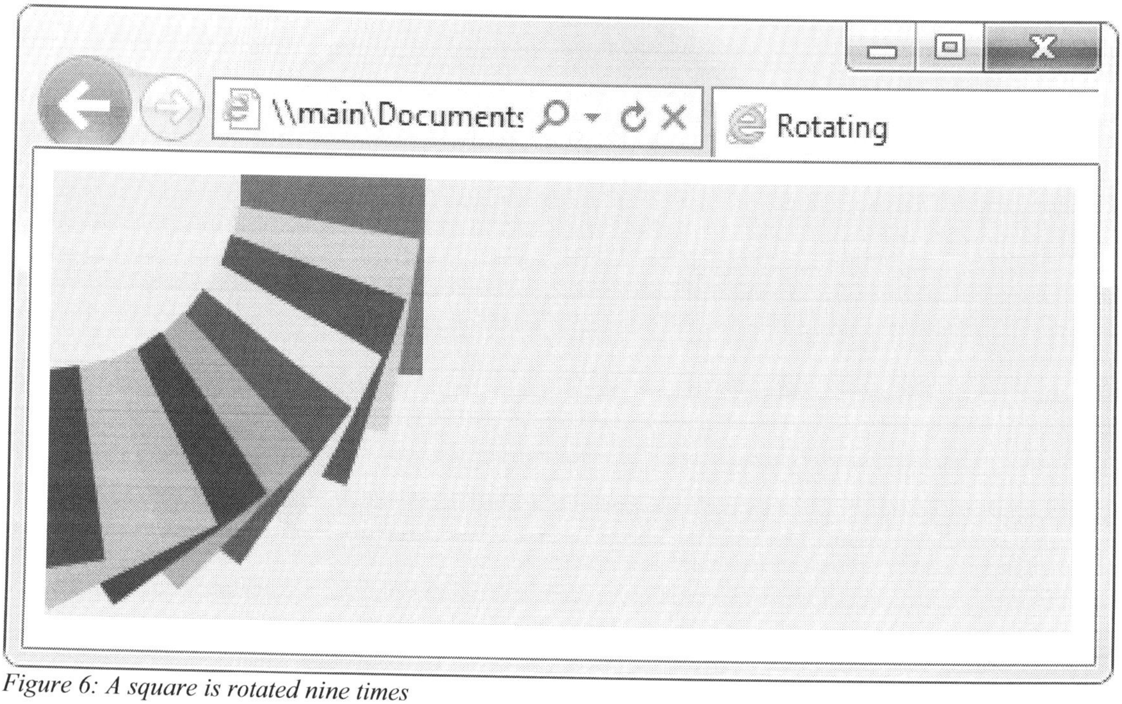

Figure 6: A square is rotated nine times

```
context.fillStyle = 'green'
context.fillRect(75, 0, 75, 75)

context.rotate(Math.PI / 20)
context.fillStyle = 'pink'
context.fillRect(75, 0, 75, 75)

context.rotate(Math.PI / 20)
context.fillStyle = 'blue'
context.fillRect(75, 0, 75, 75)

context.rotate(Math.PI / 20)
context.fillStyle = ' yellow '
context.fillRect(75, 0, 75, 75)

context.rotate(Math.PI / 20)
context.fillStyle = 'red'
context.fillRect(75, 0, 75, 75)

context.rotate(Math.PI / 20)
context.fillStyle = 'violet'
context.fillRect(75, 0, 75, 75)

context.rotate(Math.PI / 20)
context.fillStyle = 'purple'
```

```
context.fillRect(75, 0, 75, 75)

context.rotate(Math.PI / 20)
context.fillStyle = 'lime'
context.fillRect(75, 0, 75, 75)

context.rotate(Math.PI / 20)
context.fillStyle = 'plum'
context.fillRect(75, 0, 75, 75)

context.rotate(Math.PI / 20)
context.fillStyle = 'brown'
context.fillRect(75, 0, 75, 75)
```

Because the `rotate()` function is called prior to each call to `fillRect()` the rotation factor is increased for each one. The place around which the rotation takes place is the origin of the canvas, at location `0,0`.

The `translate(x,y)` Function

If you prefer to rotate an object around another axis such as the object's center you need to also call the `translate()` function to move the origin of the canvas to a new location, around which the element can rotate, like this line for example (which sets it to the coordinates `100,100`):

```
context.translate(100, 100)
```

Let's use this in a simple example similar to the previous one, but in which the squares will rotate around their centers, like this (as shown in Figure 14-7):

```
context.translate(280, 85)
context.fillStyle = 'green'
context.fillRect(-60, -60, 120, 120)

context.rotate(Math.PI / 10)
context.fillStyle = 'pink'
context.fillRect(-60, -60, 120, 120)

context.rotate(Math.PI / 10)
context.fillStyle = 'blue'
context.fillRect(-60, -60, 120, 120)


context.rotate(Math.PI / 10)
```

```
context.fillStyle = 'yellow'
context.fillRect(-60, -60, 120, 120)

context.rotate(Math.PI / 10)
context.fillStyle = 'violet'
context.fillRect(-60, -60, 120, 120)
```

If you look closely at the code in this example you'll see some negative values. This is because the origin of the canvas is no longer at location `0,0` – it has been translated to the location `280, 85`.

Therefore all function calls that address the canvas must now bear this new origin in mind and, since the squares are 120 pixels wide and deep, to place their centers over the new origin position, they must be located at a point relative to the origin of `-60,-60`.

***Note**: After translating the origin of the canvas you may wish to restore it to `0,0` for future access of the canvas, or you can use the `save()` and `restore()` functions in appropriate places to automatically restore the context.*

The `transform(h,vs,hs,v,x,y)` Function

Finally, in this part of the course on the HTML5 canvas, comes the most complicated and possible most powerful feature of all, the `transform()` function, with which you can stretch and transform elements in many different ways using matrixes.

Interestingly, the previous functions that manipulate elements all actually use matrixes to achieve their effects, and you can do the same yourself using the `transform()` method to either emulate or improve on the built-in functions, or create your own new transforms.

For example, you can emulate the `scale()` function by issuing the following command:

```
context.transform(1.6, 0, 0, 1.6, 0, 0)
```

This is equivalent to the following call because the first and fourth parameters represent the horizontal and vertical scaling respectively:

```
context.scale(1.6, 1.6)
```

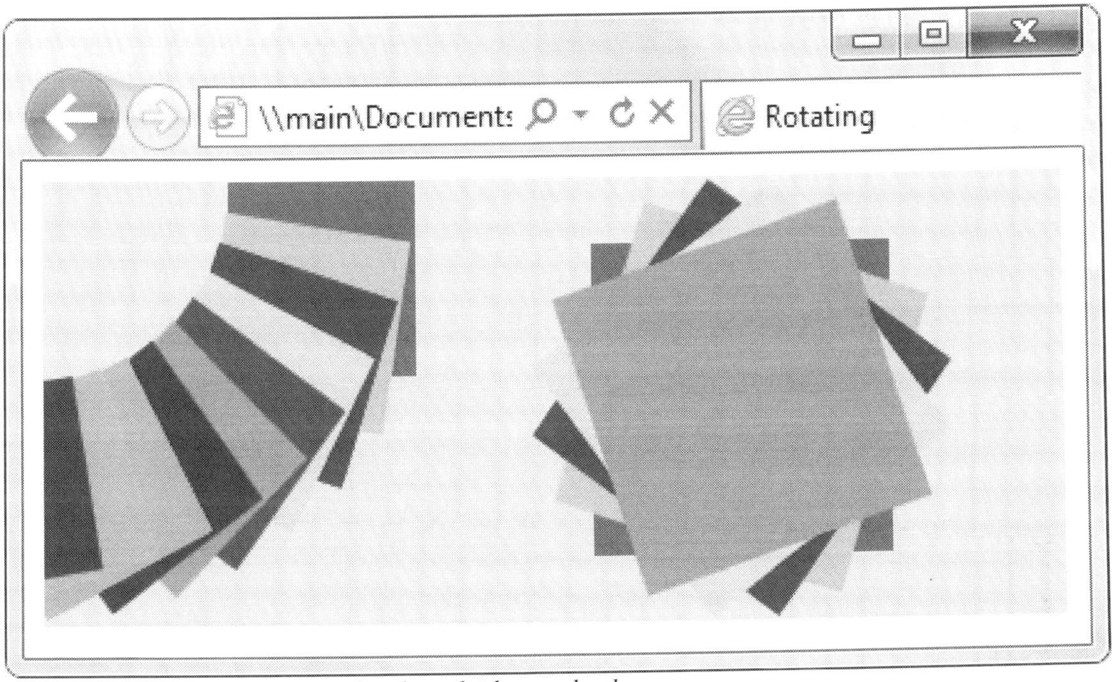

Figure 7: Five squares are rotated and overlaid on each other

Here's some code using the function that first draws a 50 by 50 pixel square in green, then applies a scaling factor of 2 in the horizontal direction and 1.5 vertically and redraws the same square, as shown in Figure 14-8.

```
context.fillStyle = 'green'
context.fillRect(35, 35, 50, 50)
context.transform(2, 0, 0, 1.5, 0, 0)
context.fillStyle = 'blue'
context.fillRect(35, 35, 50, 50)
```

This is the same as using the following command:

```
context.scale(2, 1.5)
```

The second and third parameters to the `transform()` function control shearing of the element. For example, to sheer the original square downwards (and not use any scaling) you could issue a command such as this:

```
context.transform(1, 0.7, 0, 1, 0, 0)
```

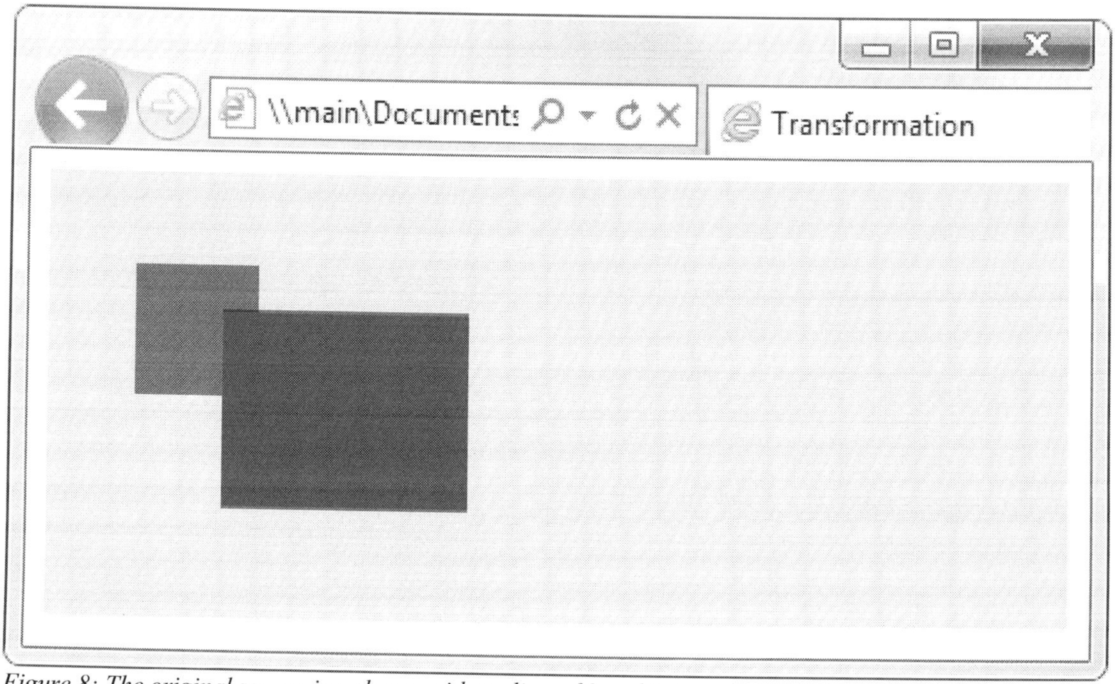

Figure 8: The original square is redrawn with scaling of 2 and 1.5

To sheer to the right you might use a command like this:

```
context.transform(1, 0, 0.7, 1, 0, 0)
```

And to sheer in both directions you might use a command such as this:

```
context.transform(1, 0.7, 0.7, 1, 0, 0)
```

In fact here's some example code that illustrates all three of these sheers at once, as shown in Figure 14-9:

```
context.fillStyle = 'green'
context.fillRect(35, 35, 50, 50)

context.restore()
context.save()

context.transform(1, 0.7, 0, 1, 0, 0)
context.fillStyle = 'orange'
context.fillRect(35, 35, 50, 50)

context.restore()
```

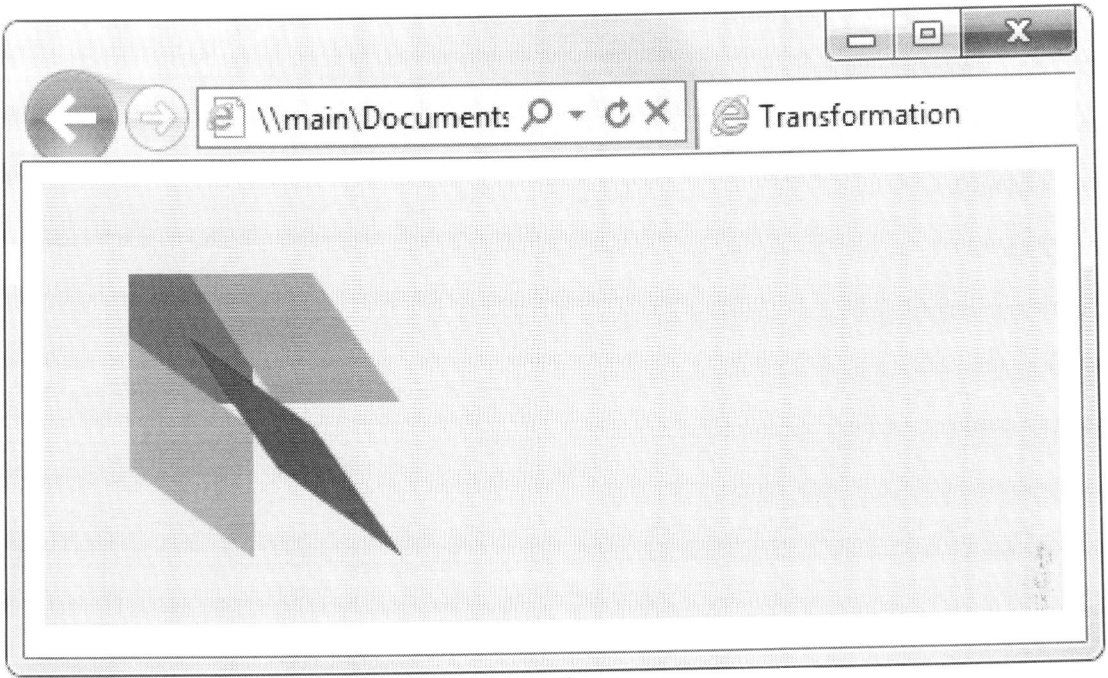

Figure 9: Three different sheers have been applied to the square

```
context.save()
context.transform(1, 0, 0.7, 1, 0, 0)
context.fillStyle = 'violet'
context.fillRect(35, 35, 50, 50)

context.restore()
context.save()
context.transform(1, 0.7, 0.7, 1, 0, 0)
context.fillStyle = 'red'
context.fillRect(35, 35, 50, 50)
```

The first section of code creates the initial square. Then `save()` and `restore()` are used for the following sections to ensure the context is returned for reuse after each. In the first `transform()` call the bottom left shape is created.

The top right one is created next, and then the bottom right shape is created out of a combined horizontal and vertical sheer.

Note: You may use different values than 0.7 in these functions, and that includes negative values to sheer in the opposite direction.

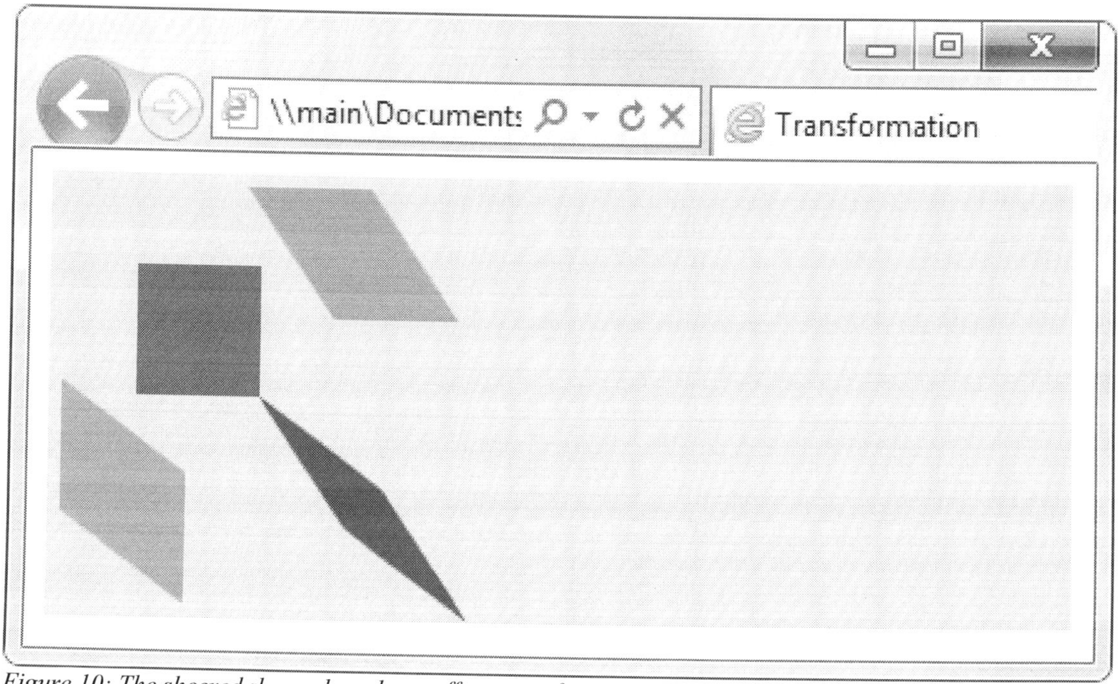

Figure 10: The sheered shapes have been offset away from the original

The final two arguments to the function are the horizontal and vertical offset to apply to the element when it is drawn on the canvas. These may be negative as well as positive values.

Therefore the following three lines of code modify the `transform()` calls in the previous example to move the bottom left shape to the left by 30 and down by 20 pixels.

The top right shape is moved to the right by 20 and up by 30 pixels, and the bottom right shape is moved both down and to the right by 25 pixels, as shown in Figure 14-10:

```
context.transform(1, 0.7,   0, 1, -30,  20)
context.transform(1,   0, 0.7, 1,  20, -30)
context.transform(1, 0.7, 0.7, 1,  25,  25)
```

The `setTransform(h,vs,hs,v,x,y)` Function

As well as using the `save()` and `restore()` functions, you can reset the transform matrix at any time by issuing this call:

```
context.transform(1, 0, 0, 1, 0, 0)
```

Then you are ready to issue a new transform of your choosing, like this, for example:

```
context.transform(1, 1.2, -1.2, 1, -20, 20)
```

However, rather than issuing two separate calls you can make just one call to the `setTransform()` function instead. This has the effect of resetting the transform matrix and then applying the requested new transform. So, in place of the two preceding calls, for example, you can simply make the following call:

```
context.setTransform(1, 1.2, -1.2, 1, -20, 20)
```

***Note**: For more information about transformation matrixes there's a comprehensive article at:* wikipedia.org/wiki/Transformation_matrix.

Summary

This concludes your introduction to the world of the HTML5 canvas. I hope you have found it enlightening and will use the functions it provided to create some weird and wonderful and compelling web pages. In the next lecture we'll move on to seeing how a browser can identify your location, and what you can use this information for.

LECTURE 15

HTML5 GEOLOCATION

By following this lecture you will:

✓ *Understand what is meant by the term geolocation.*

✓ *Know how to use geolocation on enabled browsers.*

✓ *Be able to create a Google map based on a browser's location.*

WITH THE INCREDIBLE rise in popularity of smartphones the ability to determine the location of a device has become almost essential, particularly for running interactive maps and navigation software, and even for finding local Wi-Fi hotspots, or services such as restaurants or cash dispensing machines, and so on.

Geolocation is also being used more and more to try and sell you services by offering promotions in stores that are near to you, and a little more benevolently in enabling you to know whether friends or acquaintances are within your near vicinity.

Thankfully you are in control of when you allow your location information to be revealed, so you can minimize any privacy or security risks the technology could create.

In this lecture I will show you how to use JavaScript to determine the location of any geolocation-enabled device, as long as the user allows you.

Note*: The examples from this lecture are in the* Lecture 15 *folder of the* examples.zip *file at* tinyurlcom/html5ccexamples.

Accessing Geolocation With JavaScript

There are no two ways about it, many of the HTML5 features are so advanced that they cannot be accessed by simple HTML. Instead you do have to learn a little JavaScript.

So far in this course I have done my best to teach you only the fewest parts of JavaScript you need in order to work through the examples. And the same goes for this lecture.

However, there is no substitute for getting a good book or taking a course on JavaScript if you wish to make full and professional use of features such as geolocation.

The `geolocation` Property

The first thing you must do when accessing geolocation is to determine whether or not it is available by testing the `geolocation` property, like this (preceding the property with the `navigator` object name):

```
if (typeof navigator.geolocation == 'undefined')
{
   alert("Sorry, no geolocation support.")
}
else
{
   // Geolocation code goes here
}
```

This code uses a JavaScript `if()` statement in which the first part of the code is executed if geolocation is not supported. Typically you will inform the user that their browser doesn't support geolocation, provide some other kind of message, or perhaps simply do nothing. In this instance I have chosen to pop up an `alert()` message window with a short message.

If geolocation is supported the part of code after the `else` statement is executed, and that's where your code that uses the geolocation information should go, as follows.

The `getCurrentPosition(y,n)` Function

Once you know that a browser supports geolocation you may ask it for its current position using the `getCurrentPosition()` function, like this:

```
navigator.geolocation.getCurrentPosition(granted,
  denied)
```

This line of code calls the browser's geolocation software passing it the names of two new functions called `granted()` and `denied()`. Because the function names (and not the actual function contents) are being passed to the `getCurrentPosition()` function, no curly brackets are placed after the names.

One or the other of these two functions will be called back by the browser according to whether the user grants or denies you the use of its location data. Therefore both of these routines must be written by you. Luckily here are a couple I made earlier.

A `granted()` Function

Here's what an example `granted()` function might look like:

```
function granted(position)
{
  alert("You are at location: "
    + position.coords.latitude + ","
    + position.coords.longitude)
}
```

In this instance I have opted to simply display the returned location information in an `alert()` message window. You will be more likely to display a map or perform other functions based on this information. As for the user's location data, this is returned in the following two properties:

```
position.coords.latitude
position.coords.longitude
```

The former property holds the latitude value and the latter the longitude.

A `denied(e)` Function

If the user has chosen not to allow the browser's location data to be revealed to your code then your `denied()` function will be called, and an error code will be given to state why.

Here's an example `denied()` function:

```
function denied(error)
{
```

```
    var message

    switch(error.code)
    {
      case 1: message = 'Permission Denied'; break
      case 2: message = 'Position Unavailable'; break
      case 3: message = 'Operation Timed Out'; break
      case 4: message = 'Unknown Error'
    }
    alert("Error with geolocation: " + message)
}
```

This code is a little longer because it processes the value in `code`, which is a property of the `error` object that is passed to the function by JavaScript, and which can be a number between 1 and 4, as follows:

1. *Permission Denied*
2. *Position Unavailable*
3. *Operation Timed Out*
4. *Unknown Error*

Again, I have chosen a simple `alert()` message to provide this information. In your code (if you choose to give a message at all), you may wish to display a simpler and more friendly phrase such as "Geolocation request denied".

In The Real World

Here's some code you can use to display a Google map of a user's current location in an `<iframe>` tag, based on the coordinates returned by the browser's geolocation software. If permission is not given or the browser doesn't support geolocation then a message stating that is provided by writing directly into the contents of the `<div>` tag with the `id` of `status` using its `innerHTML` property.

```
<div id='status'></div><br />
   <iframe id='map' width='640' height='320'></iframe>

   <script>
     // The O() and S() functions go here, as usual

      if (typeof navigator.geolocation == 'undefined')
      {
        alert("Geolocation not supported.")
```

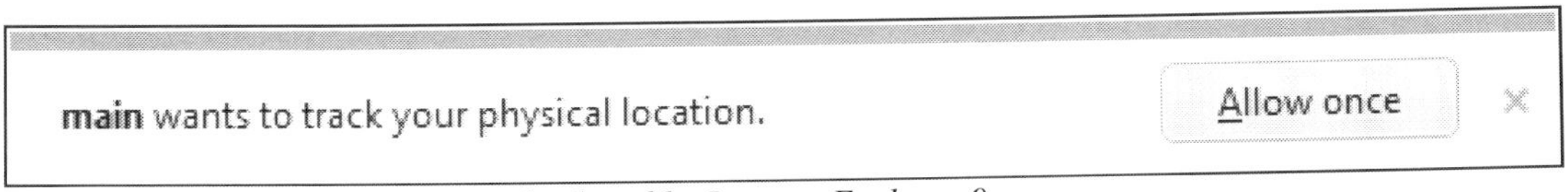

Figure 1: The geolocation request displayed by Internet Explorer 9

```
    }
    else
    {
      navigator.geolocation.getCurrentPosition(granted,
        denied)

      function granted(position)
      {
        O('status').innerHTML = 'Permission Granted'
        var gmap = 'http://maps.google.com/maps?q='
          + position.coords.latitude + ','
          + position.coords.longitude
        O('map').src = gmap
      }

      function denied(error)
      {
        var message

        switch(error.code)
        {
          case 1: message = 'Permission Denied'; break;
          case 2: message = 'Position Unavailable';break;
          case 3: message = 'Operation Timed Out'; break;
          case 4: message = 'Unknown Error'; break;
        }

        O('status').innerHTML = message
      }
    }
  </script>
```

When a web page containing this is loaded into a browser the first thing that happens is a request is made to the user. Depending on the browser and operating system in use this may be presented in a variety of different ways. On Internet Explorer 9, for example, it looks like Figure 15-1.

If permission is not given then only a short message will be displayed, but if it is then the result will be similar to Figure 15-2.

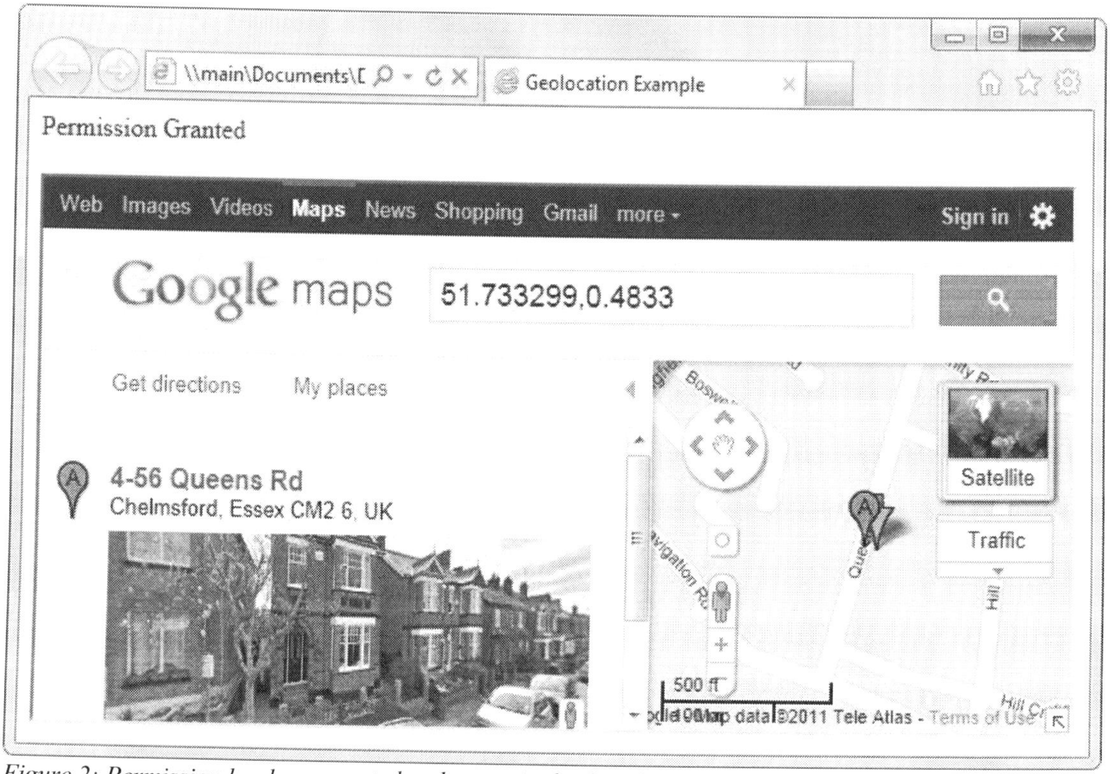

Figure 2: Permission has been granted and a map is displayed

The GPS Service

The GPS (Global Positioning Satellite) service consists of multiple satellites orbiting the earth whose positions are very precisely known. When a GPS-enabled devices tunes into these satellites, the different times at which signals from these various satellites arrive at it enable the device to know where it is to within just a few feet.

This is achieved by the fact that the speed of light (and radio waves) is a known constant, and the time it takes a signal to get from a satellite to a GPS device precisely indicates the satellite's distance.

By making a note of all the different times at which signals arrive from different satellites, a simple calculation lets the device derive each of the satellite's positions relative to each other, and therefore very closely triangulate the position of the device relative to the satellites.

Many mobile devices such as phones and tablets have GPS chips and can provide this information. But some don't, others have them tuned off, and others may be used indoors where they are shielded from the GPS satellites, and therefore cannot receive any signals. In these cases additional techniques may be used to attempt to determine your location.

Other Location Methods

Firstly, if your device has mobile phone hardware it may attempt to triangulate its location by checking the timings of signals received from the various communication towers with which it can communicate (and whose positions are very precisely known). If there are a few towers, this can get almost as close to your location as GPS. But where there's a single tower the signal strength is used to determine a radius around the tower, and the circle it creates represents the area in which you are likely to be located. This could place you anywhere within a mile or two of your actual location, down to within a few tens of feet.

Failing that, there may be known Wi-Fi access points within range of your device whose positions are known, and since all access points have a unique identifying address called a MAC (Media Access Control) address, a reasonably good approximation of location can be obtained, perhaps to within a street or two.

And if that fails the IP (Internet Protocol) address used by your device can be queried and used as a rough indicator of your location. Often though, this provides only the location of a major switch belonging to your Internet provider, which could be dozens or even hundreds of miles away. But at the very least, your IP address can (usually) narrow down the country, and sometimes the region you are in.

***Note**: Your IP address is commonly used by media companies that restrict playback of their content by territory. However, some people are able to set up proxy servers that use a forwarding IP address in the country that is blocking them to fetch and pass content through the blockade directly to their browser. Therefore you should be aware that if you locate someone by IP address it is not 100% accurate that you do, in fact, have the right country for them.*

Using geolocation will enable you to improve the features you offer to your web visitors but in my experience it's a little early to rely on them too heavily. For example, in Figure 15-2 my address was returned as somewhere in Chelmsford, Essex (about 100 miles away from where I ran the test) because the device I used had no GPS, Wi-Fi or mobile phone hardware. So a service that offers to locate a good local pizza company will not work for me based on that data (which is evidently the location of a switch used by my Internet provider)

Nevertheless, used sensibly and perhaps even in conjunction with asking your users directly to correct any such misinformation in order for you to provide better service, geolocation is a great feature. And if you know your user has an iPhone or Android phone, you can be almost certain that you're receiving accurate data.

Summary

And that's all there is to geolocation, so this is a short and sweet lecture, but hopefully one you have found very useful. In the next lecture I'll take you through the extensions that HTML5 has made to HTML forms.

LECTURE 16

HTML5 FORMS

By following this lecture you will:

- ✓ *Learn about all the new form tags and attributes.*
- ✓ *Discover the power of popup data pickers.*
- ✓ *Learn about HTML5 input validation.*

IF YOU'VE EVER used HTML forms you'll be aware of how limiting they can be. Alright they provide the facility to create different types of fields and buttons, but that's about it.

There are no date pickers for easy selection of dates from popup menus. There's no built in verification (or validation) of data types such as numbers, strings or email addresses and there's no built-in ability to match patterns in regular expressions.

But with HTML5 all these problems and several more have been addressed, making completing forms easier than ever for users, and also much simpler for web developers to create.

***Note**: The examples from this lecture are in the* Lecture 16 *folder of the* examples.zip *file at* tinyurlcom/html5ccexamples.

Form Attributes

As you will see from the following, HTML5 is still very much an evolving specification that browsers are implementing only piecemeal. Therefore some features are available in some browsers, and others in different ones.

And it's not always the same browsers that haven't yet caught up with the spec because, as of this writing, all of the latest versions of all the main browsers omit at least three of these attributes, and some as many as ten.

Nevertheless, as time passes browsers will implement more and more of the HTML5 spec, and therefore the information you need for using these features follows.

The `autocomplete` Attribute

This attribute can be applied to the `<form>` tag or any of the `color`, `date`, `email`, `password`, `range`, `search`, `tel`, `text` or `url` types of the `<input>` tag. Valid arguments for this attribute are `on` (the default) and `off`.

When `autocomplete` is `on`, any field with an `id` that has previously had an input entered will remember its value and offer it as a suggested value, saving you from having to enter it again.

When `autocomplete` is `off` this behavior is disabled. When applied to a `<form>` tag the attribute affects all relevant fields within a form. When applied to an `<input>` tag only that field is affected. Here are two examples of using the attribute:

```
<form action='prog.php' method='post' autocomplete='on'>
  <input type='text' name='field1' autocomplete='off' />
</form>
```

***Note**: This feature is supported by the latest versions of all major browsers and is safe to use.*

The `autofocus` Attribute

The `autofocus` attribute can be applied to any `<input>` tag to give its field automatic focus when a page loads.

This has the effect of placing the cursor in an input field ready to type, or selecting any other type of field ready to change it. It is activated like this:

```
<input type='text' name='field' autofocus='autofocus' />
```

***Note**: This feature is supported by the latest versions of all major browsers except for Internet Explorer, but is safe to use in your web pages because IE still runs perfectly well anyway, it just doesn't provide the extra usability of autofocussing any fields.*

Autofocus And Internet Explorer

You can achieve the same effect as autofocus in Internet Eexplorer by adding some JavaScript to the `<body>` tag of your web page, like this:

```
<body onload='document.forms.myform.myfield.focus()'>
```

Then make sure your form looks something like this:

```
<form id='myform' action='prog.php' method='post'
   autocomplete='on'>
  <input id='myfield' type='text' name='field'
     autofocus='autofocus' />
</form>
```

To make this work both the `<form>` and the `<input>` tags must each be given a unique `id`. In this case I chose the name `myform` for the form and `myfield` for the field. These are then easily referenced in the argument to the `onload` event of the `<body>` tag, which calls the `focus()` function on the field when the web page has loaded.

The `form` Attribute

With this attribute it is not necessary for you to place `<input>` tags within the form to which they apply. Instead, as long as you give a form an `id` you can specify that value as the argument for a `form` attribute.

For example, the following code creates a form with the `id` of `form1`, only after which is the `<input>` tag `field` attached to it:

```
<form id='myform' action='form.php' method='get'>
  <input type='submit' />
</form>

<input form='myform' type='text' name='field' />
```

***Note**: This feature is currently available only in the Opera and Chrome browsers and therefore I recommend you do not use it until the other major browsers follow suit.*

Form Overrides

Several new attributes have been added to HTML in version 5 that allow you to override various form settings such as the `action` and `enctype` properties, but so far only a few browsers have implemented them. They are listed following.

***Note**: Form overrides work with either of the `submit` or `image` types of the `<input>` tag, but are currently supported only by the Opera, Firefox and Chrome browsers. Therefore I do not recommend using them until the other main browsers catch up.*

The `formaction` Attribute

This attribute is a form override that lets you change the action attribute to a different destination. For example, in the following code, the form will not post to the program *prog.php* as specified in the `<form>` tag, and will instead post to *prog2.php*:

```
<form action='prog.php' method='post'>
  <input type='text' name='field' />
  <input type='submit' formaction='prog2.php' />
</form>
```

This attribute can be particularly useful when you wish to provide more than one submit button, each with a different destination program to which the form should submit. (Currently Opera, Firefox and Chrome browsers only).

The `formenctype` Attribute

This attribute is a form override that lets you change the encoding type of a form (the `enctype` attribute), in a similar manner to the `formaction` override. (Currently Opera, Firefox and Chrome browsers only).

The `formmethod` Attribute

This attribute is a form override that lets you change the posting method (the `post` or `get` argument of the `method` attribute), in a similar manner to the `formaction` override. (Currently Opera, Firefox and Chrome browsers only).

Figure 1: Resizing an image used in an input

The `formnovalidate` Attribute

This attribute is a form override that lets you change the `novalidate` attribute, in a similar manner to the `formaction` override. (Currently Opera, Firefox and Chrome browsers only).

The `formtarget` Attribute

This attribute is a form override that lets you change the `target` attribute, in a similar manner to the `formaction` override. (Currently Opera, Firefox and Chrome browsers only).

The `height` and `width` Attributes

These attributes can be applied to the image type of the `<input>` tag to change its height and width. You use the attributes like this, with a result such as that in Figure 16-1:

```
<input type='image' src='finger.png'
  width='117' height='100' />
```

***Note**: This feature is available in the latest versions of all major browsers and is safe to use.*

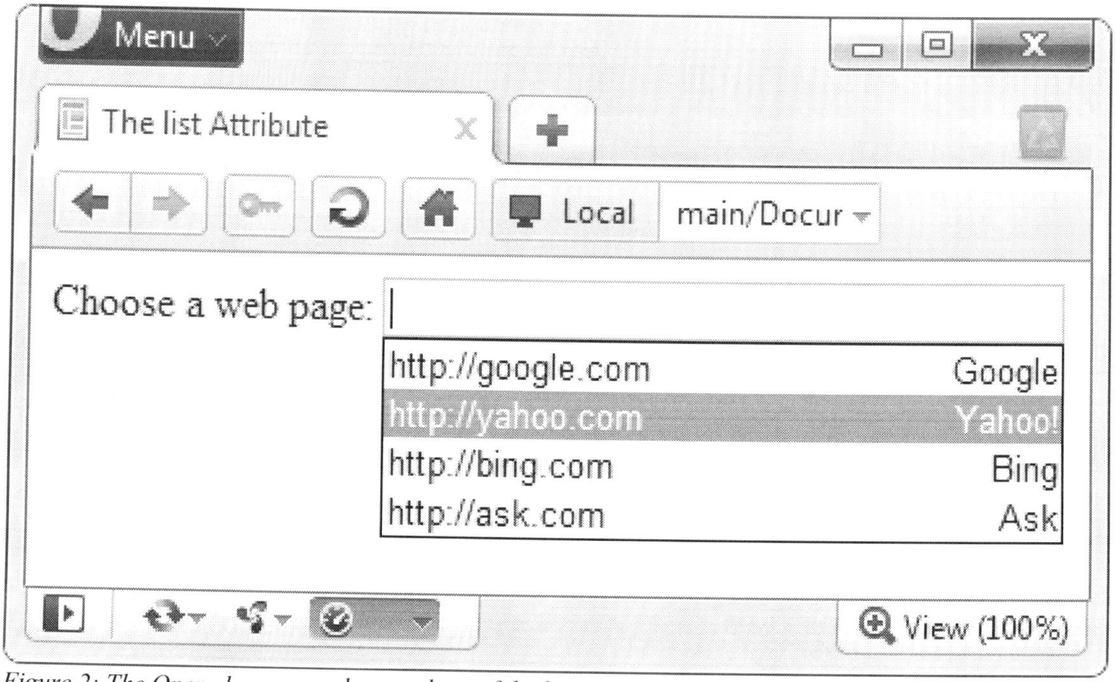

Figure 2: The Opera browser makes good use of the list attribute

The `list` Attribute and `<datalist>` and `<option>` Tags

Some input fields support lists and this attribute can be used to reference them. For example, the following code uses this attribute, along with the new `<datalist>` tag to offer up a selection of URLs from which to choose:

```
Choose a web page: <input type='url' name='site'
  list='links' />

<datalist id='links'>
  <option label='Google' value='http://google.com' />
  <option label='Yahoo!' value='http://yahoo.com'  />
  <option label='Bing'   value='http://bing.com'   />
  <option label='Ask'    value='http://ask.com'    />
</datalist>
```

The value supplied to the `list` attribute should be the id name of a `<datalist>` tag. This feature works a bit like the `autocomplete` attribute, except that you define the list of suggested choices that appear when the input is given focus.

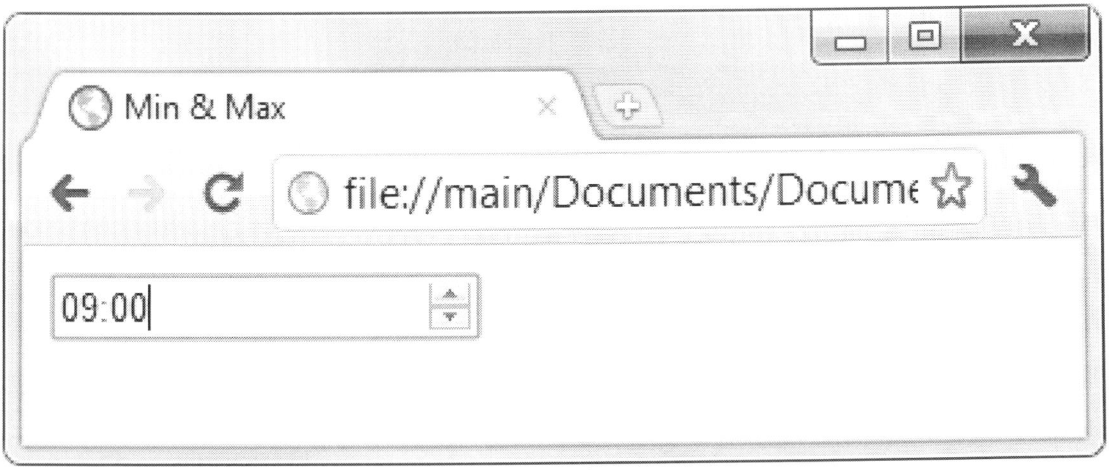

Figure 3: Using the min and max properties in Google Chrome

***Note**: Currently the feature is supported only by the Opera (as shown in Figure 16-2) and Firefox browsers, but you can still use it in your web pages because other browsers will simply not display the list of suggestions but, over time, as other browsers adopt this attribute, your web forms that use it will become quicker to fill in.*

The `min` and `max` Attributes

These attribute are used to specify minimum and maximum value for input types that contain numbers or dates.

Here is an example (the result of which being used in the Google Chrome browser can be seen in Figure 16-3, in which the up and down selectors can be seen to the right of the input):

```
<input type='time' name='deliver' value='09:00'
  min='09:00' max='17:00' />
```

As well as using the mouse to change the input up or down (within the minimum and maximum values), a valid input between these values can be directly entered, or the up and down keyboard buttons can be used to scroll through the supported values.

***Note**: I don't recommend you rely on this type of validation yet, though, since only Google Chrome and the Opera browsers support its use.*

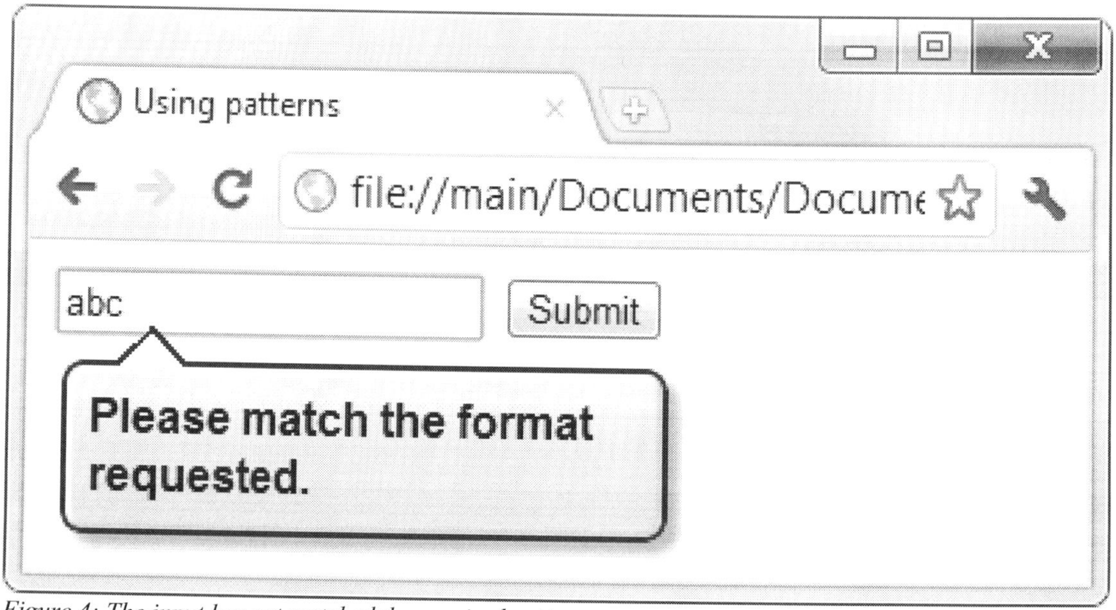

Figure 4: The input has not matched the required pattern

The `multiple` Attribute

This attribute allows you to accept multiple values for an `<input>` tag that uses either the `email` or `file` type. It works in the latest versions of all major browsers except for Internet Explorer and Opera. You will enable it like this:

```
<input type='file' name='images' multiple='multiple' />
```

Then, when the browse box pops up, multiple files can be selected at a time (normally in conjunction with the `Ctrl` key). On browsers that don't yet support this feature only single files can be selected.

***Note**: Because Internet Explorer and Opera will only allow single items to be selected, until it also supports it this feature is not safe to use if you are requiring multiple inputs (rather than simply allowing them). Better still use the attribute but also allow single uploads multiple times.*

The `novalidate` Attribute

This attribute specifies that a form should not be validated when it is submitted. It accepts values of `true` or `false` but is, however, not yet implemented in any major browser.

When browsers do support it, the attribute will be applicable to the `<form>` tag and any of the `color`, `date`, `email`, `password`, `range`, `search`, `tel`, `text` or `url` types of the `<input>` tag. You use it like this:

```
<input type='text' name='field' novalidate='true' />
```

***Note**: Since HTML5 validation is not a well-supported feature across all major browsers I don't recommend using it yet. Therefore there's also no reason to use this attribute to turn validation off (since you won't have it on yet, anyway).*

The `pattern` Attribute

This attribute lets you specify a regular expression with which an input field should be evaluated. It can be applied to any `<input>` tag that uses any of the `email`, `password`, `search`, `tel`, `text` or `url` types. For example, to allow only alphanumeric characters, and the dash and underline in a

field, you might use the following HTML which displays differently according to whether the browser supports the attribute, but similar to Figure 16-4 (a grab from Google Chrome) in browsers that do:

```
<input type='text' name='username'
  pattern='[\w\-]{6,16}' />
```

The pattern `'[\w\-\_]{6,16}'` tells the browser to accept only the following:

- **`\w`** The letters `a-z` and `A-Z`, the digits `0-9` and the underline character
- **`\-`** The dash character
- **`{6,16}`** Between `6` and `16` characters inclusive

***Note**: Currently this feature works only with the Opera, Firefox and Chrome browsers and therefore it cannot be relied upon for reliable in-browser validation until Internet Explorer and Safari catch up.*

The `placeholder` Attribute

This attribute lets you place a helpful hint in any blank input field, with which you can help explain to users what they should enter. You use it like this:

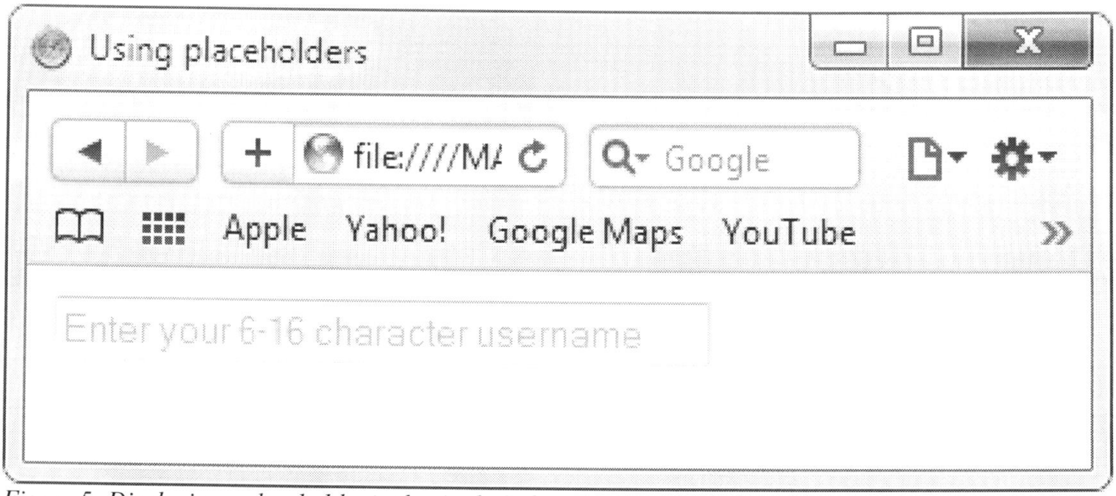

Figure 5: Displaying a placeholder in the Apple Safari web browser

```
<input type='text' name='username' size='35'
  placeholder='Enter your 6-16 character username' />
```

The `size` attribute value of 35 ensures that there's enough room for the placeholder text which, as long as nothing has yet been entered into a field, is displayed in a light color, as shown in Figure 16-5, a screen grab from Apple Safari.

As soon as the field is given focus the prompt disappears ready for text to be input. This attribute can be applied to any of the `email`, `password`, `search`, `tel`, `text` and `url` types of the `<input>` tag.

Note: *The `placeholder` attribute is available in the latest versions of all major browsers except for Internet Explorer. However it is safe to use as it is simply ignored by IE.*

The `required` Attribute

The required attribute is used to ensure that a field has been completed before a form is submitted. You use it like this:

```
<input type='number' name='age' required='required' />
```

Note: *As with many other validation features, the `required` attribute is currently available only in the Google Chrome, Firefox and Opera web browsers and therefore is not reliable for in-browser validation of all web forms.*

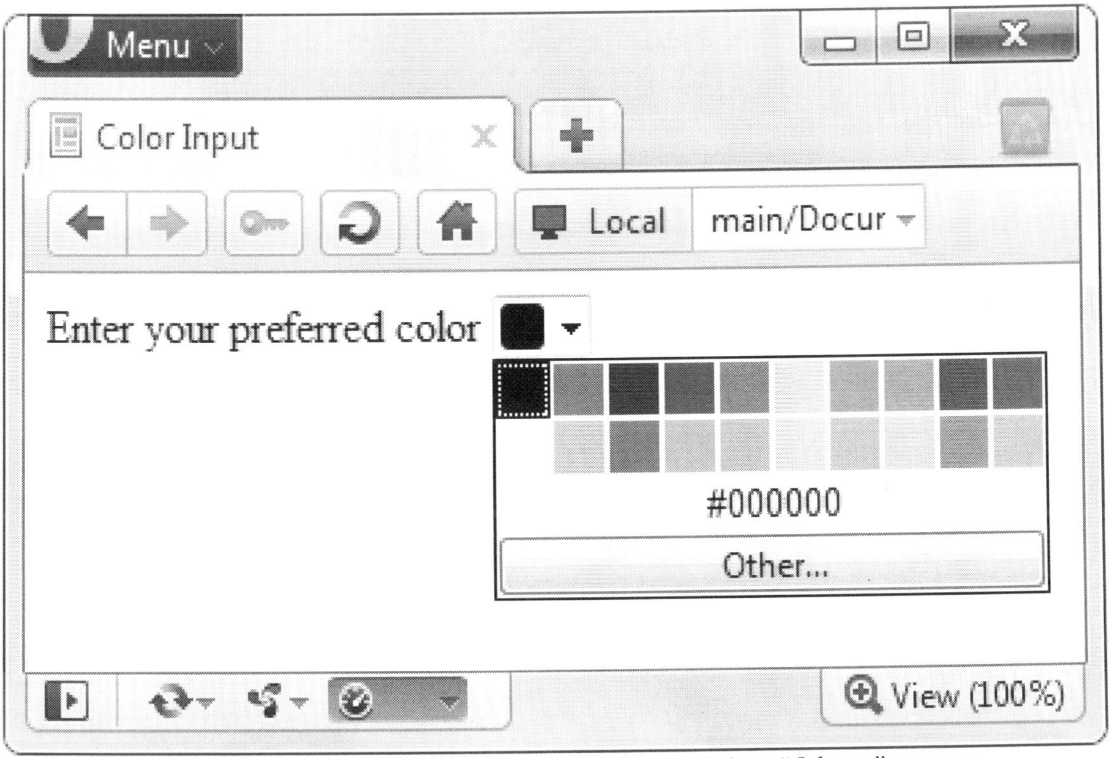

Figure 7: The Opera color picker – more colors are available by clicking "Other..."

The `step` Attribute

This attribute is used to specify a step value for input types that contain numbers or dates, and is also supported only by Google Chrome and the Opera browser. Here's how you might use it in conjunction with the `min` and `max` attributes:

```
<input type='time' name='deliver' value='09:00'
  min='09:00' max='17:00' step='3600' />
```

The value can be any positive integer and, in the case of times, its value is in seconds. By clicking on the up and down icons to the field's right, or by using the up and down cursor keys, it is possible to scroll through the hours to make a selection.

***Note**: Since the `step` attribute is supported only by Google Chrome and the Opera browsers it won't work on any other browsers, but neither will the use of this tag break*

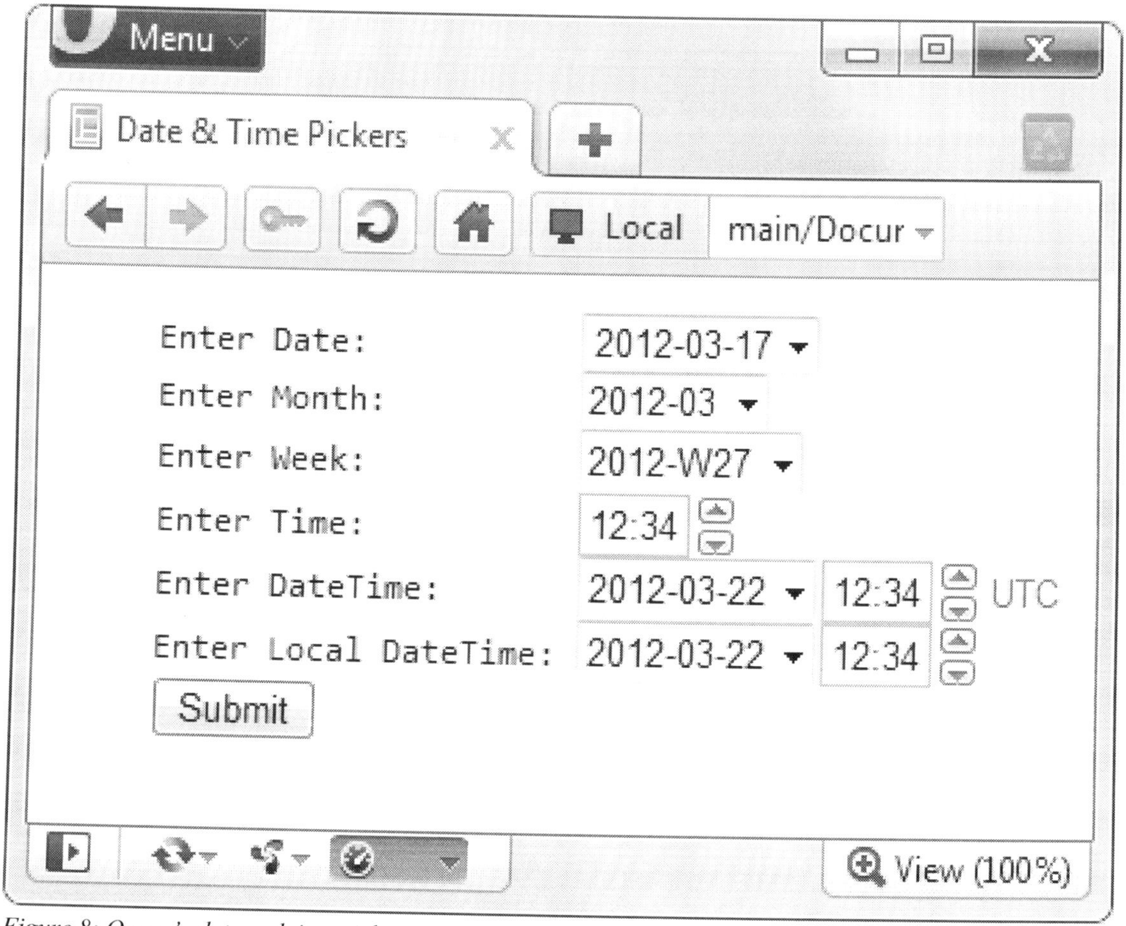

Figure 8: Opera's date and time pickers

any of your HTML, so you can use it if you don't rely on always receiving the values you expect from an input until all browsers support the attribute.

The `color` Input Type

The `color` input type calls up (or should call up) a color picker so that you can simply click on the color of your choice, but right now it works only on Opera (as shown in Figure 16-7). You use it like this:

```
Enter your preferred color
<input type='color' name='favcolor' />
```

Note: *This input type works well on Opera where a color picker pops up, and it used to work (sort of) on Google Chrome in that it operated like a* `required` *attribute by refusing* *to submit a form unless a color name was entered. However in recent tests even this functionality appears broken and Chrome seems to refuse any type of input that uses this attribute. For these reasons I do not recommend using this feature until all the other browsers catch up with Opera.*

Date and Time Pickers

Date and time pickers are similar to the color input type in that eventually you'll be able to click on one and a calendar will pop up, from which you can select a date or time, as shown in Figure 16-8.

***Note**: Currently these date and time pickers work only in Opera (which pops up a handy calendar) and Google Chrome (which doesn't pop up any type of picker, and you can only click the up and down icons, or press the up and down cursor keys, to change a selection). Nevertheless, on browsers that don't recognize these input types, a standard input is displayed, meaning these are safe to use now in your pages. Just don't rely on the dates submitted being valid, so do your own validation.*

The date Input Type

This input type selects a date and is used like this:

```
<input type='date' name='thedate' />
```

The returned value will be of the form `YYYY-MM-DD`. If you wish to seed the date you can use HTML such as this:

```
<input type='date' name='thedate' value='2012-03-17' />
```

The `month` Input Type

This input type selects a month and is used like this:

```
<input type='month' name='themonth' />
```

The value returned is of the form `YYYY-MM`. If you wish to seed the month you can use HTML such as this:

```
<input type='month' name='themonth' value='2012-03' />
```

The `time` Input Type

This input type returns a time in the 24-hour form `HH:MM`. You use it like this:

```
<input type='time' name='thetime' />
```

To seed the time you can use code such as this:

```
<input type='time' name='thetime' value='12:34' />
```

The `week` Input Type

This input type returns the week in the form `YYYY-WNN` (for example `2011-W06`). You use it like this:

```
<input type='week' name='theweek' />
```

To seed the time you can use code such as this:

```
<input type='week' name='theweek' value='2012-W27' />
```

The `datetime` Input Type

This input type returns the date and time in UTC (Coordinated Universal Time), which will be almost the same as Greenwich Mean Time, give or take a second. The returned value will be of the form `YYYY-MM-DDTHH:MMZ` (for example `2011-10-15T15:35Z`). You use it like this:

```
<input type='datetime' name='dateandtime' />
```

To seed the time you can use code such as this:

```
<input type='datetime' name='dateandtime'
  value='2012-03-22T12:34Z' />
```

The `datetime-local` Input Type

This input type returns the user's local date and time. The returned value will be of the form `YYYY-MM-DDTHH:MM` (for example `2011-10-15T15:35`). You use it like this:

```
<input type='datetime-local' name='localdateandtime' />
```

To seed the time you can use code such as this:

```
<input type='datetime-local' name='localdateandtime'
  value='2012-03-22T12:34' />
```

The `email` Input Type

This validation type ensures that only email addresses that are in a valid format can be entered. You use it like this:

```
<input type='email' name='emailaddress' />
```

***Note**: The email validation type is currently supported only by Google Chrome, Mozilla Firefox and Opera and so should not be relied on for validation in all cases.*

The `number` Input Type

This input type causes a pair of up and down icons to be placed to the right of the input with which you can click to increment or decrement the input, or use the up and down cursor keys.

Or you can enter a value directly from the keyboard. You use it like this:

```
<input type='number' name='age' />
```

***Note**: Only Chrome and Opera support this input type and neither browser tests to ensure that a number has been entered, so this input type's use in its (currently limited) implementations is somewhat debatable. In the future it may become useful when all browsers implement it, and they also ensure that only a number is entered.*

The `range` Input Type

This input type causes a range widget to be displayed that you can slide to select any value between a minimum and maximum, and with a specified start and step value, as shown in Figure 16-9, and is used like this:

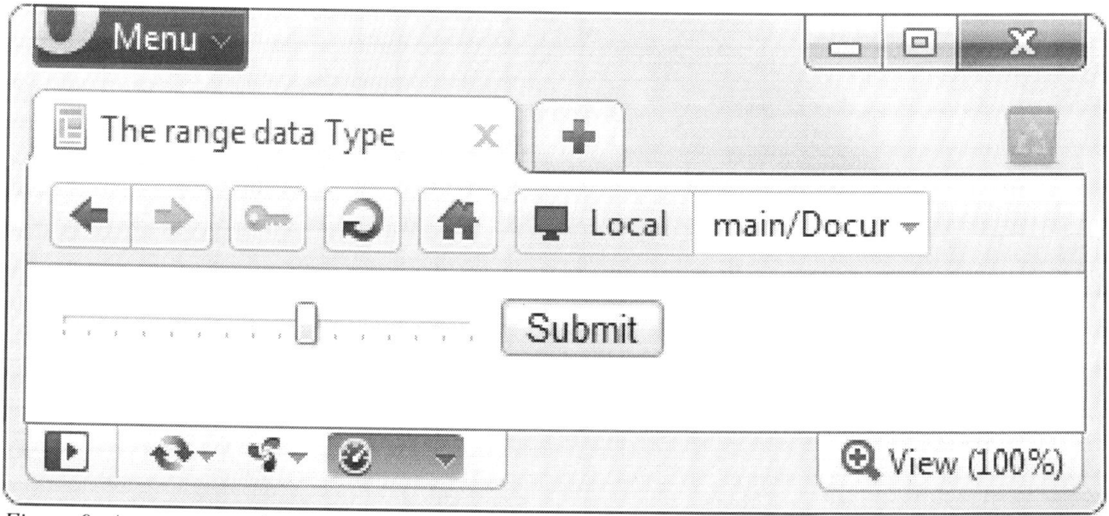

Figure 9: A range control as presented by Opera

```
<input type='range' name='num' min='0' max='255'
  value='128' step='1' />
```

***Note**: This feature works only on the latest versions of Opera, Chrome and Safari. In other browsers a plain text input field is displayed, into which the user should directly enter a number, so you probably won't want to use this input type until IE and Firefox catch up and the interface presented will then be the same on all browsers.*

The `search` Input Type

By specifying the search type browsers are supposed to tailor the input box to provide features that might include search suggestions (in a similar way to Google search), an icon with which to empty the field, and possibly styling changes to alert you to the type of input. You use the attribute like this:

```
<input type='search' name='searchphrase' />
```

***Note**: Currently you probably see nothing different when you use this feature as it has been implemented only very lightly on Safari and Chrome, and the only enhancements are an* `x` *icon for clearing the input, and a rounded input field (on Mac Safari only). But there's no harm in you using this input type right now as other browsers simply display a text field, but when they support the feature your web pages will already be enhanced for it.*

Summary

And that is the state of play as far as the enhancements to HTML5 forms goes. As you can see we are only partly on the way on what looks likely to be a long and winding road of browser uptake of these features, so I recommend you keep testing new releases of browsers to see which features have been added, so that you can then cross off those that I recommend holding back on, once they are adopted by all the main browsers. In the following lecture, the last of this part of the course before moving onto audio and video, I'll show you how you can access local storage for saving much more data than simply the contents of cookies to users' devices.

LECTURE 17

HTML5 LOCAL STORAGE

By following this lecture you will:

- ✓ *Learn how to use local storage for saving data.*
- ✓ *Understand how this storage is accessed.*
- ✓ *Be able to restore and delete any stored data.*

YOU ARE PROBABLY quite familiar with cookies; small units of data that are stored locally by your browser, and which contain information helpful to using a website, such as your login details (to save you continuously reentering them), and which are often also used somewhat more intrusively to track your surfing habits.

Local storage is similar to cookies, but it supports storing much larger amounts of data and also supplies a local database engine to make saving and retrieving data much easier.

The benefits of this are more powerful web apps, with more data residing on your computer, rather than on servers somewhere else in the world. For example, a website that manages your TV viewing could store all your favorite programs in a local database, so that when you open the app it only has to check a website of listings to see when these programs are on next, and on which channels. This takes a strain off the web server by leaving the data distributed among users.

Another benefit is that such local databases can be accessed from a local web page using JavaScript, meaning that the data can be used by the app even where there is no Internet connection (in this example case, as long as the TV listings have also been downloaded).

***Note**: The examples from this lecture are in the* Lecture 17 *folder of the* examples.zip *file at* tinyurlcom/html5ccexamples.

Using Local Storage

In the past the only way you could store data on a user's computer was with cookies, which were limited in number and could hold only 4K of data in each. They also have to be passed back and forth on every page reload and, unless your server uses SSL (Secure Sockets Layer) encryption, each time a cookie is transmitted it travels in the clear.

But with HTML5 you have access to a much larger local storage space (typically between 5MB and 10MB per domain depending on the browser) that remains over page loads and between website visits (and even after powering a computer down and back up again), and which is not sent to the server on each page load.

You handle the data in pairs comprising a *key* and its *value*. The key is the name assigned for referencing the data and the value can hold any type of data, but it is saved as a string.

All data is unique to the current domain. Any local storage created by websites with different domains is separate to the current local storage for security reasons, and is not accessible by any domain other than the one that stored the data.

Storing and Retrieving Local Data

To access local storage you use methods of the `localStorage` object such as `setItem()`, `getItem()`, `removeItem()` and `clear()`. For example, to locally store a user's username and password you might use code such as this:

```
localStorage.setItem('username', 'BObama')
localStorage.setItem('password', 'IAmThePrez')
```

If the size of the value is larger than the disk quota remaining for the storage area, an "Out of memory" exception is thrown. Otherwise, when another page loads or when the user returns to the website, these details can be retrieved to save the user entering them again, like this:

```
username = localStorage.getItem('username')
password = localStorage.getItem('password')
```

If the key doesn't exist then the `getItem()` function returns a value of `null`.

You don't have to use these function names if you don't want to, and can access the localStorage object directly because the two following statements are equivalent to each other:

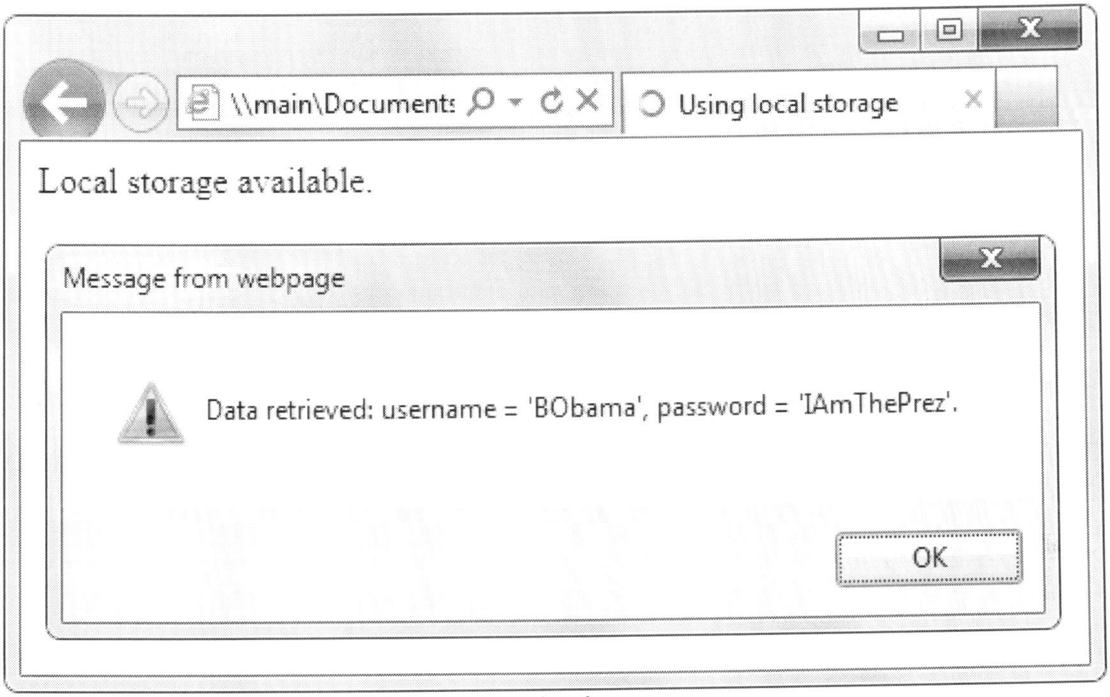

Figure 1: Data has been save to and retrieved from local storage

```
localStorage.setItem('key', 'value')
localStorage['key'] = 'value'
```

And the two following statements are therefore also equivalent to each other:

```
value = localStorage.getItem('key')
value = localStorage['key']
```

Figure 17-1 shows an `alert()` message window displaying these values being retrieved from local storage, using the following code:

```
if (typeof localStorage == 'undefined')
{
  document.write("Local storage unavailable.")
}
else
{
  document.write("Local storage available.")

  localStorage.setItem('username', 'BObama')
  localStorage.setItem('password', 'IAmThePrez')
```

```
    username  = localStorage.getItem('username')
    password  = localStorage.getItem('password')

    alert("Data retrieved: username = '"
      + username + "', password = '"
      + password + "'.")
  }
```

The first part of code within the `if()` statement writes an error message to the web page if local storage is not supported in the browser. This is determined by examining the `localStorage` object and, if it is undefined, then local storage is unavailable. In the `else` part of the code a message is first written to the web page indicating that local storage is supported. Then the username and password are saved to local storage with the `setItem()` function.

Next these values are retrieved from local storage into the variables `username` and `password`. Finally an `alert()` message window is popped up which displays the retrieved values.

Note*: Until they are erased, these values will remain in the local storage once saved, and you can verify this by trying the preceding code for yourself, running it once, commenting out the two lines of code that call* `setItem()`*, and then running it again – the alert window will still report the same vales.*

Removing and Clearing Local Data

To remove an item of data from the local storage all you need to do is issue a command such as this:

```
username = localStorage.removeItem('username')
```

This serves to retrieve the item of data and place it into a variable (in this case username), and then deletes the data from local storage. If you don't need to first read the data you are removing, you can simply call the function on its own, like this:

```
localStorage.removeItem('username')
```

You can also completely clear the local storage for the current domain by issuing this command:

```
localStorage.clear()
```

***Note**: Try any of these methods on the preceding example and run it again and you'll find that the values have been erased.*

Saving and retrieving data is starting to take us into the realms of much more complicated JavaScript programming, somewhat beyond the scope of this book. So the information in this lecture is mostly of use to programmers working with large amounts of JavaScript program code.

So if you are a beginner to JavaScript it's best to simply be aware of the possibilities of local storage, and come back here to refresh your memory about how it works when your programming is sufficiently advanced and you find the need for it.

Summary

That concludes this part of the course on some of the more advanced aspects of HTML5 that you can use now. In the next two lectures I'll show you how to have fun with adding HTML5 audio and video to your web pages.

LECTURE 18

HTML5 AUDIO

By following this lecture you will:

- ✓ *Understand what codecs are and how they are used.*
- ✓ *Learn the tags and attributes used for HTML5 audio.*
- ✓ *Be able to support older browsers with audio too.*

IN THIS SECTION of the course (this and the following lecture) I'll introduce two the of most popular additions to HTML5, the `<audio>` and `<video>` tags. In fact they are probably going to be even more used that the amazing `<canvas>` tag due to the ability to play media directly within the browser, without the need for an external plug-in such as the Flash player.

So in this lecture I'll show you how easy it is to add HTML5 audio to your pages, which I think you'll find is a remarkably easy thing to do, as long as the browser is a recent one.

As you work through the lecture please remember that the technology is still young and the file formats supported are constantly evolving (and vary by browser for patent reasons), but the following explains all you need to know to get started with embedding audio using HTML5.

***Note**: Flash is a programming environment best suited for creating animations and games, but which has mostly been adopted for playing video. However it is likely that HTML will supersede it, partly due to Apple not including it by default on new Macs and banning it from iOS devices, and also because the* `<canvas>` *tag provides everything a programmer previously would have needed Flash for.*

Understanding Codecs

Note*: The examples from this lecture are in the* Lecture 18 *folder of the* examples.zip *file at* tinyurlcom/html5ccexamples.

The term codec stands for enCOder/DECoder and describes the functionality provided by software that encodes and decodes media such as audio and video. In HTML5 there are currently a number of different sets of codecs available, depending on the browser used. Here are the codecs currently in use by the HTML5 `<audio>` tag (and also when audio is attached to HTML5 video):

- **AAC** This audio codec, which stands for Advanced Audio Encoding, is the one used by Apple's iTunes store, and is a proprietary patented technology supported by Apple, Google and Microsoft.

- **MP3** This audio codec, which stands for MPEG Audio Layer 3, has been available for many years and the term is often (incorrectly) used to refer to any type of digital audio, however it is a proprietary patented technology that is supported by Apple, Google and Microsoft.

- **PCM** This audio codec, which stands for Pulse Coded Modulation, stores the full data as encoded by an analog to digital convertor, and is the format used for storing data on audio CDs. Due to not using compression it is called a lossless codec and its files are generally many times larger than AAC or MP3 files. It is supported by Apple, Mozilla and Opera.

- **Vorbis** Sometimes referred to as Ogg Vorbis, due to it generally using the *.ogg* file extension, this audio codec is unencumbered by patents and free of royalty payments. It is supported by Google Chrome, Mozilla Firefox and Opera.

The following list details the major operating systems and browsers, along with the audio types they support by default:

- **Apple iOS** AAC, MP3, PCM

- **Apple Safari** AAC, MP3, PCM

- **Google Android 2.3+** AAC, MP3, Vorbis

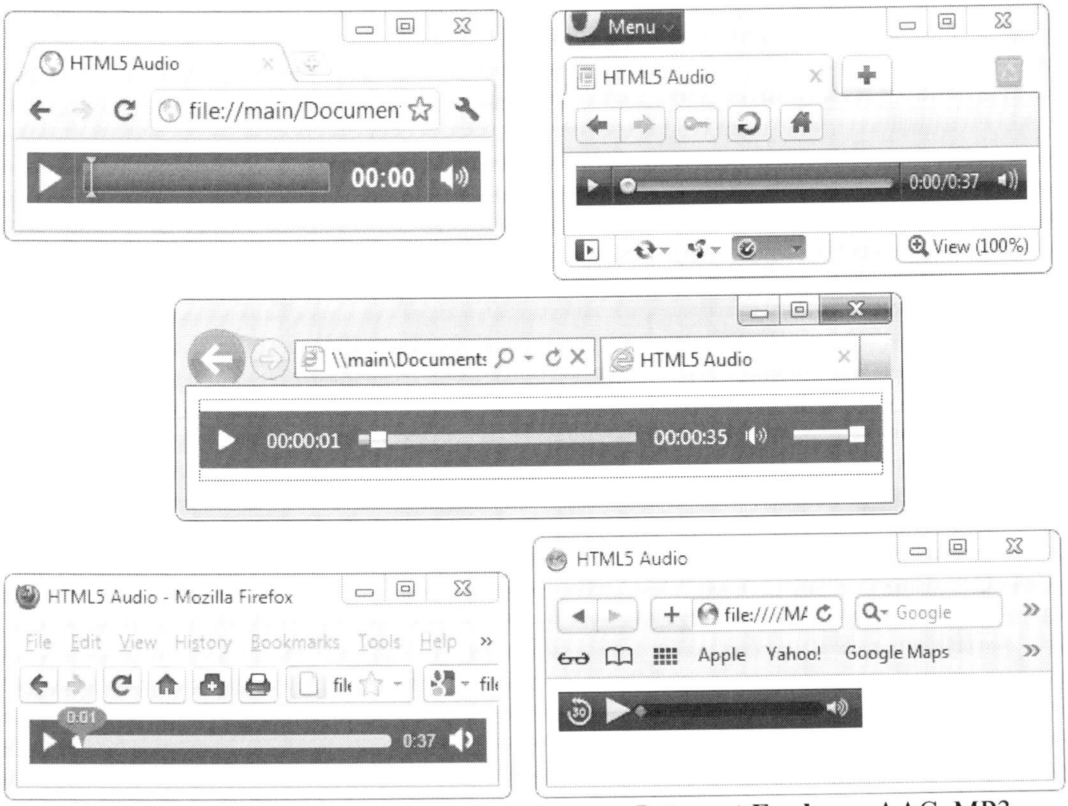

Figure 1: How the five main browsers display HTML5 audio

- **Internet Explorer** AAC, MP3
- **Google Chrome** AAC, MP3, Vorbis
- **Mozilla Firefox** PCM, Vorbis
- **Opera** PCM, Vorbis

If you study this list you'll see that none of these codecs is shared by all browsers and platforms, which is rather inconvenient. The problem occurs because browsers such as Firefox and Chrome choose to not employ the licensable codecs for both financial and moral reasons.

***Note**: Apple Safari for Windows requires the Apple QuickTime media player to be installed in order for HTML5 audio and video to play, so you may wish to use browser detection JavaScript software to alert your Windows Safari users of this, particularly since the only error they may otherwise get is any message you include inside the* `<audio>` *tags.*

Figure 2: The fallback Flash audio player

The <audio> and <source> Tags

However there's a simple (if inconvenient solution), which is to record your content using multiple codecs and then list them all within an `<audio>` and `</audio>` tags, like this, the result of running which in all the main browsers can be seen in Figure 18-1:

```
<audio controls>
  <source src='audio.m4a' type='audio/aac' />
  <source src='audio.mp3' type='audio/mp3' />
  <source src='audio.ogg' type='audio/ogg' />
</audio>
```

***Note**: Perform an Internet search to find suitable programs to create the file types you need – there are plenty of them – both paid and free.*

The <audio> and <source> Tag Attributes

In the preceding example you may have noticed that I applied an attribute with the name `controls` to the `<audio>` tag. This had the effect of causing a set of controls to appear, as displayed in Figure 18-1.

If that attribute is omitted then the controls will not display (and you'd either have to use another attribute called `autostart` or some JavaScript to make the audio play).

Here's the complete list of audio attributes supported by HTML5:

- **`autoplay`** Causes the audio to commence playing as soon as it is ready.
- **`controls`** Causes the control panel to be displayed.
- **`loop`** Sets the audio to play over and over.
- **`preload`** Causes the audio to begin loading even before the user selects Play.
- **`src`** Specifies the source location of an audio file
- **`type`** Specifies the codec used in creating the audio.

By selecting the attributes you require, and encoding audio in the right formats, you can ensure that it will play on all HTML5 compatible browsers, and you'll never have to worry about loading in a Flash or other audio player again, unless you intend to also support older browsers, as follows.

Supporting Older Browsers

Older browsers that do not recognize the `<audio>` tag can still play audio as long as they allow the embedding of an object that can play audio, such as a Flash program file. Assuming you have access to a Flash player called *audioplayer.swf* (there is one in the *examples.zip* file for this course) you can use code such as the following to do this:

```
<audio controls>

  <object type="application/x-shockwave-flash"
    data="audioplayer.swf" height="30" width="300">
    <param name="FlashVars"
      value="mp3=audio.mp3&showstop=1&showvolume=1">
  </object>

  <source src='audio.m4a' type='audio/aac' />
  <source src='audio.mp3' type='audio/mp3' />
  <source src='audio.ogg' type='audio/ogg' />

</audio>
```

On a non-HTML5 audio enabled browser the code within the `<object>` and `</object>` tags will load in the Flash program file *audioplayer.swf*, and pass it the MP3 filer *audio.mp3*, which can then be played by selecting the play button. Figure 18-2 shows what the player looks like – not bad compared to the HTML5 ones, so it's a pretty good fallback.

Summary

Once you complete this lecture you will have all the tools you need in order to play audio in your web pages, whether or not the browser supports HTML5 (but as long as it at least supports Flash). In the next lecture I'll show you how to do the same with video.

LECTURE 19

HTML5 VIDEO

By following this lecture you will:

- ✓ *Know all about the various video codecs.*
- ✓ *Be able to create your own HTML5 video player.*
- ✓ *Understand how to support non-HTML5 browsers with video too.*

ADDING HTML5 VIDEO to your pages is almost as easy as audio but there are some differences, and I'll point out the things you need to concern yourself with.

The main thing to realize, though, is that HTML5 video is still in its infancy and that specifications and codecs may change over times, as may the best ways to code and display your video. Still, following the advice in this lecture you'll be able to add video to any HTML5 enabled browser that's supports the `<video>` tag, and also some other or earlier browsers that do not (as long as they support the Flash plug-in)

***Note**: The examples from this lecture are in the* Lecture 19 *folder of the* examples.zip *file at* tinyurlcom/html5ccexamples.

The Video Codecs

As explained in the previous lecture the term codec stands for enCOder/DECoder and describes the functionality provided by software that encodes and decodes media such as audio and video.

For video, though, codecs are placed with containers, which may be any of the following:

- `MP4` A license-encumbered multimedia container format standard specified as a part of MPEG-4, supported by Apple, Microsoft and, to a lesser extent Google, since it has its own WebM container format.

- `OGG` A free, open container format maintained by the *Xiph.Org* Foundation. The creators of the Ogg format state that it is unrestricted by software patents and is designed to provide for efficient streaming and manipulation of high quality digital multimedia.

- `WebM` An audio-video format designed to provide a royalty-free, open video compression format for use with HTML5 video. The project's development is sponsored by Google.

In the HTML5 `<video>` tag there are currently a number of different sets of codecs available, depending on the browser used:

- `H.264` A patented proprietary video codec for which playback is free for the end user, but which may incur royalty fees for all parts of the encoding and transmission process. Consequently Apple and Microsoft support it, but browsers that use only open source or that do not have the financial ability to license it do not.

- `Theora` This is a video codec unencumbered by patents, and which is free of royalty payments at all levels of encoding, transmission and playback. This codec is supported by Google Chrome, Mozilla Firefox and Opera.

- `VP8` This video codec is similar to Theora but is owned by Google, which has published it as open source, making it royalty free. It is supported by Google Chrome, Mozilla Firefox and Opera.

The following list details the major operating systems and browsers, along with the video containers and video types they support by default:

- **Apple iOS** MP4 / H.264

- **Apple Safari** MP4 / H.264

- **Google Android 2.3+** MP4, OGG, WebM / Theora, VP8

- **Google Chrome** MP4, OGG, WebM / Theora, VP8

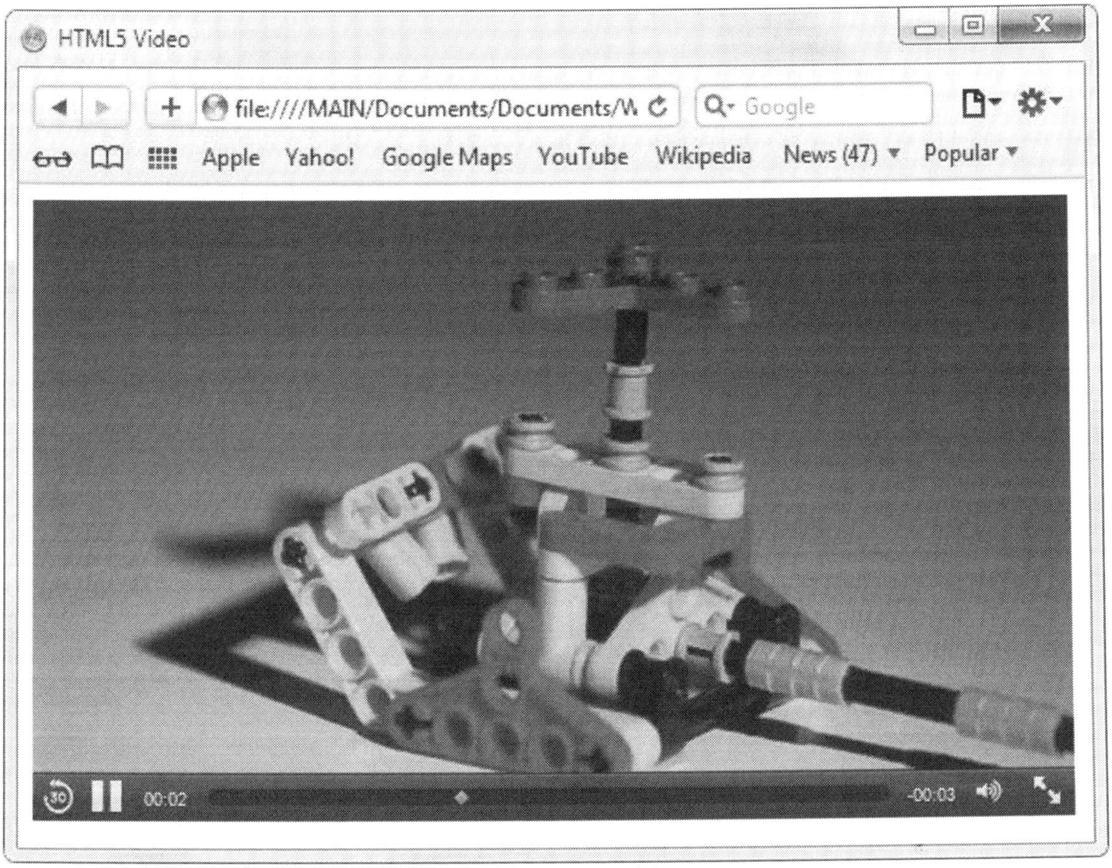

Figure 1: Playing an HTML5 video (file courtesy: www.808.dk)

- **Internet Explorer** MP4 / H.264
- **Mozilla Firefox** OGG, WebM / Theora VP8
- **Opera** OGG, WebM / Theora VP8

As with HTML5 `<audio>` there is no single container and/or codec for the `<video>` tag common to all browsers and platforms, because browsers such as Firefox and Chrome choose to not employ the licensable codecs for both financial and moral reasons.

What's more Google is trying to establish a new standard with the WebM format. However, Microsoft has come to the rescue by releasing plug-ins for the Firefox and Chrome browsers, available at the following URLs:

tinyurl.com/wmpforchrome
tinyurl.com/wmpforfirefox

Therefore one solution with which you can gain a wide level of compatibility is to use JavaScript to detect the browser in use and possibly offer these URLs to the relevant users in order to get them upgraded to be able to play MP4 / H.264 video. Then only users of Opera (Less than 1% of all users) will be unable to view your video.

The `<video>` and `<source>` Tags

Of course you may prefer not to exclude anyone, and choose to encode your video twice, using both MP4 / H.264 and WebM / Theora, so that all HTML5 browsers can play it. And that's the solution used as follows, in which three different video formats are offered to the browser, as shown in the Safari screen capture in Figure 19-1:

```
<video width='560' height='320' controls>
  <source src='video.mp4'  type='video/mp4'  />
  <source src='video.webm' type='video/webm' />
  <source src='video.ogv'  type='video/ogg'  />
</video>
```

Note: *If you don't have access to any you can search the Internet for a range of free and paid video conversions and compression tools.*

The `<video>` and `<source>` Tag Attributes

In the preceding example I applied the attribute with the name `controls` to the `<audio>` tag. This had the effect of causing a set of controls to appear, as displayed in Figure 19-1. If that attribute is omitted then the controls will not display (and you'd either have to use another attribute called `autostart` or some JavaScript to make the video play).

Here's the complete list of video attributes supported by HTML5:

- **`autoplay`** Causes the video to commence playing as soon as it is ready.
- **`controls`** Causes the control panel to be displayed.
- **`height`** Specifies the height at which to display the video.

- **`loop`** Sets the video to play over and over.
- **`poster`** Lets you choose an image to display where the video will play.
- **`preload`** Causes the video to begin loading before the user selects Play.
- **`src`** Specifies the source location of a video file
- **`type`** Specifies the codec used in creating the video.
- **`width`** Specifies the width at which to display the video.

Supporting Older Browsers

By selecting the attributes you require and encoding video in the right formats you can ensure that it will play on all HTML5 compatible browsers, and you'll never have to worry about loading in a Flash or other video player again, unless you intend to also support older browsers, as follows:

```
<video width='560' height='320' controls>

  <object width='560' height='320'
    type='application/x-shockwave-flash'
    data='flowplayer.swf'>
     <param name='movie' value='flowplayer.swf' />
     <param name='flashvars'
       value='config={"clip": {"url":
         "http://tinyurl.com/html5video-mp4",
         "autoPlay":false, "autoBuffering":true}}' />
  </object>

  <source src='video.mp4'  type='video/mp4'  />
  <source src='video.webm' type='video/webm' />
  <source src='video.ogv'  type='video/ogg'  />

</video>
```

The preceding code displays like Figure 19-2 in browsers that do not support the `<video>` tag but do have Flash installed.

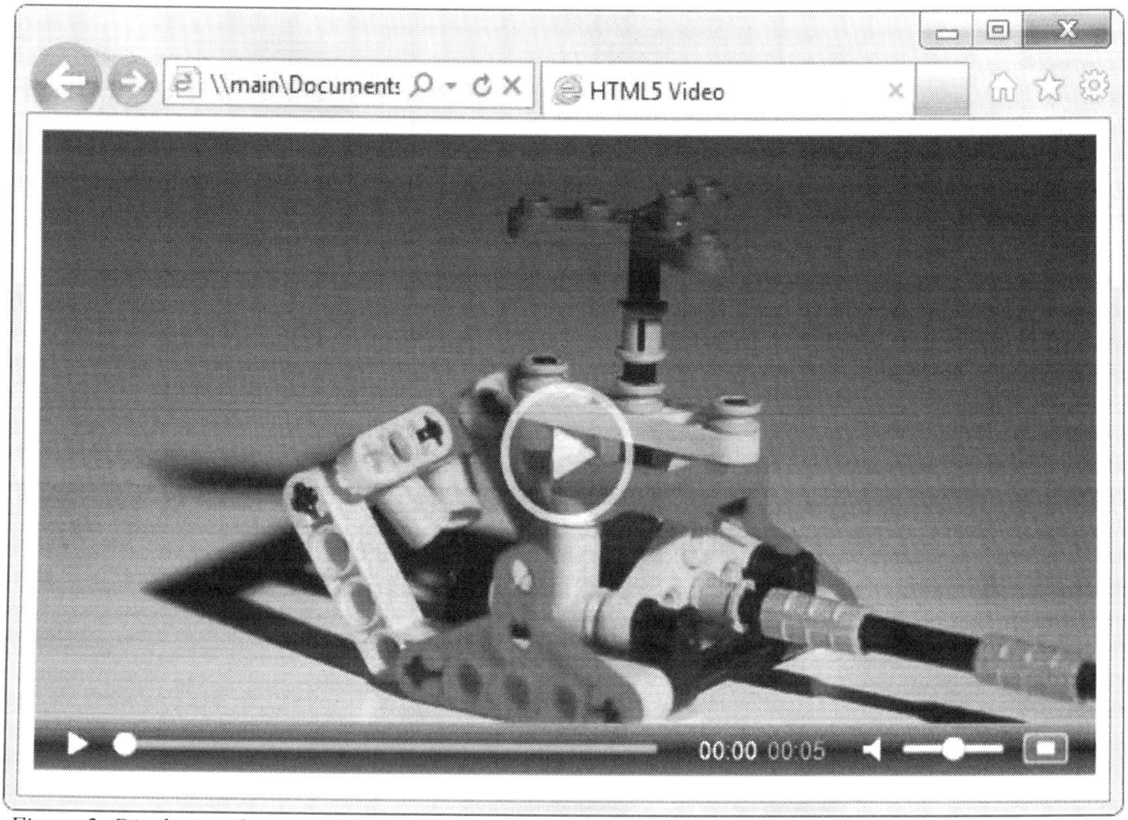

Figure 2: Displaying the same video using a Flash player

Using the code in the `<object>` and `</object>` tags you can ensure that non HTML5 enabled browsers can still play your mp4 videos as long as they have the Flash plug-in loaded.

The *flowplayer.swf* files required to do this are included in the *examples.zip* file on the accompanying website, but you can check for newer versions at the *flowplayer.org* website. If you download a newer version ensure you match the code to the filenames, which will have numeric extensions such as -3.2.7 (which I removed for simplicity), and so on.

***Note**: The* flowplayer.swf *file restricts the playing of files directly from a local hard disk on a computer, therefore you must supply it with the full Internet URL of a file, as in the example, which uses a URL at the* nixonpublishing.com *website (but shortened via the* tinyurl.com *service).*

Summary

Now that you've completed this lecture you will have all the audio and video tools you need in order to play media in your web pages, whether or not the browser supports HTML5 (but as long as it at least supports Flash). You have now learned almost everything that is currently usable in HTML5.

In the final lecture I'll explain the features that are included in HTML5 but which have so far been poorly implemented (if at all), but which you should know about because they will be adopted by the major browsers over the coming months and years.

LECTURE 20

MICRODATA, WEB WORKERS & WEB APPLICATIONS

By following this lecture you will:

- ✓ *Understand the other major features coming to HTML5.*
- ✓ *Be able to use some of these features even before being widely adopted.*
- ✓ *Know how HTML is planned to develop in the future.*

THE FACT IS that HTML5 is a development project that is proceeding gradually. Many of its tags and features have already been implemented by the major browsers, while, as you've seen, others are only partly supported on some browsers.

So I have reserved the final lecture in this course for discussion of the remaining HTML5 features that have yet to be fully (or even properly) implemented, some of which are going to turn out extremely powerful when they become available, and some of which it may actually benefit you to start using already.

Where possible I'll show you how they work (or are planned to work), although aspects of some parts of the implementation could develop or be improved over time as HTML5 is really more of a bundling of a group of unrelated features that developers want to add to HTML.

Note*: The examples from this lecture are in the* Lecture 20 *folder of the* examples.zip *file at* tinyurlcom/html5ccexamples.

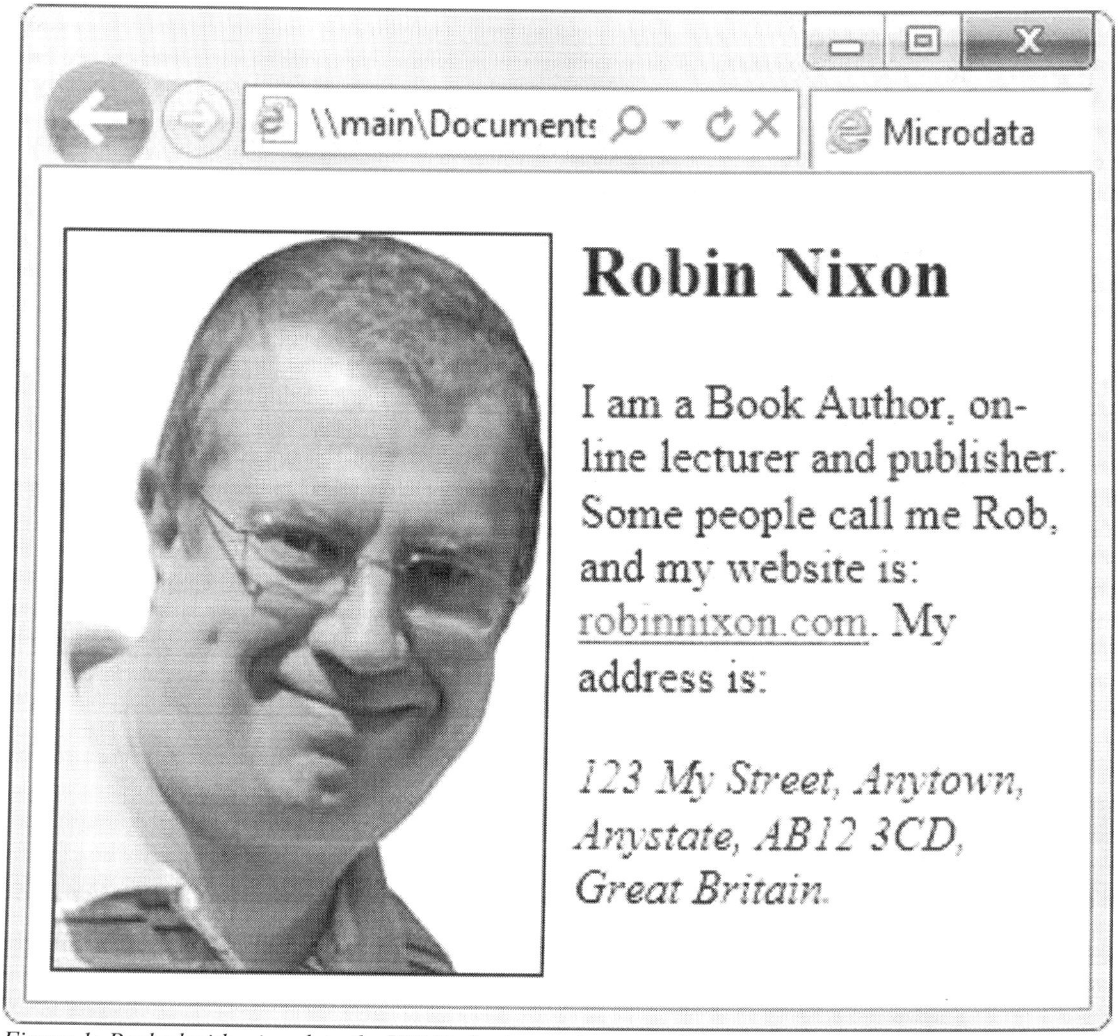

Figure 1: Packed with microdata the HTML displays quite normally

Microdata

The first of these features is called microdata, which is a subset of HTML designed for making a document have meaning to machines by providing meta data, just as it has meaning to a reader of the document.

What it does is make available the following new tag attributes: `itemscope`, `itemtype`, `itemid`, `itemref` and `itemprop`. Using them you will be able to clearly define the properties of an item such as a book, providing a range of information that a computer can use to understand, for example, its authors, publishers, contents and so on.

Here's how HTML code looks that incorporates microdata, and Figure 20-1 shows how this HTML displays:

```
<section
  itemscope
    itemtype='http://data-vocabulary.org/Person'>

  <img itemprop='photo' src='robin.jpg'
    alt='Robin Nixon' align='left'/
    style='margin-right:10px' />

  <h2 itemprop='name'>Robin Nixon</h2>

  <p>I am a <span itemprop='role'>Book Author, On-line
    Lecturer and
      <span itemprop='title'>Publisher</span>.
    Some people call me
      <span itemprop='nickname'>Rob</span>,
    and my website is: <a itemprop='url'
    href='http://robinnixon.com'>robinnixon.com</a>.

   My address is:</p>

  <address
    itemscope
      itemtype='http://data-vocabulary.org/Address'
    itemprop='address'>

    <span itemprop='street-address'>23 My Street</span>,
    <span itemprop='locality'>Anytown</span>,
    <span itemprop='region'>Anystate</span>,
    <span itemprop='postal-code'>AB12 3CD</span>,
    <span itemprop='country-name'>Great Britain</span>.

  </address>
</section>
```

As you might expect the adding of microdata has done nothing to alter the display of the HTML in any way. But it has provided a wealth of information to any browsers or search engines that can read the microdata and understand what it represents.

If you study the example code (recommended) you'll see a couple of references to URLs at the *data-vocabulary.org* web server. That's because this is where all the information you need for using microdata can be found, and from which you can choose the microdata types to use in your HTML – I strongly recommend you check the website out.

However, the in-browser DOM (Document Object Model) functions for managing microdata appear not to have been implemented yet by any major browser publisher.

When the API is incorporated into the major browsers the microdata scripts will be able to use the microdata to expose information to the user, for example offering it in a form that can be used by other applications.

Very likely there will also be mouseover and other information revealed when mousing over text which has microdata attached. So from that point of view there's not a lot of reason to use microdata; not yet, anyway.

Because the API will use the function `getItems()` you can test whether a browser supports it or not using the following code, which pops up a message telling you:

```
<script>
  if (!!document.getItems)
       alert("Microdata supported")
  else alert("Microdata not supported")
</script>
```

The specs for microdata are available at *tinyurl.com/microdataspecs*, so take a look if you want to know what to expect, and how to use the `getItems()` function when browsers start to support it.

***Note**: The first big users of microdata will actually be the search engines and it has been reported that some microdata information is already turning up in Google's index. Therefore you* do *(after all) have a very good reason to start using microdata immediately, because anything you can do to legitimately improve your rankings in the search engines is important to implement.*

Web Workers

Normally, to achieve background processing in JavaScript, you need to set up a timer that is constantly called, supplying slices of processor time to one or more functions, and these functions must then quickly do a small piece of work and return, in order to not slow down the browser and make it seem sluggish.

Web Workers, however, will provide a standard way for browsers to run multiple JavaScript threads in the background that can pass messages to each other, in much the same manner as the threads running in an operating system. You will simply call up a new worker script which will sit there in the background waiting for messages to be sent to it, which it will then act upon.

On the whole the aim of this is to achieve a 2-3 times speed increase over regular background JavaScripts, although getting to grips with programming requires a longer rather than shorter learning curve.

***Note**: At the moment Internet Explorer is the only major browser not to use web workers. However, I have experienced difficulties getting Google Chrome to work correctly, even though it apparently supports web workers. Therefore, since these two browsers represent a large portion of the market between them, I do not recommend you implement web workers until these browsers do. If you are capable of using web workers, you are easily able to continue using timed interrupts for the time being.*

If you want to learn how to use web workers using browsers other than Internet Explorer, take a look at this code:

```
<script>
  if (!!window.Worker)
       alert("Web workers supported")
  else alert("Web workers not supported")
</script>
```

This script simply alerts you as to whether or not web workers are supported by the browser you are using. Once you have determined that the browser will use them then you can run code such as the following, which calculates prime numbers in the background:

```
<p>The highest prime number discovered so far is:
  <output id='result'></output></p>
<script>
  // O() & S() functions go here

  var worker = new Worker('worker.js')

  worker.onmessage = function (event)
  {
    O('result').innerHTML = event.data;
  }
</script>
```

This script displays some text and creates an element with the `id` of `'result'` into which the highest prime number found so far is continuously written. This is achieved by creating the new object called `worker` by calling the `Worker()` function, passing it the name of an external JavaScript file called *worker.js* (explained shortly).

The `onmessage` event of the `worker` object is then attached to. This triggers only when there is a new message to display, and the code that is called copies the data in `event.data` into the `innerHTML` property of the `'result'` element. After the code exits it will not be called again until another message is ready to display. The code that does the prime number calculation is saved separately in the file *worker.js*, and looks like this:

```
var n = 1

search: while (true)
{
  n += 1

  for (var i = 2; i <= Math.sqrt(n); i += 1)
    if (n % i == 0) continue search;

  postMessage(n)
}
```

This is a simple iterative piece of code that increases the value of `n`, starting from 1. After each increase, all values of 2 up to the square root of `n` are tested to see if they are a factor of `n`. If any of them is, then `n` cannot be prime and so the `continue` keyword forces execution to go back to the start of the `search:` loop to see if `n+1` is prime, and so on.

But if `n` is found to have no factors then it is prime and the `continue` keyword is not encountered. In which case program flow drops through to the `postMessage()` call, which posts the value `n`, creating an `onmessage` event on the `worker` object in the preceding code. The result of running this code is a line of text at the top of the browser that continuously updates and looks like this:

The highest prime number discovered so far is: 42737

Together an HTML page and associated JavaScript file can work away in the background performing all manner of tasks, something which was achievable in the past only by manually creating events to run the code a few instructions at a time before returning to allow the web page to have some processor cycles, after which another event is created to let the program code run a few more cycles, and so on.

As you might imagine, the old way is rather tricky and can be cumbersome. It can also mess with smooth animations on your web page if you don't get the event timings and time sharing exactly right.

But with web workers you can forget all about these things and simply place your background code into its own file – just ensure the code calls the `postMessage()` function whenever it has something to say.

For full details on the web worker specifications you can check out the official website at *tinyurl.com/webworkerspecs*.

***Note**: Although Google Chrome says that is supports Web Workers, it does not run this example code. Also the Opera browser initially runs the code a little slower (maybe 10%) than Firefox, but then seems to get faster (by up to 30%) after a few minutes, while the Apple Safari browser seems to run up to ten times faster than either Firefox or Opera. Therefore, where timing is critical (perhaps you are writing a game in JavaScript), this is another reason why web workers may not yet be ready for primetime.*

Offline Web Applications

The idea of offline web applications is that once you visit a website, it tells your browser about all the files it uses so that the browser can download them all and you can then run the web application locally, even without an Internet connection.

There is a slight complication with offline web applications in that they may require a web server to set up with the correct MIME types (originally known as Multipurpose Internet Mail Extensions, but the word *Mail* has since been replaced with *Media*), in order for a browser that understands offline web applications to make use of the feature and fetch the files it needs.

If you are using web server that is not Apache, consult your manuals for how to add the `text/cache-manifest` MIME type for `.appcache` file extensions, in order for your server to send the manifest file using the correct type. Otherwise for Apache users there's a neat shortcut you can use, which is to create a file called *.htaccess* in the same folder as the files to be made available offline, with the following contents:

```
AddType text/cache-manifest .appcache
```

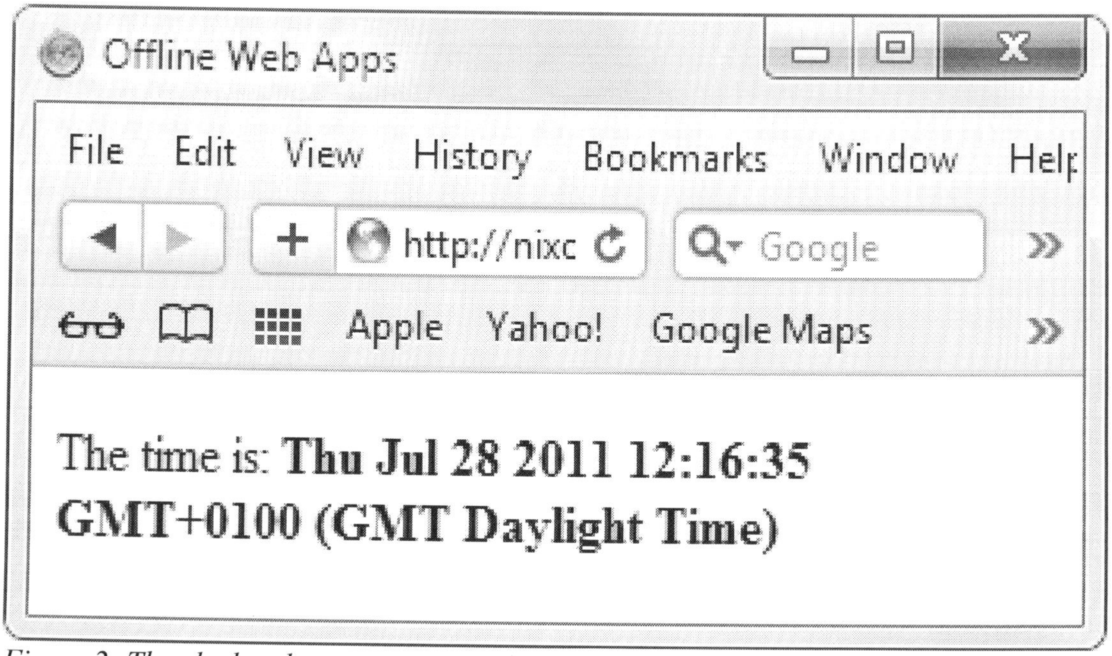

Figure 2: The clock web app running in the Safari browser

***Note**: On Windows you cannot create a file that starts with a period, so call the file something like* a.htaccess *and then rename it to* .htaccess *after uploading it. On some FTP programs the file will then seem to disappear because it is a system file.*

How Offline Web Apps Work

Here's how offline apps are supposed to work. You start with a manifest file that contains all the files you'd like to offer for offline use, like the following, which is saved with the filename *clock.appcache*:

```
CACHE MANIFEST
clock.htm
clock.css
clock.js
```

The three files detailed in the manifest are then as follows, starting with *clock.htm*:

```
<!DOCTYPE html>
<!-- saved from url=(0014)about:internet -->
<html manifest='clock.appcache'>
  <head>
```

```
    <title>Offline Web Apps</title>
    <script src='clock.js'></script>
    <link rel='stylesheet' href='clock.css'>
  </head>
  <body>
    <p>The time is: <output id='clock'></output></p>
  </body>
</html>
```

Here's *clock.css*:

```
output { font-weight:bold; }
```

And this is *clock.js*:

```
// The O() & S() functions go here

setInterval(function ()
{

  O('clock').innerHTML = new Date()
}, 1000)
```

The idea of offline web apps is that, thanks to the manifest, all these files will be downloaded and made available for use offline to use in any environment. Between them they simply create a simple clock that looks like Figure 20-2. The code that does the work is in the *clock.js* file. It starts with the `O()` and `S()` function definitions and then sets up a regular interval with `setInterval()` such that the code within it is called every 1,000 milliseconds (or once a second). This code simply copies the date and time into the `innerHTML` property of the `'clock'` element.

***Note**: All major browsers except Internet Explorer support offline web applications, although I have received mixed results with some browsers that don't always behave in the way I would expect. Therefore I recommend plenty of testing before you release offline enabled web pages to the world, and probably you may want to wait until Internet Explorer catches up because, even though it does quite a good job of offline caching using its own technology, it doesn't work the HTML5 offline web application way, and so may well be incompatible with your code.*

For full details on the offline web applications specifications you can check out the official website at *tinyurl.com/offlinewebapps*.

Drag And Drop

There are seven events associated with drag and drop in HTML5: `dragstart`, `drag`, `dragover`, `dragenter`, `dragleave`, `drop`, and `dragend`.

These must all be attached to using JavaScript and then code written to decide what to do depending upon each action.

Firefox, Safari and Internet Explorer all have pages explaining how to use HTML5 drag and drop, but none of the examples appear to be interoperable with other browsers.

Because of this, and since the use of these events requires some quite advanced JavaScript, it is beyond the scope of this course. However, you may wish to explore HTML5 drag and drop further yourself by visiting the following web sites:

dev.w3.org/html5/spec/dnd.html
hacks.mozilla.org/2009/07/html5-drag-and-drop
msdn.microsoft.com/en-us/library/ms537658(VS.85).aspx
quirksmode.org/blog/archives/2009/09/the_html5_drag.html

Cross Document Messaging

This is another highly advanced specification designed to make it easier for documents to communicate with each other but, again, it is really beyond the scope of this course.

However, there is more information available at these websites:

en.wikipedia.org/wiki/Cross-document_messaging
whatwg.org/specs/web-apps/current-work/multipage/comms.html
dev.w3.org/html5/postmsg/

Other HTML5 Tags

There are a number of other new HTML5 tags that have not yet been implemented in any browser, and which I therefore won't detail (particularly since their specs could change).

But, for the sake of completeness, these tags are: `<article>`, `<aside>`, `<command>`, `<details>`, `<figcaption>`, `<figure>`, `<footer>`, `<header>`, `<hgroup>`, `<keygen>`,

<mark>, <meter>, <nav>, <output>, <progress>, <rp>, <rt>, <ruby>, <section>, <summary>, <time> and <wbr>. You can get more information on these and all other HTML5 tags at:

dev.w3.org/html5/markup

Summary

Congratulations! You've just completed this course on HTML5. Thanks for taking it! I hope you've enjoyed the process and have learned plenty of useful things from the course but, before you go, you may be interested in visiting my website at *robinnixon.com* to see my other books and courses, which cover both web technology and motivational and personal improvement topics. And thanks once again for taking the course!

INDEX

21419410R00168

Made in the USA
Lexington, KY
11 March 2013